Internet Censorship and Regulation Systems in Democracies:

Emerging Research and Opportunities

Nikolaos Koumartzis
Aristotle University of Thessaloniki, Greece

Andreas Veglis
Aristotle University of Thessaloniki, Greece

A volume in the Advances in Information Security, Privacy, and Ethics (AISPE) Book Series

IGI Global
PUBLISHER of TIMELY KNOWLEDGE

Published in the United States of America by
IGI Global
Information Science Reference (an imprint of IGI Global)
701 E. Chocolate Avenue
Hershey PA, USA 17033
Tel: 717-533-8845
Fax: 717-533-8661
E-mail: cust@igi-global.com
Web site: http://www.igi-global.com

Library of Congress Cataloging-in-Publication Data

Names: Koumartzis, Nikolaos, 1984- author. | Veglis, Andreas, author.
Title: Internet censorship and regulation systems in democracies : emerging research and opportunities / by Nikolaos Koumartzis and Andreas Veglis.
Description: Hershey PA : Information Science Reference, 2020.
Identifiers: LCCN 2019014122| ISBN 9781522599739 (hardcover) | ISBN 9781522599753 (ebook) | ISBN 9781522599746 (softcover)
Subjects: LCSH: Internet--Law and legislation.
Classification: LCC K4345 .K68 2020 | DDC 343.09/944--dc23 LC record available at https://lccn.loc.gov/2019014122

This book is published in the IGI Global book series Advances in Information Security, Privacy, and Ethics (AISPE) (ISSN: 1948-9730; eISSN: 1948-9749)

British Cataloguing in Publication Data
A Cataloguing in Publication record for this book is available from the British Library.

For electronic access to this publication, please contact: eresources@igi-global.com.

Advances in Information Security, Privacy, and Ethics (AISPE) Book Series

ISSN:1948-9730
EISSN:1948-9749

Editor-in-Chief: Manish Gupta, State University of New York, USA

MISSION

As digital technologies become more pervasive in everyday life and the Internet is utilized in ever increasing ways by both private and public entities, concern over digital threats becomes more prevalent.

The **Advances in Information Security, Privacy, & Ethics (AISPE) Book Series** provides cutting-edge research on the protection and misuse of information and technology across various industries and settings. Comprised of scholarly research on topics such as identity management, cryptography, system security, authentication, and data protection, this book series is ideal for reference by IT professionals, academicians, and upper-level students.

COVERAGE

- Security Classifications
- Technoethics
- Risk Management
- Telecommunications Regulations
- Electronic Mail Security
- Tracking Cookies
- Data Storage of Minors
- IT Risk
- Device Fingerprinting
- Internet Governance

IGI Global is currently accepting manuscripts for publication within this series. To submit a proposal for a volume in this series, please contact our Acquisition Editors at Acquisitions@igi-global.com or visit: http://www.igi-global.com/publish/.

The Advances in Information Security, Privacy, and Ethics (AISPE) Book Series (ISSN 1948-9730) is published by IGI Global, 701 E. Chocolate Avenue, Hershey, PA 17033-1240, USA, www.igi-global.com. This series is composed of titles available for purchase individually; each title is edited to be contextually exclusive from any other title within the series. For pricing and ordering information please visit http://www.igi-global.com/book-series/advances-information-security-privacy-ethics/37157. Postmaster: Send all address changes to above address.

Titles in this Series

For a list of additional titles in this series, please visit:
http://www.igi-global.com/book-series/advances-information-security-privacy-ethics/37157

Handbook of Research on Multimedia Cyber Security
Brij B. Gupta (National Institute of Technology, Kurukshetra, India) and Deepak Gupta (LoginRadius Inc., Canada)
Information Science Reference • © 2020 • 372pp • H/C (ISBN: 9781799827016) • US $265.00

Security and Privacy Applications for Smart City Development
Sharvari C. Tamane (MGM's Jawaharlal Nehru Engineering College, India)
Information Science Reference • © 2020 • 300pp • H/C (ISBN: 9781799824985) • US $215.00

Cyber Security of Industrial Control Systems in the Future Internet Environment
Mirjana D. Stojanović (University of Belgrade, Serbia) and Slavica V. Boštjančič Rakas (University of Belgrade, Serbia)
Information Science Reference • © 2020 • 374pp • H/C (ISBN: 9781799829102) • US $195.00

Digital Investigation and Intrusion Detection in Biometrics and Embedded Sensors
Asaad Abdulrahman Nayyef (Sultan Qaboos University, Iraq)
Information Science Reference • © 2020 • 320pp • H/C (ISBN: 9781799819448) • US $235.00

Handbook of Research on Intrusion Detection Systems
Brij B. Gupta (National Institute of Technology, Kurukshetra, India) and Srivathsan Srinivasagopalan (AT&T, USA)
Information Science Reference • © 2020 • 407pp • H/C (ISBN: 9781799822424) • US $265.00

For an entire list of titles in this series, please visit:
http://www.igi-global.com/book-series/advances-information-security-privacy-ethics/37157

IGI Global
PUBLISHER of TIMELY KNOWLEDGE

701 East Chocolate Avenue, Hershey, PA 17033, USA
Tel: 717-533-8845 x100 • Fax: 717-533-8661
E-Mail: cust@igi-global.com • www.igi-global.com

Table of Contents

Foreword vii

Preface ix

Acknowledgment xi

Introduction xiv

Section 1
Literature Review: The Internet Regulation Phenomenon Worldwide

Chapter 1
Online Filtering Policies Around the World 1

Chapter 2
Internet Users and Internet Regulation: Enemies or Allies? 29

Section 2
How an IRS Works: A Currently and Already Implemented Paradigm

Chapter 3
How an IRS Works: UK's CleanFeed as a Comparative Model 56

Section 3
Measuring Public Opinion Around the World

Chapter 4
The Survey 77

Chapter 5
Research in Greece 92

Chapter 6
Research in Germany 100

Chapter 7
Research in Russia 109

Chapter 8
Research in India 117

Chapter 9
Research in Kosovo 125

Chapter 10
Research in Cyprus 134

Chapter 11
Sum Up: Statistical Analysis and General Conclusions 143

Section 4
Research, Design, and Blueprint of a Fair IRS

Chapter 12
Designing a Fair Internet Regulation System 153

Chapter 13
Putting a FIRS to the Test: The Case Study of Greece 162

Section 5
Outcome

Chapter 14
Concluding Remarks and Future Work 181

Appendix 193

Related Readings 254

About the Authors 269

Index 271

Foreword

One of the most vexed questions about the Internet concerns its regulation. To begin with, Internet regulation is as much about the technology as it is about the contents facilitated and carried by the technology and about the end users of both the technology and its contents. It covers questions of technical infrastructure, protocols, and conventions of interoperability and at the same time it has to deal with the communicative contents supported by the various applications that use the Internet as well as take into account the various categories of users that will be accessing them. And if this is not complex enough, the Internet operates globally while regulation tends to operate at the local, national or regional level. Some aspects of regulation, those concerning the technological protocols, have to be agreed by everyone and to operate globally. Others, for example those concerning certain categories of contents and certain categories of users, are regulated differently in different national and regional contexts.

Another layer of complexity emerges out of ideological issues and positions. A crucial source of tension emerges out of the constituent set of ideas that made the Internet, namely ideas revolving around the freedom of circulation of information, and the pragmatic problems that have emerged recently in the context of the various kinds of problematic and occasionally malicious information that have been found circulating unchallenged. A second source of tension emerges out of the averseness to regulate large ICT corporations because of the belief that this may interfere with the operation of free market principles. The complexity and difficulty of regulating the Internet is perhaps at the root of the reluctance with which liberal democracies approach the subject. But this will not make the issues go away. We still must talk about regulation.

This contribution by Andreas Veglis and Nikolaos Koumartzis is doing precisely this: they are placing the question of regulation at the centre. They examine regulation primarily from the perspective of users: if the Internet is to be regulated, then those affected by this regulation must have a say and an input. Hence, rather than developing top down normative ideals for its implementation, they begin with users, whose views and opinions are often ignored, disregarded and misrepresented. Rather than focusing on one cultural setting, they study views on regulation across different cultures. By conducting a cross-cultural study, the authors are able to identify what is specific to certain cultural settings and what is more universally valid. This information can then feed into the development of a blueprint for fair regulation. While it is important to take into account users' views, expert opinion may contribute to understanding the potential limitations and broader implications of regulation. The authors therefore include expert interviews that add depth and perspective to the user surveys. A final consideration is that any regulatory system must be dynamic as the Internet is itself extremely dynamic and constantly evolving. Combining all insights developed from bibliographical and empirical research, the authors propose a dynamic Fair Internet Regulation System (FIRS) that relies on dynamic lists of URLs to be blocked, updated and revised on the basis of continuous user feedback.

There is little doubt that any regulation must be attentive to the needs of end users, and to be continuously open to these needs. This is a crucial parameter that the authors identified and built into the design of the system; the dynamism of the designed blueprint guarantees that the system is able to follow the evolution of the Internet and the shifting views of its users. While broader complex questions of what and how to regulate may persist, the FIRS proposed by the authors which incorporates the views of end users shows a way out of the regulatory impasse we currently find ourselves.

Eugenia Siapera
University College Dublin, Ireland
March 2019

Preface

This book discusses the phenomenon of Internet regulation in general, and the use of Internet Regulation Systems (IRSs) by authoritarian regimes and western democracies. The authors explore these two topics through different scopes (technical, design, ethical, and so on), before proposing a blueprint for the development and implementation of a Fair Internet Regulation System (FIRS). The book is based on original research conducted by the authors from 2008 until 2017 on seven countries.

This research is based partly on literature review, partly on former research of the authors in the UK, partly on technical analysis of the current IRSs, and partly on surveys that were conducted by the authors in different countries around the world.

More specifically, in the introductory chapter, the authors present in brief the topic of the book and what an Internet Regulation System (IRS) is. What's more, they present the main key areas of interest that their research focuses on, its research aims and objectives, and the research methods, along with the limitations they have faced.

In Chapter 1, the authors proceed with an introduction to the global phenomenon of Internet regulation, the development of online censorship, and they discus the need for Internet regulation, along with the role that Internet users can actually play.

Chapter 2 examines if Internet users are against any kind of Internet regulation policy or not. In their endeavour, they begin with a literature review of older related surveys, and then proceed by presenting their UK-related survey that was conducted in 2007-2008, focusing on the UK's IRS, i.e. BT's CleanFeed.

In Chapter 3, the authors describe in detail the UK's CleanFeed design and the blocking mechanisms that it is using. The description presented is based mainly on two papers by Dr. Clayton of Cambridge Computer Laboratory, while many figures are presented in order for CleanFeed's design to be more understandable to a broader public.

Chapter 4 discusses the design of the authors' questionnaire and how it was evolved from the initial 2007 UK questionnaire to the one that was used for conducting surveys in six different countries. This chapter presents the procedure that was used for collecting responses and what kinds of "safeguard" measures were taken in order to avoid deterioration of the gathered survey data.

Chapter s5 to 10 present data gathered by initial surveys conducted by the authors in Greece (Chapter 5), Germany (Chapter 6), Russia (Chapter 7), India (Chapter 8), Kosovo (Chapter 9), and Cyprus (Chapter 10) during 2010, 2011, and 2012.

In Chapter 11, the authors present the trends and associations between the aforementioned surveys, thanks to a series of statistical analysis that lead to valuable conclusions. Among the others, the authors used Pearson Chi-square analysis, Kruskal-Wallis H and Mann-Whitney U tests.

Taking into consideration the IRSs, older surveys and authors' surveys results discussed in previous chapters, Chapter 12 presents a Fair Internet Regulation System (FIRS) that was designed by the authors.

In Chapter 13, the authors implement their Fair Internet Regulation System (FIRS) blueprint, using Greece as a case study. They discuss the results of Greece initial survey, and they present all the improvements that were implemented in the initial questionnaire. The improved questionnaire was then used for Greece's Mass Survey that was conducted in October 2013, gathering 446 responses, the results of which are being presented here. Taking the results of Greece's Mass Survey into account, the authors proceed with choosing the content and categorisation that FIRS will target and the technical aspects based on the aims and the budget.

Last, in Chapter 14, the authors present their concluding remarks, along with their thoughts about future work regarding the need for a Fair Internet Regulation System (FIRS) to be developed, and implemented in different countries.

Acknowledgment

A proper research cannot be conducted based solely on the researcher's skills, knowledge, technological expertise, and key contacts. In order to achieve the latter, the researchers have to discuss, be advised and corrected by experts in various fields, get in touch with researchers around the world and organise coordinated research endeavours.

This is the case with this book, as well: it is a multicultural and international joint effort in different countries moderated by the authors with the aid of the Media Informatics Lab at Department of Journalism and Mass Communications (Aristotle University of Thessaloniki).

Thanks must go to Dr. Georgios Kalliris too, for initiating helpful discussions during our research.

We owe special thanks to our colleagues abroad who helped us to collect valuable data that played a crucial role in our research.

More specifically, for the "Germany Survey," we would like to thank Johannes Fritz (PhD Candidate and Researcher assistance at Friedrich-Alexander Universität Erlangen in Nürnberg, Germany), for the "Russia Survey" Evgeniy Efimov (Head Teacher at Volgograd State Technical University, Russia), and for the "Kosovo Survey" Artan Rogova (Research Fellow at the Group for Legal and Political Studies). The "India Survey" was a collaborative effort with Anshul Tewari and Astik Sinha (journalists, India) carrying most of the work, Sumit Kalra (publisher, India) for playing a key role in the initial stage of the survey, and Astik Sinha for his help at the beginning. The "Cyprus Survey" was conducted in a similar way with Dr. Lia-Paschalia Spyridou (Research Associate at the Department of Communication and Internet Studies, Cyprus University of Technology) playing a key role during the first stage of the survey, and Andreas Andreou having a crucial part in gathering all the needed responses.

Moreover, thanks must go to all the researchers with whom we have collaborated in the past for similar surveys that have not managed to receive the needed responses: Cigdem Erdal (PhD Candidate, Marmara University, Turkey), Giorgos Dermentzis (PhD Candidate, University of Innsbruck, Austria), Keren Nachmias (Western Galilee College, Israel), and so on.

Special reference must be made to Angelina Bitziouni (graduate MA student of the Dept. of Journalism & Mass Media, Aristotle University of Thessaloniki) for her valuable contacts in finding willing researchers across the world for the survey part of this research. Another reference must be made to Dr. Alexandros Baltzis, who helped us improve and enrich the survey's questions in order to form the final questionnaire for the massive survey in Greece.

Moreover, special thanks must go to the people that helped us carry out the first steps of our research on Internet regulation in the United Kingdom. Part of this book is based on findings from our research at LCC. So, regarding this time period, we would like to thank MA Publishing course director Desmond O'Rourke, who helped us focus on the right aspects of censorship, and played a key role in our initial engagement with this research field. Secondly, Dr. David Penfold (LCC former professor) helped a lot by proposing the right contacts with IT experts.

From the very first stage of our UK based research, Dr. Richard Clayton of Cambridge University Computer Laboratory accepted our invitation for an interview, but in the end we proceeded to a discussion via emails as he was able to answer almost immediately every enquiry we made.

Also, Family Online Safety Institute's Chief Technical Officer Phil Archer was more than positive in explaining to us the point of view of family and children institutions regarding UK's CleanFeed system, while his answers to our enquiries were more than helpful concerning our research. Moreover, Internet Archive's Office Manager Paul Forrest Hickman's response to our specialised enquiries was immediate and as detailed as it had to be in order to proceed with specific parts of our research.

Concerning the initial 2007 online survey conducted in the UK, Dr. David Penfold's and Keith Martin's advice was very important before the uploading of the questionnaire, while many different people helped us with the collection of the necessary responses. We would like to thank especially Kimon Polichroniadis (MSc Software Engineering graduate, University of York) for his aid in this part of our research.

Last, my first efforts to understand filtering methods and technology in use for Internet regulation were during my UK-based research, and the aid from Maria Sarigiannidou (MSc Intelligent Web Technologies graduate, Queen Mary University) and Charilaos Thomos (MSc graduate, King's College University) was significant.

Introduction

In this introductory chapter, the authors present very briefly the topic of the book and what an IRS is. What's more, they present the main key areas of interest that their research focuses on its research aims and objectives and the research methods, along with the limitations they have faced.

One of the author, Nikolaos Koumartzis, was first engaged with this research field as an MA student back in 2007-08. Back then, he analysed a specific IRS that was implemented in the United Kingdom, and proposed improvements from a technical and an ethical point of view. In 2010, the authors decided to proceed with further research, not focusing on one country, but targeting many by conducting related surveys. By combining 2007-08 findings with the latter research, the authors' ultimate objective is to propose a Fair Internet Regulation System, i.e. a system that each country's Internet users will be able to interact with, improve, and control.

Due to the fact that the authors' research began in 2007, their initial motivation discussed here is based on events that occurred during that period of time.

MOTIVATION

"Proposals to regulate the Internet are often presented as 'new' solutions to deal with modern problems." E. Ehrlich, 2014

It was in 2004 when for the first time a western democracy openly implemented an Internet Regulation System (IRS), an action that opened a great on-going discussion among researchers focusing on the development of the Internet. This IRS was called CleanFeed, an online mandatory content blocking system that went online in June 2004, and it was implemented by the UK government and British Telecommunications (BT).

From the very beginning, some ethical problems arose from its usage (Bright, 2004· Thompson, 2004) and technical weaknesses showed its ineffectiveness (Clayton, 2005).

Design Issues: Silent vs. Open Model of Internet Censorship

From the very first days of its implementation, various British journalists pointed out ethical issues that would arise or had already arisen from the usage of CleanFeed. Martin Bright of the Observer stated that CleanFeed was *"[...] the first mass censorship of the web attempted in a Western democracy"* (Bright, 2004).

Blocking websites is something highly controversial around the world, and until then such an action was used only by oppressive regimes, such as Saudi Arabia and China (Zittrain & Edelman, 2003· Hermida, 2002).

According to B. Thompson's statements at BBC News, there are two different ways for online censorship: the open way and the silent way (Thompson, 2004). The Saudi Arabian government uses the "open way," which means that the user can understand that a website is blocked and even react to that action. More specifically, in Saudi Arabia, when a website is blocked, the user sees a page that informs him that the access to that website has been denied. Moreover, he can fill an online form stating why he thinks the website should be unblocked in order for the government's Internet Services Unit to consider his request. As B. Thompson states: *"It is censorship, but it is honest censorship [...]"* (Thompson, 2004).

The above comes in contrast to other countries, like China, where a user gets an error massage. This means that he doesn't know if the site is blocked or if there is something wrong with the connection (Bright, 2004). The UK government uses the latter method (the "silent way"), as well.

Among the main questions that had arisen from the design of CleanFeed software were: why is the user not informed that the website he is trying to access is blocked? What is the procedure if someone believes that a website which is blocked should not be? Who will be responsible if a website without illegal content will be blocked?

Apart from the reactions of individual journalists or IT experts, in July 2004 many technically literate, including ISPA (the trade group for the UK's ISPs), drew a sceptical response to the release of CleanFeed's stats from BT (Hunter, 2004). More specifically, even ISPA stated: *"It would be better if CleanFeed stated that the website is blocked and cannot be accessed"* (Richardson, 2004).

Researchers, Child Abusers, and Accusations

According to B. Thompson (2004), for all the above reasons, CleanFeed system set a dangerous precedent for the Internet freedom of speech as it is very simple to start, including the blocking list websites with other content.

On the other hand, BT stated that there were "no plans to extend the project beyond child porn sites." So, was there really a need for further research upon CleanFeed? According to Family Online Safety Institute's Chief Technical Officer Phil Archer: "I guess the only argument [regarding CleanFeed's use] is whether it should be more transparent – should you know that you've been blocked from a site because it contains illegal material. Possibly, but doing so would, of course, advertise its presence and thereby potentially serve to encourage circumventing CleanFeed (which is pretty easy to get round anyway, to be honest). [...] The area of most concern is 'mission creep'. Might BT and others choose to use CleanFeed to legal but – in someone's eyes – undesirable content? I'm satisfied that this is very unlikely" (see appendix 9).

But, on the other hand, UK Home Office's latest statements came in contrast with the initial statements of BT regarding blocking of only child abuse content. According to Professor Lilian Edwards of University of Southampton: "The Home Office has already admitted that it considered asking ISPs to block sites that 'glorified terrorism', even before such content was criminalised by the Terrorism Act 2006 – and that it likes to retain 'flexibility' for such action. If CleanFeed-style technology is imposed on all UK ISPs - by law or voluntarily – it could be the most perfectly invisible censorship mechanism ever invented" (Edwards, 2006; OPSI, 2003).

Technical Weaknesses

Despite all the above ethical and design problems, in November 2005, a very important technical paper by Dr Richard Clayton of University of Cambridge Computer Laboratory was published concerning the technical weaknesses of CleanFeed. Among the others, it proved that the system had many weak points from which an end user or a content provider can circumvent it (Clayton, 2005). But the most important disadvantage of CleanFeed, according to this paper, was that it could be used as an "oracle" by the end user in order to extract a list of the blocked websites (Clayton, 2005).

Following the publication of this paper, BT's Director of Internet Operations Mike Galvin stated that: "We've built a system that won't stop the hardened paedophile [...] CleanFeed's main aim is to stop accidental access from users following links, such as those in spam email" (Mathieson, 2005). Soon, similar statements followed by IWF, too (Grossman, 2006).

Cleanfeed as a Comparative Model

Cleanfeed played a key role in this research and it was the initial motivation for the authors. Among the others, through its analysis and comparison with other IRSs that are implemented by authoritarian regimes around the world, the authors set this book main question: is it possible for a democratic country to design, develop, and implement an IRS that will be accepted by the country's Internet users?

Through technical analysis, historical research, and surveys in different countries around the world, the authors managed to set the key points for the development of their Fair Internet Regulation System (FIRS).

AIMS AND OBJECTIVES

Based on the aforementioned starting point and the already presented motivations, this research aims to develop a blueprint for a Fair Internet Regulation System (FIRS).

FIRS development and implementation scheme will be concluded through literature review of existing IRSs and filtering methods implemented in authoritarian regimes, a thorough analysis of the UK's CleanFeed design (as the first "silent" IRS implemented in western democracy), ethical and technical weaknesses of current IRSs, and surveys conducted around the world.

More specifically, the objectives of the current research are to give answers to three key area inquiries: a. how the current IRSs implemented around the world can be improved, b. what actually the Internet users believe, and c. can a Fair IRS really be developed and implemented? (see Figure 1)

These three key area inquiries can be further broken down into these questions or research approaches:

1. Literature review, historical analysis, and comparative analysis of Internet Regulation Systems

2. Can Internet users accept an Internet Regulation System? Literature review of older related surveys.
3. What kind of online content should a FIRS focus on? Design and run surveys in different countries around the world, in order to use their results as a guide to specifically design a FIRS for each country.
4. How a Fair IRS can be designed? Present and discuss the importance of well-designed surveys, categorisation of targeted online content, technical aspects of FIRS development, ways to circumvent an IRS and possible solutions.
5. How will a Fair Internet Regulation System will work? The ultimate objective of this book is to propose a blueprint for a FIRS development and implementation.

The outcome of this research is multifaceted as this book covers issues and proposes solutions in favour of more than one recipient; future researchers, Internet users, current IRSs, western democracies' governments willing to implement an "open" IRS, and so on.

Figure 1. Research aims and objectives.

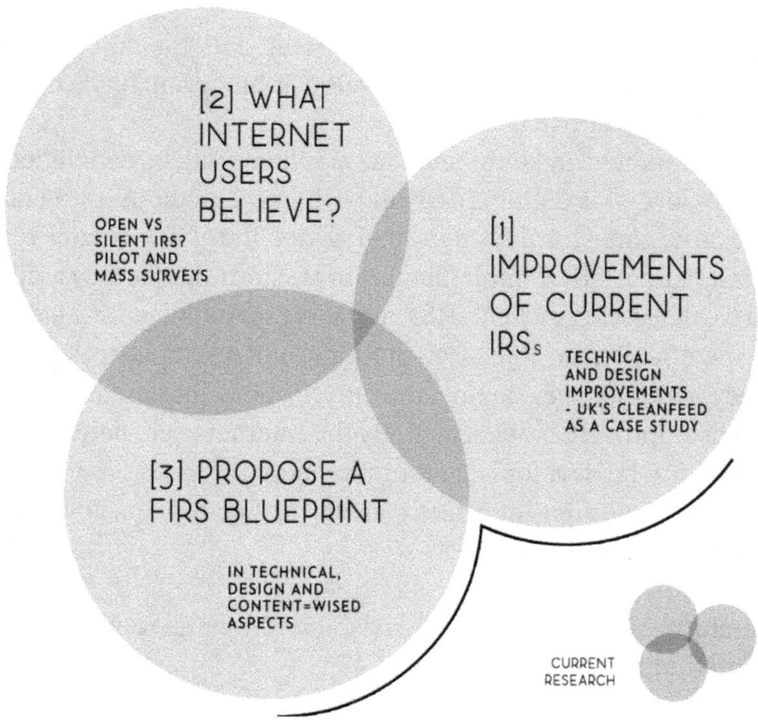

RESEARCH METHODS

As part of this research, several research methods were used.

- First, historical research on the development of online censorship and specific IRSs in use by authoritarian regimes and western democracies.
- Secondly, literature review of technical research papers focused on CleanFeed system that were published, and selected papers focused on past and current content blocking systems that were used to propose specific changes for the UK's CleanFeed and current IRSs in general.
- Thirdly, online questionnaires were set up and surveys were run gathering data and measuring public opinion in 6 different countries. Via the questionnaires, Internet users were asked about several things related to ethical issues that arise from the usage of a IRS. Closed type questions were used in order to extract quantitative results. Based on the feedback, statistical analysis was made in order to provide answers for the 2nd and the 3rd key area stated on section 0.2 above.
- Last, interviews were conducted with academic experts on this topic, in order for this research to keep up-to-date with current technology of today's content blocking systems, and propose specific changes for an IRS in technical terms. For this reason, Dr Richard Clayton of Cambridge University Computer Laboratory was interviewed regarding technical weaknesses of CleanFeed, and Family Online Safety Institute's Chief Technical Officer Phil Archer was interviewed regarding how child protection institutions see content blocking systems of this scale. Moreover, the researcher came in touch with the UK's Internet Archive's Office Manager Paul Forrest Hickman in order to discuss the issue of using this service to circumvent the UK's CleanFeed and current IRSs in general.

Below, all the research methods that were used by the authors are being presented in figure 2.

LIMITATIONS

During their research, the authors faced several limitations based mainly on lack of funds and access to key information of IRSs that are currently implemented around the world.

Figure 2. Research methods used.

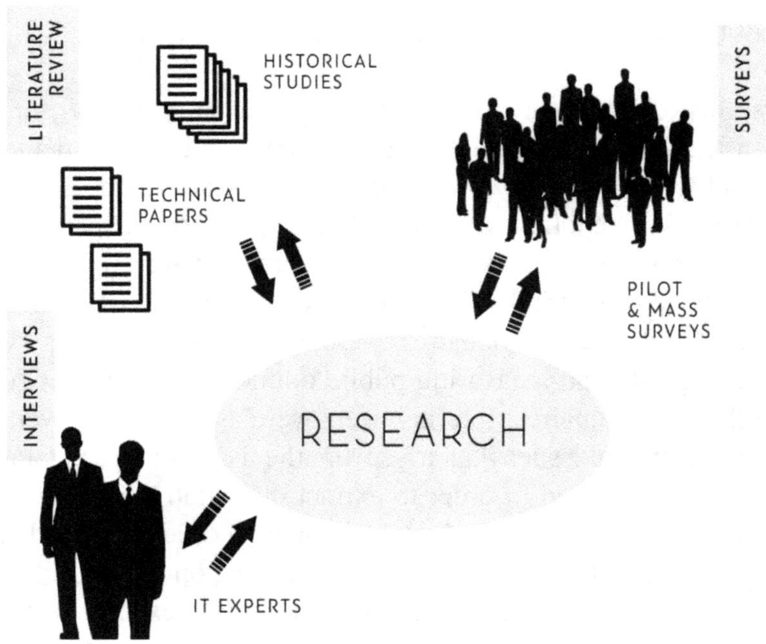

More specifically, extensive research funding can be used to run massive scale surveys in the same or even more countries around the world. Furthermore, access to the code of already implemented IRSs can help understand and solve many issues that these IRSs are facing today.

Taking into account these limitations, the current research was designed and run for almost a decade (2007 to 2016).

STRUCTURE

This book includes 14 chapters and twenty-one appendices. In general, authors' literature review is being presented in Chapter 1, while all the other chapters are the authors' contribution to the research field.

To be more descriptive, this book begins with "Section 1: Literature Review" that includes Chapter 1. Chapter 1 is a literature and history review regarding online censorship, Internet Regulation Systems, and filtering policies around the world, both in authoritarian regimes and western democracies.

Next, the authors continue with the "Section 2: How an IRS Works: A Current and Already Implemented Paradigm" that contains two chapters. In Chapter 2, the authors discuss the widespread misconception that Internet users are undeniably against the implementation of any kind of Internet Regulation System or filtering policies. By presenting results from their initial research in the United Kingdom, the authors highlight the need to measure Internet users' opinion around the world. In Chapter 3, an in-depth analysis of the UK's CleanFeed is being presented, as an example of how a modern IRS in a western democracy works and interacts with the Internet user.

"Section 3: Measuring Public Opinion Around the World" includes eight chapters. In Chapter 4, this book discusses many aspects of the surveys that were conducted by the authors: questionnaire design issues, how the participants were selected, how the data was analysed, the possibility of biased questions, and so forth. In Chapters 5 to 11, valuable survey data is being presented. The results were extracted from six surveys that were conducted around the world: Greece, Germany, Russia, India, Kosovo, and Cyprus. Public opinion in each country is being presented through graphical representation (pies and charts) and thorough statistical analysis (Pearson χ^2, gamma and Kendal's tau-b methods).

Next, this book continues with "Section 4: Research, Design, and Blueprint of a Fair IRS" that includes Chapters 12 and 13. In Chapter 12, a blueprint of a Fair Internet Regulation System (FIRS) is being proposed, with detailed plans about the steps prior to its implementation, and moreover how such a system can interact with Internet users in order for the latter to enrich it according to their needs. In Chapter 13, the authors proceed with the theoretical implementation of the FIRS to Greece, by explaining how a survey can lead to a better questionnaire for the later mass survey, and how the collected data can be translated to specific characteristics of the final FIRS, and so on.

Last, "Section 5: Outcome" includes Chapter 14 in which the authors discuss their conclusions and final remarks, along with proposals for future work.

Finaly, it is important to state that this book is based on research conducted from 2008 until 2017 in seven specific countries: United Kingdom, Greece, Germany, Russia, India, Kosovo and Cyprus. In that sense, this original research and its outcome is being presented in this publication. For readers/researchers interested in the current state (i.e. 2020) of the global phenomenon of Internet Regulation, below you can find an indicative list of recent selected publications and papers to start from:

Aceto, G., Montieri, A., & Pescapé, A. (2017, May). Internet censorship in italy: An analysis of 3g/4g networks. In 2017 IEEE International Conference on Communications (ICC) (pp. 1-6). IEEE.

Acharya, H. B., Ramesh, A., & Jalaly, A. (2019, April). The World from Kabul: Internet Censorship in Afghanistan. In IEEE INFOCOM 2019-IEEE Conference on Computer Communications Workshops (INFOCOM WKSHPS) (pp. 1061-1062). IEEE.

Agrawal, V., & Sharma, P. (2019). Internet Censorship in India. In Proceedings of 10th International Conference on Digital Strategies for Organizational Success.

Al-Saqaf, W. (2016). Internet censorship circumvention tools: Escaping the control of the Syrian regime. Media and Communication, 4(1), 39-50.

Banerjee, A. (2017). Internet censorship in India: the law and beyond. In Digital Democracy in a Globalized World. Edward Elgar Publishing.

Busch, A., Theiner, P., & Breindl, Y. (2018). Internet Censorship in Liberal Democracies: Learning from Autocracies?. In Managing democracy in the digital age (pp. 11-28). Springer, Cham.

Chen, I. C. (2020). Government Internet Censorship Measures and International Law (Vol. 26). LIT Verlag Münster.

Clark, J. D., Faris, R. M., Morrison-Westphal, R. J., Noman, H., Tilton, C. B., & Zittrain, J. L. (2017). The shifting landscape of global internet censorship.

Darer, A., Farnan, O., & Wright, J. (2018, May). Automated discovery of internet censorship by web crawling. In Proceedings of the 10th ACM Conference on Web Science (pp. 195-204).

Dixon, L., Ristenpart, T., & Shrimpton, T. (2016). Network traffic obfuscation and automated internet censorship. IEEE Security & Privacy, 14(6), 43-53.

Druzin, B., & Gordon, G. S. (2018). Authoritarianism and the Internet. Law & Social Inquiry, 43(4), 1427-1457.

Du, Y. R. (2016). Same events, different stories: Internet censorship in the Arab Spring seen from China. Journalism & Mass Communication Quarterly, 93(1), 99-117.

Faust, M. (2019). Does the democratic West 'learn'from the authoritarian East? Juxtaposing German and Chinese Internet censorship and filter bubbles. East Asian Journal of Popular Culture, 5(1), 55-78.

Gebhart, G., & Kohno, T. (2017, April). Internet censorship in Thailand: User practices and potential threats. In 2017 IEEE European symposium on security and privacy (EuroS&P) (pp. 417-432). IEEE.

Giuseppe Aceto and Antonio Pescapé. 2015. Internet Censorship detection: A survey. Computer Networks 83, C, 381--421.

Khattak, S. (2017). Characterization of Internet censorship from multiple perspectives (No. UCAM-CL-TR-897). University of Cambridge, Computer Laboratory.

Nisbet, E. C., Kamenchuk, O., & Dal, A. (2017). A psychological firewall? Risk perceptions and public support for online censorship in Russia. Social Science Quarterly, 98(3), 958-975.

Shen, F., & Tsui, L. (2016). Public opinion toward Internet freedom in Asia: A survey of Internet users from 11 jurisdictions. Berkman Center Research Publication, (2016-8).

Shi, G. (2019). MultiProxy: a collaborative approach to censorship circumvention.

Ververis, V., Isaakidis, M., Loizidou, C., & Fabian, B. (2017, December). Internet censorship capabilities in Cyprus: An investigation of online gambling blocklisting. In International Conference on e-Democracy (pp. 136-149). Springer, Cham.

Wang, Z., Cao, Y., Qian, Z., Song, C., & Krishnamurthy, S. V. (2017, November). Your state is not mine: a closer look at evading stateful internet censorship. In Proceedings of the 2017 Internet Measurement Conference (pp. 114-127).

Zhongjie Wang, Yue Cao, Zhiyun Qian, Chengyu Song, and Srikanth V. Krishnamurthy. 2017. Your state is not mine: a closer look at evading stateful internet censorship. In Proceedings of the 2017 Internet Measurement Conference (IMC '17). Association for Computing Machinery, New York, NY, USA, 114–127. DOI:https://doi.org/10.1145/3131365.3131374

Zittrain, J. L. et al (2017). The Shifting Landscape of Global Internet Censorship, Berkman Klein Center Research Publication No. 2017-4

REFERENCES

Bright, M. (2004, June 6). BT puts block on child porn sites. *The Observer*.

Clayton, R. (2005). Anonymity and Traceability to Cyberspace (Technical Report UCAM-CL-TR-653). *University of Cambridge, Computer Laboratory*. https://www.cl.cam.ac.uk/techreports/UCAM-CL-TR-653.html

Edwards, L. (2006). From child porn to China, in one Cleanfeed. *SCRIPTed - A Journal of Law. Technology in Society*, *3*(3).

Grossman, W. M. (2006). IWF reforms could pave way for UK net censorship. *The Register*. https://www.theregister.co.uk/2006/12/29/iwf_feature/

Hermida, A. (2002). *Saudis Block 2000 websites*. BBC News.

Hunter, P. (2004). Computer Fraud & Security 2004(8). Amsterdam: Elsevier.

Mathieson, S. A. (2005). Back door to the black list. *The Guardian*.

OPSI. (2003). Terrorism Act 2006. *Office of Public Sector Information - National Archives*. http://www.legislation.gov.uk/ukpga/2006/11/contents

Richardson, T. (2004). *ISPA seeks analysis of BT's "CleanFeed" stats – Web filtering figures "could be misleading"*. The Register.

Thompson, B. (2004, June 11). Doubts over web filtering plans. *BBC News*.

Zittrain, J., & Edelman, B. (2003). *Documentation of Internet Filtering Worldwide*. Cambridge, MA: Harvard Law School.

Section 1

Literature Review: The Internet Regulation Phenomenon Worldwide

Chapter 1
Online Filtering Policies Around the World

ABSTRACT

In this chapter, the authors begin by providing definitions about the basic terms in use and then proceed with an introduction to the global phenomenon of internet regulation. Furthermore, the development of online censorship is being presented, and the need for internet regulation is being discussed, along with the role that internet users can actually play. Additionally, the chapter provides a brief history of internet regulation systems (IRSs) around the world, and the authors examine the technical aspects of accessing the internet today and in previous years. Moreover, the reasons that initiate internet regulation policies are being reviewed. Next, the authors present and compare two contradictory kinds of IRSs: open vs. silent IRSs. Last, the authors explain how existing IRSs can be used as a guide in an effort to design and present a blueprint for a fair IRS.

INTRODUCTION

In this chapter, the authors begin by providing definitions about the basic terms in use and then proceed with an introduction to the global phenomenon of Internet regulation In the next section, the development of online censorship is being presented, while in later the need for Internet regulation is discussed, along with the role that Internet users can actually play.

DOI: 10.4018/978-1-5225-9973-9.ch001

This chapter provides a brief history of Internet Regulation Systems (IRSs) around the world, while in the next section the authors examine the technical aspects of accessing the Internet today and in previous years. Moreover, the reasons that initiate Internet regulation policies are being reviewed.

For the first time, the authors present and compare two contradictory kinds of IRSs: Open vs Silent IRSs. The authors further focus on the UK's paradigm (as the first massive IRS that was implemented in a Western democracy), they examine and compare transparent and non-transparent systems they present opinions around the world about why silent IRSs are dangerous for the freedom of speechand how the UK's IRS might become an example for similar systems in the rest of the Western democracies.

Last, the authors explain how existing IRSs can be used as a guide in an effort to design and present a blueprint for a Fair IRS.

Basic Definitions

Former IT (Information Technology) familiarity is essential for fully understanding this book as there are many specialised terms in use throughout the whole dissertation. In this section, the authors present basic terms for the non-technically literate reader in order for the latter to be able to seek further assistance as needed.

- **Censorship:** Censorship is defined as "The suppression or prohibition of any parts of books, films, news, and so on that are considered obscene, politically unacceptable, or a threat to security" (Oxford Living Dictionaries, 2017). In other words, it is the suppression of speech, public communication, or other information that may be considered objectionable, harmful, sensitive, politically incorrect or inconvenient as determined by governments, media outlets, authorities or other groups or institutions. (Merriam-Webster Dictionary, 2017). **Internet or online censorship** is the control or suppression of what can be accessed, published, or viewed on the Internet enacted by regulators, or on their own initiative (Schmidt & Cohen, 2014).
- **Domain Name Server (DNS):** The Domain Name System (DNS) is a hierarchical decentralised naming system for computers, services, or any resource connected to the Internet or a private network. It associates various information with domain names assigned to each of the participating entities.

- **Internet Regulation:** Internet regulation is part of "media regulation" term, which is used to refer to the control or guidance of mass media by governments and other entities. Internet regulation is enforced through laws, rules, or procedures and might have different goals, i.e. intervention to protect a stated "public interest" or establishing common technical standards. Internet regulation can be implemented by both authoritarian regimes and western democracies. In that sense, Internet regulation can act in favour of society's interests.
- **Internet Regulation System (IRS):** Internet Regulation Systems (IRSs) are systems implemented at a national level by governments, delivering to Internet users filtered versions of content on the World Wide Web. A **Fair IRS (FIRS)** is a term proposed by the authors of the present book, and it is used to describe an Internet Regulation System designed, developed, and implemented by taking into account Internet user's opinion and on-going feedback. Ideally, a FIRS is accepted by the majority of each country Internet users.
- **Internet Service Provider (ISP):** An Internet service provider (ISP) is an organisation that provides services for accessing and using the Internet. Internet services typically provided by ISPs include Internet access, Internet transit, domain name registration, web hosting, Usenet service, and collocation.
- **IP address:** An Internet Protocol address (IP address) is a numerical label assigned to each device (e.g., computer, printer) participating in a computer network that uses the Internet Protocol for communication.
- **Network Host/Server:** A network host is a computer or other device connected to a computer network. A network host may offer information resources, services, and applications to users or other nodes on the network.
- **Online content blocking methods:** Internet content is subject to technical censorship methods, including Internet Protocol (IP) address blocking, Domain name system (DNS) filtering and redirection, Uniform Resource Locator filtering, Packet filtering, and so forth.
- **Proxy Server:** In computer networks, a proxy server is a server (a computer system or an application) that acts as an intermediary for requests from clients seeking resources from other servers. A client connects to the proxy server, requesting some service, such as a file, connection, web page, or other resource available from a different server and the proxy server evaluates the request as a way to simplify

and control its complexity. Proxies were invented to add structure and encapsulation to distributed systems.

- **URL:** A Uniform Resource Locator (URL), commonly informally termed a web address (a term which is not defined identically), is a reference to a web resource that specifies its location on a computer network and a mechanism for retrieving it.
- **World Wide Web (WWW):** The World Wide Web (abbreviated WWW or the Web) is an information space where documents and other web resources are identified by Uniform Resource Locators (URLs), interlinked by hypertext links, and can be accessed via the Internet.

There is a common (but sadly false) impression today that the Internet is the only media that, thanks to its nature, cannot be regulated. "The Internet treats censorship as a malfunction and routes around it," John Gilmore, co-founder of the Electronic Frontier Foundation, said more than a decade ago (Barlow, 2016). Unfortunately, since then, many things have changed in disfavour with freedom of speech on the web.

According to Reporters Without Borders, the number of Internet journalists that end up in prison each year worldwide is constantly on the rise. 66 Internet journalists were imprisoned in 2008, 95 in 2009, 116 in 2010 and the number is still rising (Reporters Without Borders, 2013). Indicative of this upward trend is that in 2016 (Reporters Without Borders, 2016), the number of the Internet journalists that were imprisoned soared to 157 (179 journalists were imprisoned in total) and an additional 9 were killed (58 journalists in total). The undoubted leader in this unofficial race is definitely China, with 89 of the 157 Internet journalists being imprisoned inside its borders.

The imprisonment of Internet journalists is the simplest and most straightforward method of Internet censorship, but not the only one in use around the globe. Nowadays, there are numerous of more technologically advanced and effective Internet regulation methods, which not only focus on journalists, but also on the Internet users at a national level.

For example, without trying to be discreet, the Egyptian government (January 2011) ordered ISPs to cut off international connections to the Internet (see graph 1.1) (Cowie, 2011). What's more, Google announced in March 2010 that it stopped complying with China Internet censorship rules, admitting officially that for many years it had been delivering censored search results to the world biggest Internet market (BBC News, 2010). Contrary to Google's actions in China, many telecommunication companies around the world tend to comply with government-level pressure to filter Internet access;

Figure 1. Internet traffic in Egypt during the recent Internet filtering actions (O'Brien, 2011).

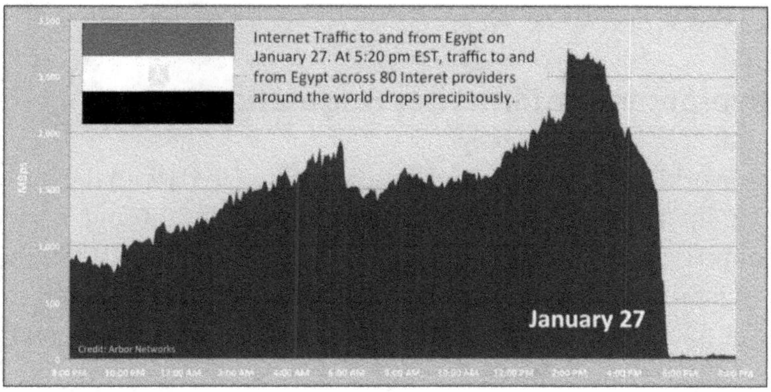

such as Research in Motion (RIM, the Canadian company well-known as the manufacturer of *BlackBerry* smartphones) that applied Internet filtering to all its users in Indonesia (ITU, 2011).

Quite a few recent examples of Internet regulation policies come from Turkey. On March 20th, 2014, Twitter was blocked due to the fact that a national court ordered "protection measures" to be applied to the service (PCWorld, 2014). Next year, on October 10th, 2015, further restrictions were imposed on Twitter by the Turkish government following the first of two bombings in Ankara (Human Rights Watch, 2016). One year later, on October 10th, 2016, Turkish authorities went even further by blocking all Internet access in a great part of the country (east and southeast part) after detaining the elected co-mayors of Diyarbakir city (Hürriyet Daily News, 2016). Turkey's government is increasingly uses Internet regulation policies as a way to suppress political incidents coverage, and prevent civil unrest. Such an example is access blocking of Facebook, Twitter, YouTube, and WhatsApp on November 4th, 2016, following the detention of 11 Free Democratic Party members of the parliament (The Independent, 2016).

Similar incidents took place in many different countries around the world. For example, on February 12th, 2014, the government of Venezuela blocked users' online images on Twitter in its attempt to limit images of protests against shortages and high inflation rate (Laya, Frier & Kurmanaev, 2014).

There are many ways to block the Internet access at a national level: through legislation, silent or open governmental interference, hacking, technologically advanced methods, and so on. This book focuses on one of the most sophisticated technological methods of Internet regulation in use today: the Internet Regulation Systems (IRSs) implemented at a national level by governments, which deliver to each country's Internet users a filtered version of the World Wide Web.

The Development of Internet Regulation

When the World Wide Web was initially set up in 1990 (with the introduction of HTML), Internet users were able to access websites through a very simple and direct procedure as shown in figure 2. Until the end of 1994, there were already 3.2 million hosts-computers connected to the Internet and 3,000 websites online that Internet users could access freely, no matter where they were connected (Penn State University, 2017). Soon afterwards, the freedom of Internet access was about to change in a different way from country to country; in 1990, China banned 100 websites, and Germany attempted for the first time to block a website (EFA, 2002).

Figure 2. Usual way of accessing the Internet (no content blocking system in the middle)

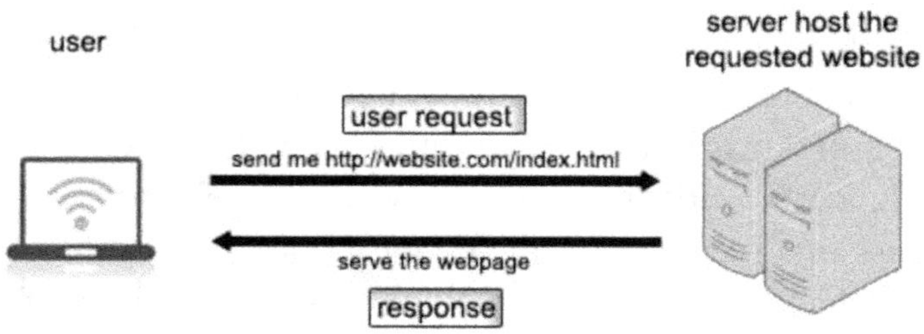

From then until now, more countries have begun to replace the simple way of accessing a website with more sophisticated procedures that give ISPs the opportunity to regulate Internet traffic with ease and efficiency (Koumartzis, 2008).

Over the last decade, Internet regulation is on the rise: in 2006, OpenNet Initiative stated that at least 26 countries were using content blocking systems (ONI, 2008), in 2009 Reporters Without Borders stated that "some sixty countries experienced a form of Web censorship, which is twice as many as in 2008" (Reporters Without Borders, 2010), while within 2010 the OpenNet Initiative became more specific by documenting Internet filtering policies by governments in over forty countries worldwide (Noman & York, 2011).

According to the "Freedom on the Net" survey results of OpenNet Initiative (ONI, 2016), the next years up to 2016 the countries that were identified as "Partly free" or "Not free" were constantly more than 70 percent of the surveyed countries. More specifically, the rates were: 79 percent of 37 surveyed countries in 2011, 71 percent of 47 countries in 2012, 71 percent of 60 countries in 2013, 71 percent of 65 countries in 2014, and 72 percent of 65 countries in 2015.

At the epicentre of this Internet regulation worldwide battle is China: a country that has the world's largest Internet population (approximately 721 million Internet users in 2016 with penetration rate at 52.2 percent, according to InternetLiveStats 2016) and at the same time, as OpenNet Initiative stated quite early, "the world's most advanced Internet censorship and surveillance regime in cyberspace" (Norman & York, 2011). This particular IRS is already being used as a guide for the implementation of similar IRSs in other countries. More specifically, Russia's "Red Web" is the outcome of the "unprecedented cyber collaboration between the countries" (Soldatov & Borogan, 2016).

Following more recent data (Freedom House, 2015), over 3 billion people who had access to the Internet in 2015, 61 percent lived in countries where criticism of the government, military, or ruling family was subject to censorship. What's more, 38 percent lived in countries where popular social media or messaging apps were blocked and 34 percent lived in countries where governments disconnected Internet in 2014-2015 mainly for political reasons.

All the above facts reveal the gradual implementation of Internet regulation systems (manual or more sophisticated IRSs) at a national level that control what it is accessed by each country's citizens. At the dawn of the 21st century, the implementation of IRSs was the case only for authoritarian regimes, but after a decade many western democracies have implemented or tried to implement Internet Regulation Systems (Reporters Without Borders, 2008).

The Need for Internet Regulation and the Role of Internet Users

Internet regulation at a national level is not only possible, but it is already a reality, according to Segura-Serrano (2006), who stated more than ten years ago that "this reality can be confirmed if we take a look at any country's existing regulations in this field." For example, U.S. related laws are numerous: Children's Internet Protection Act of 1998 (FCC, 2000) and Computer Crime Enforcement Act (U.S. Congress, 2000), to name but a few.

Figure 3. Brief History of Internet and its regulation
(party based on Koumartzis 2012, Fake 2008 & EFA 2002).

1969
Internet is born

1971
1st email send

1984
DNS introduced 1000

1990
World Wide Web is born - HTML introduced

1994
3.2 millions hosts - 3000 websites

1996
China bans 100 websites - GERMANY 1st

1997
19.5 millions hosts - 1.2 million websiteshosts

1999
Saudi Arabia government regulates Internet

2000
UK Government's Communications White Paper - no third-party regulation

2004
Norway launches an Internet filtering system - BT launches CleanFeed in UK

2005
Sweden launch an Internet filtering system

2008
95% of UK ISPs blocks banned websites (IWF list)

2009
60 countries experienced a form of Web censorship, which is twice as many as in 2008

2010
Over 40 countries worldwide implement Internet filtering policies

2011-2015
Constantly more than 70% of the surveyed countries are identified as "Partly free" or "Not free" (OpenNet Initiative)

2016
Russia and China collaborates to develop Russia's Red Web

At an international level, U.S.'s Digital Millennium Copyright Act of 1998 (GPO.org, 2010) and E.U.'s Electronic Commerce Directive 2000/31/EC (EUR-Lex, 2002) introduced to the international Internet community a highly criticised process called "notice and take-down" (Gallagher, 2002; Article 19, 2013), while the highly controversial Trans Pacific Partnership Agreement (USTR.gov, 2015) that was signed in February 2016 tackles numerous issues regarding Internet regulation on a global scale (Isfeld, 2015; Binder, 2016; Sutton, 2015).

Taking into account regional and international legislation, there is definitely a need for certain online information to be regulated. Hate-speech & defamatory content (both tackled by the International Covenant on Civil and Political Rights 1966), copyright infringement (tackled by various national and international copyright laws), child pornography content (tackled by the United Nations Convention on the Rights of the Child 1989) are just a few topics that are widely censored worldwide in all traditional media; online media cannot be an exception.

Based on all the above, many university researchers, IT experts, and media representatives are engaged in a discussion regarding what kind of censorship must be implemented: transparent (open) to the user or non-transparent (silent). Surprisingly, even though such policies affect Internet users the most, there are very few surveys being conducted regarding what users think about the implementation of IRSs.

According to older related surveys conducted on a massive scale, Internet users are split in half regarding where they stand about Internet regulation (GlobalScan Incordporeated, 2010), while smaller surveys (premised upon limited but highly educated samples) show that the majority of Internet users prefer the implementation of some short of "open" Internet regulation systems (i.e. systems that they will be able to interact with, enrich, or even correct their database) to no Internet regulation whatsoever (Koumartzis & Veglis, 2010· Koumartzis, 2008).

As stated by John Palfrey, executive director of the Berkman Centre for Internet and Society at Harvard Law School, this issue is an open question as "Some people would say that certain kinds of information should be banned" (Blau, 2007). There is a worst-case scenario, though, as described by Hamade in which "filtering creeps into the system in an ad hoc way without formal evaluation of the standards [...]" (2008).

This debate is further explored in Chapters 5 to 11, where several specialised surveys around the world are being discussed, and valuable data is being presented, along with an in-depth statistical analysis.

A Brief History of Internet Regulation Systems Around the World

Internet regulation systems have a long history of development and implementation in many countries worldwide, as it is stated in various sources (Zittrain & Edelman, 2003· Ramachander, 2008· Libertus, 2008).

China used to spend every year extensive resources, trying to build one of the largest and most sophisticated filtering systems worldwide (ONI, 2009), while Saudi Arabia State uses (starting from 2004) a web proxy system to block requests for banned websites from a list created by citizen's URL reports (Internet Services Unit, 2004). Concerning European countries, Norwegian Telenor and KRIPOS (the Norwegian National Criminal Investigation Service) introduced a child pornography blocking system in Norway in October 2004, which sends to the user a web page containing information about the filter and a link to KRIPOS (Telenor Norge, 2004). Moreover, Telenor introduced a content blocking system in Sweden too in 2005, based on Norway's system (Telenor, 2005). Similar content blocking systems are also implemented in many European countries, such as Denmark, Finland, Netherlands, Switzerland, Italy, and others (Libertus, 2008).

Despite the fact that many countries individually started a limited and voluntary implementation of ISP-level blocking programs, as mentioned above, the landmark model to a large-scale blocking era came from the UK with the implementation of the CleanFeed model (Ramachander, 2008). It was created in 2003 by BT (British Telecom) in consultation with the UK Home Office and was implemented in BT's network on June 9 2004 (Bright, 2004). The UK government gave Internet Service Providers (ISPs, i.e. BT, Virgin, etc.) a deadline in 2008 to block all access to websites that host illegal images of child abuse (Ballard, 2006).

Soon, many other countries followed the UK's model. In 2006, Canada's largest ISPs announced the launch of Project CleanFeed Canada (CTV News, 2006) based on the UK CleanFeed model in order to block access to child pornography websites. In 2007, Australia's Telecommunications Minister Stephen Conroy announced that a mandatory content blocking system will be implemented and that it will focus on child abuse content and "inappropriate material" (ABC, 2007). The CleanFeed model was abandoned in Australia after 2010 elections.

More recent examples include Turkey (2014, Turkish Prime Minister Recep Tayyip Erdoğan vowed to "wipe out Twitter" and Turkey's ISPs complied by blocking access to Twitter), Brazil (2015, Brazilian government blocked WhatsApp for 16 hours), and so on. Neither of the last two countries used sophisticated IRSs, but rather simple systems using Internet regulation methods, such as DNS poisoning.

Technical Aspects: Accessing Internet Now and Then

In this section, the chapter analyses the issue from a technological point of view. Concerning Internet regulation policies, there are many different ways to control what Internet users can access online: from sophisticated systems that filter search results from search engines (Meiss & Menczer, 2008· Moroi & Yoshiura, 2008), to the simplest and most efficient way of having and monitoring a few government controlled access points inside a country (such as in Cuba· ONI, 2009).

But the most common in use great-scale system among countries with authoritarian regimes and even more among western democracies is content blocking (or content filtering) mechanism using "blacklists." There are many different such mechanisms used in the past around the world, but three of them can be considered the basic and most commonly used by ISPs and network operators: a) *packet dropping*, b) *DNS poisoning,* and c) *content filtering* (Clayton, 2005· Koumartzis, 2008).

As mentioned above, all the three mechanisms use "black lists" to determine what they have to block/filter. "Black lists" are lists of generic domain names or very specific URLs that are created manually by humans. The exact procedure for creating those "black lists" differs from country to country. For example, authoritarian regimes prefer to have government officials to prepare those lists, while Western democracies (such as the United Kingdom) depend in some extent on Internet users' complaints about illegal online content through hotlines, and so forth.

Packet dropping mechanism described in figure 4 is considered a quite simple mechanism and its operation is based on a list consisting of the websites' IP addresses to be blocked. Users' requests for these IPs are discarded, thus no connection with the requested server is made. The main disadvantage of *packet dropping* is that it is a massive blocking system without accuracy.

A very important advantage of this mechanism is that it can identify the type of IP and thus implement selective filtering, i.e. blocks HTTP packets for a particular IP address, but leaves email unblocked. But, there is a crucial disadvantage, too. This particular kind of system blocks all the web content

Figure 4. Packet dropping system.

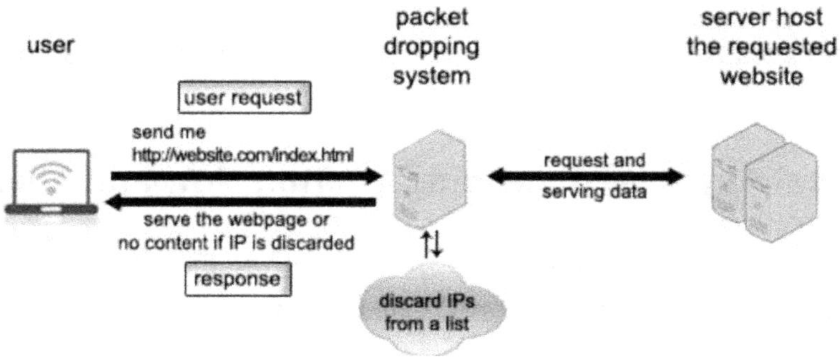

of a particular IP address as it is a massive blocking system and not accurate. For example, Edelman conducted experiments that showed that there is a significant risk of over-blocking with systems based exclusively on IP addresses (Edelman, 2003).

Systems based on *DNS poisoning* (see figure 5) are interfering in the DNS lookup process for the blocked websites' hostnames, in order to prevent the correct IP address from being returned.

Figure 5. DNS poisoning system

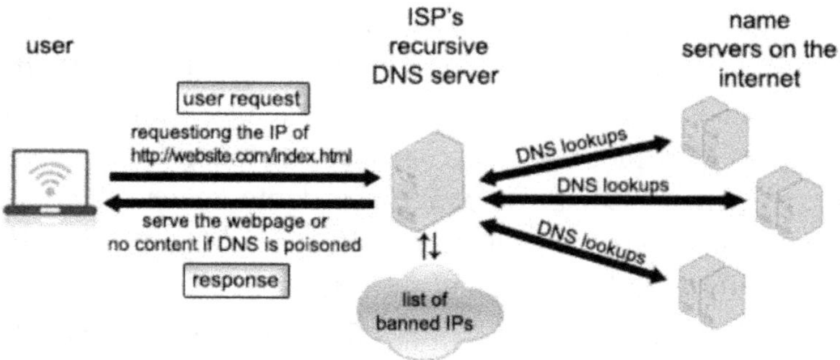

The main advantage of this mechanism, besides its simplicity, is that the blocking does not affect other domain names hosted on the same server, as in the case of the *packet dropping* system above. On the other hand, the main disadvantage of this system is that it blocks all the content of the blocked domain names (i.e. over-blocking). As Dr. R. Clayton says in his paper *Failures of a Hybrid Content Blocking System*: "Thus it would not be an appropriate solution for blocking content hosted somewhere like geocities.com; blocking one site would also block about three million others" (Clayton, 2008). Moreover, DNS poisoning blocks other services besides IP addresses, such as email. For a case of DNS poisoning over-blocking, please refer to Dornseif's research regarding right-wing and Nazi-related content in Germany (2003).

What's more, there is an issue of under-blocking in cases where a user types in an IP address and not a hostname. In this case, the browser uses the IP address and does not make a DNS lookup.

Last, *content filtering* systems (see figure 6) are based on a one by one URL examination. For this reason, they are very accurate on blocking exactly everything that is contained in a list of blocking URLs (i.e. specific images, videos, audio clips, and so on), but at the same time they are by far the most demanding in processing power and for this reason the most expensive systems.

Figure 6. Content filtering system

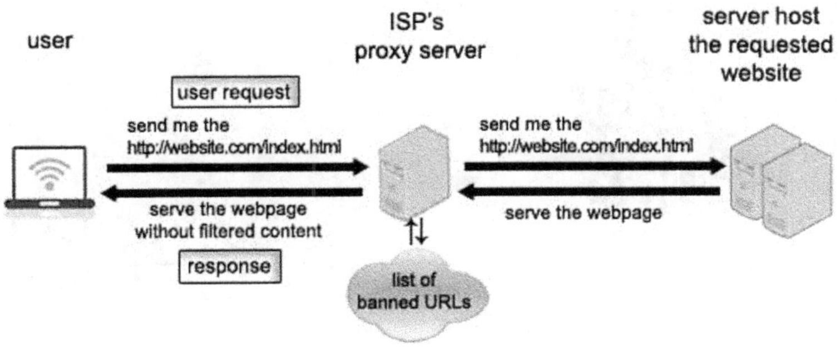

Thus, content filtering systems are not preferred by ISPs.

The crucial disadvantages that all the above systems have lead to the development of hybrid systems in order to combine the advantages of two or even three of those mechanisms. For example, thanks to Dr. Clayton's research, it is well known today that BT and UK Home Office tried through CleanFeed to develop an accurate system at a low cost, leading to a 2-stage system, using both *packet dropping* and *content filtering* mechanisms (see figure 7). In brief, the first stage resembles a packet dropping system, except that it does not discard requests, but redirects them to the second stage. In the second stage, a web proxy resembles a content filtering system. DNS poisoning was avoided in both stages in order for CleanFeed software not to affect any protocols (such as email) other than web traffic.

Figure 7. CleanFeed's design
(based on a figure in Clayton, R., 2008, Failures of a Hybrid Content Blocking System, University of Cambridge, Computer Laboratory)

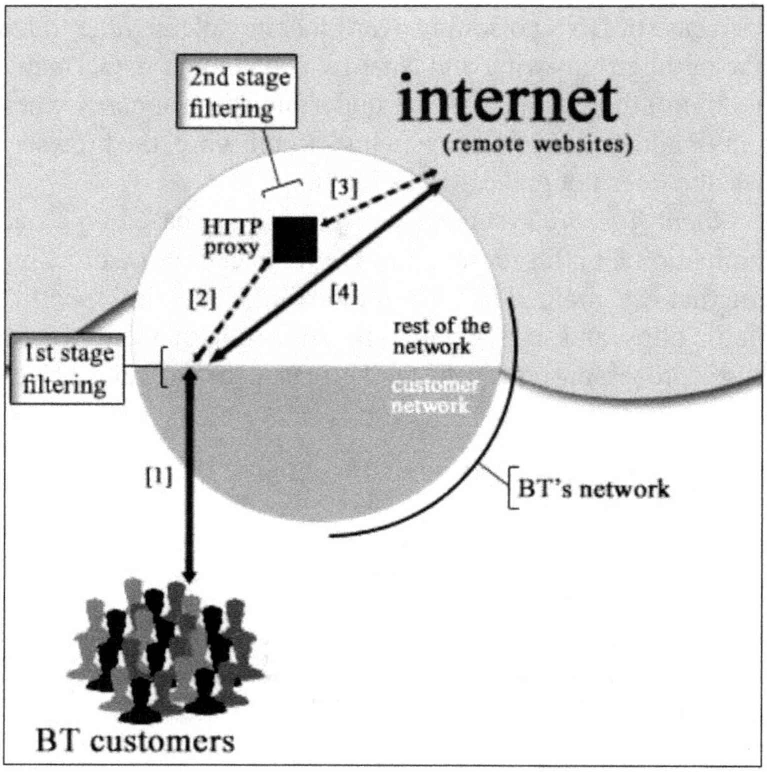

Currently, such content blocking systems (hybrid or not) are used in many countries around the world, such as China, Saudi Arabia, the United Kingdom, and Canada. According to OpenNet Initiative (ONI) research published in a book titled *Access Denied*, there were at least 26 countries in 2006 that were using content blocking systems, and ONI predicted that many more would follow in the years to come. According to Freedom House (2016b), approximately 64% of the 65 countries (that were researched) experienced some form of web censorship in 2016. What's more, this is the sixth consecutive year that Internet freedom has declined, while two-thirds of all the Internet users "live in countries were criticism of the government, military, or ruling family are subject to censorship" (FreedomHouse, 2016b).

Other well-known content blocking mechanisms (see figure 7) are: Internet Protocol (IP) address blocking (in which access to a certain IP address is denied), connection reset, networking disconnection (in which all the routers, software and hardware, are cut off), portal censorship & search results removal (for example, Google.de and Google.fr remove Neo-Nazi and other listings in compliance with German and French law), computer network attacks & denial-of-service attacks, and so forth. (ZDNet, 2015· ONI, 2015· Norman, 2011). Some of these mechanisms are quite primitive (such as networking disconnection), and some more advanced (such as search results removal).

Figure 8. Common content blocking mechanisms

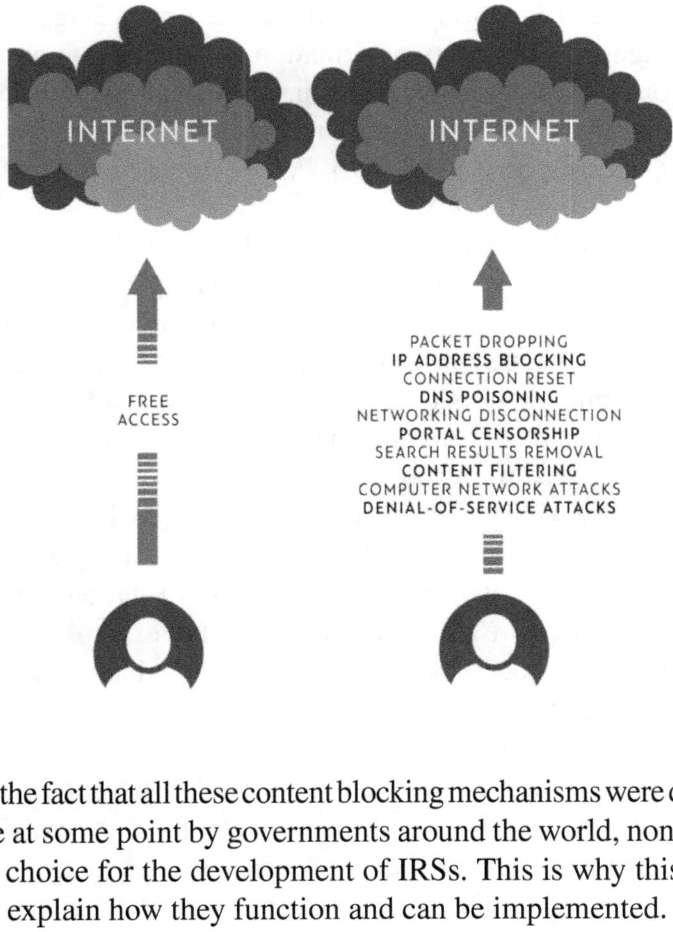

Despite the fact that all these content blocking mechanisms were documented to be in use at some point by governments around the world, none of them is a common choice for the development of IRSs. This is why this book does not further explain how they function and can be implemented.

The Reasons Behind Internet Regulation Policies

The reasons behind the implementation of such systems differ from state to state, and according to OpenNet Initiative (ONI, 2008) they can be categorised as a) political, b) social, c) conflict and security, and d) Internet tools (i.e. proxy servers, anonymisers, and so on).

For example, South Korea employs an Internet Regulation system mainly to block online content related to conflict and security reasons, while Singapore, Sudan, and Oman focus on content related to special social issues in each country. To be more specific, different Internet Regulation systems implemented around the world target online content regarding free expression and media freedom, political transformation and opposition parties, human rights, environmental issues, public health, gay/lesbian content, pornography, gambling, minority faiths, search engines, anonymisers and circumvention, hate speech, and so forth (ONI, 2008). For an extensive list, please refer to Figure 9.

While many topics are quite expected to be regulation targets, there are some that seem at least strange. For example, dating related online content is banned in Burma, Sudan, Qatar, and Yemen, while Voice over Internet Protocol (VoIP) is banned in Belize and the United Arab Emirates. The most important thing here is that, in order to understand why some topics are targets and some others are not, someone needs to study each country's political, social, and cultural context.

Regarding what kind of online content targets each country, Figure 9 presents the research of OpenNet Initiative. There are many examples where governments choose to pervasively or substantially filter only specific kinds of content, while others are left totally unfiltered. For example, Oman is doing pervasive filtering in social, but not at all in political and security content. While Libya is not filtering social, security, and Internet tools, its government substantially filters political content.

As a conclusion, there are many countries that are not filtering in general, but focus only on a very specific kind of content (i.e. Azerbaijan, Jordan, Singapore, and others), and on the other hand, there are many countries that implement Internet filtering policies extensively and without a topic-focused approach. There is a quite important difference between these two kinds of approaches.

Figure 9. Categories subject to Internet Filtering.
Reproduced from (ONI, 2010)

- Free expression and media freedom
- Political transformation and opposition parties
- Political reform, legal reform, and governance
- Militants, extremists, and separatists
- Human rights
- Foreign relations and military
- Minority rights and ethnic content
- Women's rights
- Environmental issues
- Economic development
- Sensitive or controversial history, arts, and literature
- Hate speech
- Sex education and family planning
- Public health
- Gay/lesbian content
- Pornography
- Provocative attire
- Dating
- Gambling
- Gaming
- Alcohol and drugs
- Minority faiths
- Religious conversion, commentary, and criticism
- Anonymizers and circumvention
- Hacking
- Blogging domains and blogging services
- Web hosting sites and portals
- Voice over Internet Protocol (VOIP)
- Free e-mail
- Search engines
- Translation
- Multimedia sharing
- P2P
- Groups and social networking
- Commercial sites

Figure 10. Summary of filtering
Reproduced from (ONI, 2008b)

	Political	Social	Conflict & Security	Internet tools
Azerbaijan	◆	✕	✕	✕
Bahrain	◆◆	◆	✕	◆
Belarus	○	○	✕	✕
China	◆◆◆	◆◆	◆◆◆	◆◆
Ethiopia	◆◆	◆	◆	◆
India	✕	✕	◆	◆
Iran	◆◆◆	◆◆◆	◆◆	◆◆◆
Jordan	◆	✕	✕	✕
Kazakhstan	○	✕	✕	✕
Libya	◆◆	✕	✕	✕
Morocco	✕	✕	◆	◆
Myanmar	◆◆◆	◆◆	◆◆	◆◆
Oman	✕	◆◆◆	✕	◆◆
Pakistan	◆	◆◆	◆◆◆	◆
Saudi Arabia	◆◆	◆◆◆	◆	◆◆
Singapore	✕	◆	✕	✕
South Korea	✕	◆	◆◆◆	✕
Sudan	✕	◆◆◆	✕	◆◆
Syria	◆◆◆	◆	◆	◆◆
Tajikistan	◆	✕	✕	✕
Thailand	◆	◆◆	✕	◆
Tunisia	◆◆◆	◆◆◆	◆	◆◆
United Arab Emirates	◆	◆◆◆	◆	◆◆
Uzbekistan	◆◆	◆	✕	◆
Vietnam	◆◆◆	◆	✕	◆◆
Yemen	◆	◆◆◆	◆	◆◆

◆◆◆ Pervasive filtering | ◆◆ Substantial filtering | ◆ Selective filtering |
○ Suspected filtering | ✕ No evidence

Open vs. Silent (Invisible) Internet Regulation Systems

While it is easy to understand the reasons behind the implementation of such great-scale systems in authoritarian regimes, it is quite complicated when western democracies are being considered. Many questions have to be answered, starting with: "Why do democratic governments need to use content blocking systems?" and "How did the public opinion in those countries accept in the first place the implementation of such powerful regulation tools?"

The UK's Paradigm

In order for some answers to be found, the UK's CleanFeed system (as an example of IRS implemented in a Western democracy) is analysed in depth in chapter 3. CleanFeed is a mandatory content blocking system –non-transparent for BT's users– that went online in the UK in June 2004, designed by the UK government and British Telecommunications plc (BT). It is used by the UK Internet Service Providers (ISPs i.e. BT, Virgin, and so forth) to block access to websites that host illegal child abuse content. The list of the banned websites is prepared and circulated by Internet Watch Foundation; a UK Hotline for reporting illegal online content also known as IWF (Koumartzis, 2008· Ballard, 2006).

So, while blocking websites is considered worldwide to be a highly controversial issue, it is widely accepted that many democratic countries employ similar methods to regulate specific illegal content, such as child pornography material. Therefore, what is the problem of many individual researchers and academic communities?

It was on June 6th, 2004 that Martin Bright of *Observer* stated that the UK's CleanFeed system was the first mass censorship of the web implemented in a Western democracy (Bright, 2004). What's more, according to BBC News and Thompson, CleanFeed has set a dangerous precedent for the Internet freedom of speech, as the system was already there and it was very simple to just start including in the blocking list websites with any kind of content (Thompson, 2004).

This was the beginning of implementation of non-transparent (silent) Internet regulation systems in western democracies.

Transparent vs. Non-Transparent Systems

As BBC News stated, there are two different ways of filtering online content: the open way and the silent way. The Saudi Arabian government uses the open way, which means that the user can understand that a website is blocked and even react to that action. More specifically, in the Middle Eastern country, when a website is blocked, the user sees a page that informs him that access to that website has been denied. The user can also fill an online form stating why he/she thinks the website should be unblocked. The request is sent to the government's Internet Services Unit for consideration. This form of censorship is considered to be honest censorship (Thompson, 2004).

The system above contradicts other countries' systems, like China, where the user gets an error message. The message does not inform the user whether the website has been blocked or if there was a problem with the connection. The latter method (non-transparent or silent) is used by the UK government's CleanFeed, as well.

Why Is It Dangerous?

There are many critical questions that arise from the use of silent Internet regulation systems: why does the user not get informed that the website he is trying to access is blocked? What is the procedure if someone believes that a website blocked should not be? Who will be responsible if a website without illegal content gets blocked? A sceptical response to the release of CleanFeed's stats from BT arose not only from individual journalists or IT experts, but also from many technically literate groups, including ISPA (the trade group for the UK's ISPs· Richardson, 2004).

Regarding the need for further research on the UK's Cleanfeed, there is an ongoing discussion. Family Online Safety Institute's Chief Technical Officer Phil Archer considers the possibility of BT or others to use CleanFeed to block legal but unwanted material highly unlikely (Koumartzis, 2010).

On the other hand, Professor Lilian Edwards (University of Southampton) recalls that the UK's Home Office has already admitted that it has considered asking ISPs to block sites that 'glorify terrorism', even before such content was criminalised by the Terrorism Act in 2006. Moreover, she states that Home Office retains 'flexibility' for such action, and believes that, if CleanFeed-like technology is imposed on all the UK ISPs, it will be the perfect invisible censorship mechanism ever invented (Edwards, 2006).

From the UK to Western Democracies

Having all these concerns in mind, it is quite disturbing that more democracies worldwide followed the UK model. For example, in 2006, Canada's largest ISPs announced the launch of Project CleanFeed Canada based on the UK CleanFeed model in order to block access to child pornography websites (CTV News, 2006).

In 2007, Australia's Telecommunications Minister Stephen Conroy announced that a mandatory content blocking system would be implemented focusing on child abuse content and "inappropriate material" (ABC, 2007). What's more, it was announced that IWF's list would be used as a basis for Australia's CleanFeed list, which would initially contain 9.000 websites (Pauli, 2008).

In 2009 though, regional press (citing wikileaks.org) revealed that many non-child-abuse websites were in the Australia's black list, such as a website promoting voluntary euthanasia (Earley, 2009). Due to the above, Australia's mandatory content blocking system has not been implemented yet.

CONCLUSION

Existing IRSs as a Guide

In conclusion, Internet regulation and online content blocking is already a reality for most of the part of our world. In figures 11 and 12, recent data is being presented from 2015 and 2016 Freedom of the Press Reports: citizens in 136 countries (or 68.7% of a total 198 countries that were surveyed) are facing some form of censorship. Concerning the Internet regulation aspect, many governments in different countries use content filtering mechanisms, advanced systems, or even primitive ways to control online access of their Internet users.

Therefore, in the next chapter, the authors try to ask the "right" question. Are the Internet users open to accept the implementation of a fair IRS, or do they prefer no Internet regulation at all? The answer can differ between different countries, so this book begins with the United Kingdom as the latter was the first country (from the western democracies) that an IRS was implemented.

Figure 11. 2015 Freedom of the Press
(Freedom House, 2015)

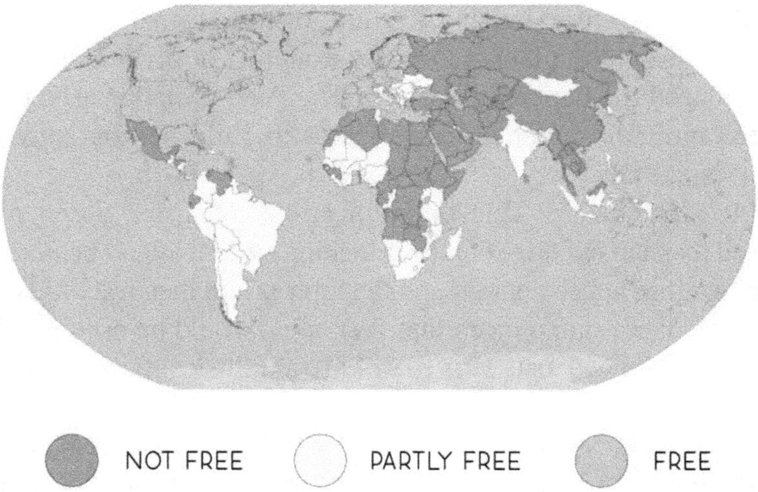

Figure 12. 2016 Freedom of the Press
(Freedom House, 2016).

REFERENCES

ABC. (2007). *Conroy announces mandatory Internet filters to protect children.* ABC News.

Article 19. (2013). *European Court strikes serious blow to free speech online.* Retrieved from https://www.article19.org/resources.php/resource/37287/en/european-court-strikes-serious-blow-to-free-speech-online

Ballard, M. (2006). *Govt sets target for blocking child porn sites.* https://www.theregister.co.uk/2006/05/18/uk_site_blocking/

Barlow, J. P. (2016). Censorship 2000. *OnTheInternet Society.* https://www.isoc.org/oti/articles/1000/barlow.html

BBC News. (2010). Google stops censoring search results in China. *BBC.* http://news.bbc.co.uk/2/hi/business/8581393.stm

Binder, K. (2016). The Trans-Pacific Partnership (TPP) Potential regional and global impacts. *EPRS | European Parliamentary Research Service, European Parliament.* https://www.europarl.europa.eu/RegData/etudes/BRIE/2016/582028/EPRS_BRI(2016)582028_EN.pdf

Blau, J. (2007, May 18). Report: More Governments Filter Online Content. *ABC News.*

Bright, M. (2004, June 6). BT puts block on child porn sites. *The Observer.*

Clayton, R. (2005). Anonymity and Traceability to Cyberspace (Technical Report UCAM-CL-TR-653). *University of Cambridge, Computer Laboratory.* https://www.cl.cam.ac.uk/techreports/UCAM-CL-TR-653.html

Clayton, R. (2008). Failures of a Hybrid Content Blocking System. In G. Danezis & D. Martin (Eds.), *Privacy Enhancing Technologies, Fifth International Workshop, PET 2005.* Berlin: Springer Verlag.

Cowie, J. (2011). *Egypt Leaves the Internet.* https://www.countercurrents.org/cowie280111.htm

CTV News. (2006, Nov. 23). New initiative will see ISPs block child porn sites. *CTV News.*

Dornseif, M. (2003). Government mandated blocking of foreign Web content, Security, E-Learning, EServices. *Proceedings of the 17 DFN-Arbeitstagung uber Kommunikationsnetze*, 617–648.

Earley, D. (2009). *Rudd's Internet blacklist includes dentist, kennel, tuckshop*. The Courier-Mail.

Edelman, B. (2003). Web Sites Sharing IP Addresses: Prevalence and Significance. *Cyber.Harvard.edu* https://cyber.harvard.edu/archived_content/people/edelman/ip-sharing/

Edwards, L. (2006). From child porn to China, in one Cleanfeed. *SCRIPTed - A Journal of Law. Technology in Society*, *3*(3).

EFA. (2002). Internet Censorship: Law & policy around the world. *Electronic Frontiers Australia*. https://www.efa.org.au/Issues/Censor/cens3.html

FCC. (2000). Children's Internet Protection Act of 1998 (CIPA) - Consumer guide. *Federal Communications Commission*. http://transition.fcc.gov/cgb/consumerfacts/cipa.pdf

Freedom House. (2015). 2015 Freedom of the Press Report. *FreedomHouse*. https://freedomhouse.org/report/freedom-press/freedom-press-2015#.WMhs23SGNAY

FreedomHouse. (2016b). Freedom on the Net 2016, *FreedomHouse*. https://freedomhouse.org/sites/default/files/FOTN_2016_BOOKLET_FINAL.pdf

Gallagher, D. (2002). New Economy; A copyright dispute with the Church of Scientology is forcing Google to do some creative linking. *The New York Times*. https://www.nytimes.com/2002/04/22/business/new-economy-copyright-dispute-with-church-scientology-forcing-google-some.html?src=pm

GlobalScan Incordporated. (2010). *Four in Five Regard Internet Access as a Fundamental Right: Global Poll*. BBC World Service.

GPO.gov. (2010). Digital Millennium Copyright Act of 1998 (DMCA) - 17 U.S.C., Chapter 5: Copyright Infringement and Remedies. *U.S. Government Printing Office*. https://www.gpo.gov/fdsys/pkg/USCODE-2010-title17/html/USCODE-2010-title17-chap5-sec506.htm

Hamade, S. N. (2008). Internet Filtering and Censorship. In *Fifth International Conference on Information Technology: New Generations*. New York: IEEE Computer Society.

Human Rights Watch. (2015). Open Letter to the Government of Turkey on Internet Blocking and Free Expression. *Human Rights Watch*. https://www.hrw.org/news/2015/10/29/open-letter-government-turkey-internet-blocking-and-free-expression

Hürriyet Daily News. (2016). CHP deputy Tanrıkulu slams internet cuts in eastern, southeastern Turkey. *Hürriyet Daily News*.

Internet Services Unit. (2004). *Local Content Filtering Procedure*. Riyadh: King Abdulaziz City for Science and Technology, Internet Services Unit.

Isfeld, G. (2015). Forget NAFTA, the TPP is the new 'gold standard' of global trade. Financial Post. Toronto: National Post. https://business.financialpost.com/news/economy/forget-nafta-the-tpp-is-the-new-gold-standard-of-global-trade

ITU. (2011). Indonesia: RIM to filter internet for BlackBerry users. International Telecommunication Union.

Koumartzis, N. (2008). *BT's CleanFeed and Online Censorship in UK: Improvements for a More Secure and Ethically Correct Systeym* (Doctoral dissertation). University of the Arts London, London College of Communication, London.

Koumartzis, N. (2010). *Greek Internet Regulation Survey*. WebObserver.net.

Koumartzis, N., & Veglis, A. (2011). Internet Regulation: The Need for More Transparent Internet Filtering Systems and improved measurement of public opinion on Internet Filtering. *First Monday, 16*(10). https://firstmonday.org/ojs/index.php/fm/article/view/3266/3071

Koumartzis, N., & Veglis, A. (2011). On the Pursue for a Fair Internet Regulation system. *Sixteenth IEEE Symposium on Computers and Communications (ISCC11)*.

Koumartzis, N., & Veglis, A. (2011). The Future of Internet Regulation: Current Trends, a Dangerous Precedent and the Role of Internet Users. *Euro-NF International Workshop on Traffic and Congestion Control for the Future Internet*.

Koumartzis, N., & Veglis, A. (2012). Internet Regulation: A New Approach: Outline of a system formed to be controlled by the Internet Users. *Computer Technology and Application, 3*(1), 16–23.

Laya, P., Frier, S., & Kurmanaev, A. (2014). *Venezuelans Blocked on Twitter as Opposition Protests Mount*. Bloomberg News.

Libertus. (2008). ISP 'Voluntary'/ Mandatory Filtering. *Libertus*.

Meiss, M., & Menczer, F. (2008). Visual comparison of search results: A censorship case study. *First Monday, 13*(7). doi:10.5210/fm.v13i7.2019

Merriam-Webster Dictionary. (2017). *Censorship – Definition*. https://www.merriam-webster.com/dictionary/censorship

Moroi, T., & Yoshiura, N. (2008). Discovering Web Pages Censored by Search Engines in Japan. In *Proceedings of 2008 International Conference on Computational Intelligence for Modelling Control & Automation*, (pp. 1171-1176). Vienna: IEEE Computer Society. 10.1109/CIMCA.2008.137

Norman, H. (2011). The Emergence of Open and Organized Pro-Government Cyber Attacks in the Middle East: The Case of the Syrian Electronic Army. *OpenNet Initiative*.

Norman, H., & York, J. C. (2011). *West Censoring East: The Use of Western Technologies by Middle East Censors 2010-2011*. OpenNet Initiative.

O' Brien, D. (2011). Watching Egypt disappear from the Internet. *Committee to Protect Journalists*. https://cpj.org/blog/2011/01/watching-egypt-disappear-from-the-internet.php

ONI. (2008). *Access Denied: The Practice and Policy of Global Internet Filtering (OpenNetInitiative)*. MIT Press.

ONI. (2008b). Table 1.5 | Summary of filtering. In *Access Denied: The Practice and Policy of Global Internet Filtering* (Vol. 19). MIT Press.

ONI. (2009). Country Report: China. *OpenNetInitiative*.

ONI. (2010). Table 2.4 | Spectrum of Cyberspace Content Controls in the CIS. In *Access Controlled* (Vol. 23). MIT Press.

ONI. (2015). Pulling the Plug: A Technical Review of the Internet Shutdown in Burma. *OpenNet Initiative*.

ONI. (2016). Internet censorship and surveillance by country. *OpenNet Initiative*.

Oxford Living Dictionaries. (2017). *Definition of censorship in English*. https://en.oxforddictionaries.com/definition/censorship

Pauli, D. (2008). *No opt-out of filtered Internet.* ComputerWorld Australia.

PCWorld. (2014). 'We'll eradicate Twitter': Turkey blocks Twitter access. *PCWorld.* https://www.pcworld.com/article/2110760/turkey-appears-to-have-blocked-twitter.html

Penn State University. (2017). Brief History of the Internet. *Psu.edu.* https://www.courses.psu.edu/ist/ist250_fja100/ist250online/Content/IHistory_T1L3.htm

Ramachander, S. (2008). Research: Europe. *OpenNet Initiative.*

Reporters Without Borders. (2010). Web 2.0 versus Control 2.0. *Reporters Without Borders.* https://rsf.org/en/news/web-20-versus-control-20

Reporters Without Borders. (2016). Press Freedom Barometer - netizens imprisoned. *Reporters Without Borders.* https://rsf.org/en/barometer

Schmidt, E. E., & Cohen, J. (2014). The Future of Internet Freedom. *New York Times.* https://www.nytimes.com/2014/03/12/opinion/the-future-of-internet-freedom.html

Segura-Serrano, A. (2006). Internet Regulation and the Role of International Law. *Max Planck Yearbook of United Nations Law, 10*, 191–272.

Soldatov, A., & Borogan, I. (2016). Putin brings China's Great Firewall to Russia in cybersecurity pact. *The Guardian.*

Sutton, M. (2015). How the TPP will affect you and your digital rights. *Electronic Frontier Foundation.* https://www.eff.org/deeplinks/2015/12/how-tpp-will-affect-you-and-your-digital-rights

Telenor. (2005). Telenor and Swedish National Criminal Investigation Department to introduce Internet child porn filter. *Telenor Media Center.*

Telenor Norge. (2004, Sept. 21). Telenor and KRIPOS introduce Internet child pornography filter. *Telenor Press Release.*

The Independent. (2016). Facebook, Twitter and Whatsapp blocked in Turkey after arrest of opposition leaders. *The Independent.*

Thompson, B. (2004). *Doubts over web filtering plans.* BBC News.

U.S. Congress. (2000). *Computer Crime Enforcement Act of 2000 - Public Law 106-572, 106th Congress.* https://www.congress.gov/106/plaws/publ572/PLAW-106publ572.pdf

USTR.gov. (2015). *Summary of the Trans-Pacific Partnership Agreement, Office of the United States Trade Representative*. https://ustr.gov/about-us/policy-offices/press-office/press-releases/2015/october/summary-trans-pacific-partnership

ZDNet. (2015). Topics – ZDNet. *ZDNet*. http://www.zdnetasia.com/news/security/0,39044215,39372326,00.htm

Zittrain, J., & Edelman, B. (2003). *Documentation of Internet Filtering Worldwide*. Cambridge, MA: Harvard Law School.

Chapter 2
Internet Users and Internet Regulation:
Enemies or Allies?

ABSTRACT

In this chapter, the authors examine if internet users are against any kind of internet regulation policy or not. In their endeavour, they begin with a literature review of older related surveys, and then proceed by presenting their UK-related survey that was conducted in 2007-2008, focusing on the UK's IRS (i.e., BT's CleanFeed). The United Kingdom CleanFeed is an ideal case study as it was the first time that an internet regulation system had been implemented to such an extent in a Western democracy. The authors' UK survey managed to collect initial valuable data that formed their further survey-based research in Greece, Germany, Russia, India, Kosovo, and Cyprus. Last, the authors discuss the need for regularly measuring internet users' opinions about the subject.

INTRODUCTION

In this chapter, the authors examine if Internet users are against any kind of Internet regulation policy or not. In their endeavour, they begin with a literature review of older related surveys and then proceed by presenting their UK-related survey that was conducted in 2007-2008, focusing on the UK's IRS, i.e. BT's CleanFeed.

DOI: 10.4018/978-1-5225-9973-9.ch002

The United Kingdom CleanFeed is an ideal case study as it was the first time that an Internet Regulation System had been implemented to such an extent in a western democracy. Authors' UK survey managed to collect initial valuable data that formed their further survey-based research in Greece, Germany, Russia, India, Kosovo, and Cyprus (see chapters 5 to 11).

Last, the authors discuss the need for regularly measuring Internet user's opinion about the subject.

Previous Related Surveys

Taking into account that the implementation of IRSs is necessary for specific reasons (such as to decrease the child-porn material circulated online), there is a need for the right conditions to be found under which such a content blocking system can be accepted in democratic societies. An option for gathering related data is to conduct surveys at a national level.

In this section, the authors discuss the results of the few related surveys already conducted around the world in order to show that Internet users in many countries are willing to accept, under conditions, the implementation of an IRS.

It is worth mentioning that the oldest related survey the authors managed to find was conducted in 1998 at GVU Center at the Georgia Institute of Technology's College of Computing (Depken, 2006). Survey's scope was to measure the demographic characteristics of the online population, but there was a question stating "I believe that certain information should not be published on the Internet". Among the US-based 4,247 respondents, 24.84 percent answered "Agree strongly" and 22.30 percent "Agree somewhat." On the other hand, the answer "Disagree somewhat" scored 15.26 percent and "Disagree strongly" 28.37 percent. Summarising, the respondents who agreed ("strongly" or "somewhat") with the non-publication of certain information online were little more (47.14 percent) than those who disagreed ("strongly" or "somewhat") (43.63 percent).

In 2007, the *Australian Broadband Survey* with 17,881 participants showed that 74.3 percent disagreed/strongly disagreed and only 13.4 percent agreed/strongly agreed with the statement "Do you support the government's policy for mandatory ISP-level content filtering (opt-out)?" (Whirlpool, 2010a). In a similar survey in 2008 (Whirlpool, 2010b), among the 19,763 participants, a staggering 88.9 percent answered "Yes" to the question "The federal Labor government plans to require ISPs to filter adult material from the Internet.

There will be the ability for customers to opt out of this filter. Would you opt out?" A similar survey conducted in 2009 by Galaxy found out that only 5 percent of 1,100 participants wanted ISPs to be responsible for protecting children online and only 4 percent wanted Australia's government to be responsible for this (Moses, 2009).

On a global scale, there was a general survey with some related questions conducted by GlobalScan Incorporated in 26 different countries for BBC World Service in 2010. Generally speaking, Internet users appear to be divided in half regarding where they stand for, as far as Internet regulation is concerned, with the percentages varying from country to country. For example, Canadians are relatively supportive of Internet regulation (51 percent disagree that the Internet should never be regulated), along with Australians and many European Union web users (such as in France, UK, Spain, Germany, Portugal, and others). On the other hand, this is not the case in Mexico (72 percent agree that no government anywhere should regulate the Internet) and other non-EU countries, such as Nigeria (77 percent), South Korea (83 percent), and others (GlobalScan Incorporated, 2010).

In 2012, the Internet Society conducted more than 10,000 online interviews with Internet users from 20 countries (Internet Society, 2012). Among others, there were quite a few related questions to Internet regulation at a national level. For example, to the question "Should the Internet be governed in some form to protect the community from harm?", 82 percent stated that they "somewhat or strongly agree."

What's more, 71 percent of the participants declared that they "somewhat or strongly agree" with the statement "Censorship should exist in some form on the Internet", 67 percent answered "somewhat or strongly agree" to the question "Each individual country has the right to govern the Internet the way they see fit," 49 percent stated "somewhat or strongly agree" to the question "Increased government control of the Internet would improve the content on the Internet," and 58 percent declared they "somewhat or strongly agree" with the statement "Increased government control of the Internet would make the Internet safe for everyone to use." Last, 61 percent declared ready to accept "a lot or somewhat" increased control/monitoring of the Internet if they gained increased safety.

In the UK, there was no "Internet regulation" survey until 2007 when a survey was conducted (Koumartzis, 2008). In summary, the survey showed that 90.21 percent of the participants were unaware of the existence of CleanFeed system and from those few who had heard about it before, only 14.81 percent understood it completely. Even fewer learned about CleanFeed by official statements of the participating bodies (11.1 percent from UK government's statements and 22.2 percent of BT's statements). What's more, 60.87 percent of the participants did not trust BT and 65.22 percent did not trust IWF either to be responsible for a silent content blocking system in the UK.

The interesting part, though, regarding UK survey was that the majority of the participants preferred an open content blocking system, rather than no Internet regulation at all. More specifically, 65.2 percent of the UK Internet users would like to see a message stating that the website is blocked, 57.3 percent to have access to a requesting form for unblocking a website, and 68.5 percent to see a better and more frequent briefing by BT, IWF, and the UK government.

As an aggregate outline of the pre-mentioned results, below are two charts showing what the Internet users believe regarding Internet regulation, both country-by-country and on a global scale. For the country-by-country results, the BBC World Service survey is being presented, as the very last massive related survey that was conducted prior to the beginning of this research. For the centralised results, two charts are being presented based on the 2012 Internet Society Survey, as the last massive related survey that took place during the early stages of this research.

It is important here to make some general observations. First, it is more than clear (thanks mainly to Figure 2) that there is a global trend in favour of the implementation of some form of Internet regulation. This is true regardless of where the country is located: America, Europe, India, Middle East, Africa, or East Asia (check Figure 3). Secondly, in Figure 1 someone can recognise that the country's location is affecting how high the percentage of agreement is, something that is confirmed in Figure 3: countries in Europe and America scores the lowest percentages to the question, while countries in Middle East, Africa, and East Asia scores the highest.

Authors' Initial Survey in the United Kingdom

As discussed in Chapter One, from the launch date of the UK's CleanFeed system many ethical issues arose regarding how transparent its usage for the UK based Internet users is, or more specifically to what extent is really a silent model of Internet censorship.

Among the questions that have arisen was: why is the user not informed that the website he is trying to access is blocked?, What is the procedure if someone believes that a website blocked should not be?, Who will be responsible if a website without illegal content will be blocked?, and so forth.

Figure 1. The Internet should never be regulated by any level of government anywhere
(GlobalScan Incorporated in 26 different countries for BBC World Service in 2010)

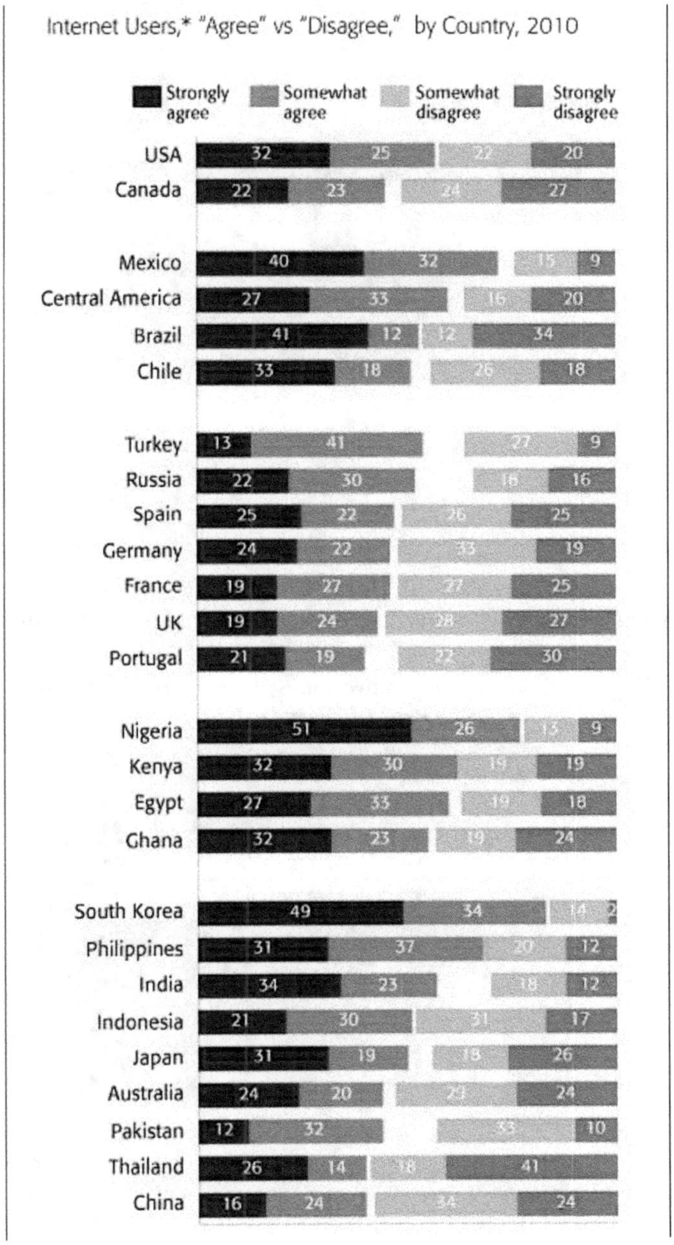

Figure 2. Do you agree that censorship should exist in some form on the Internet? *(Global Internet User Survey 2012). Results for the Internet users worldwide*

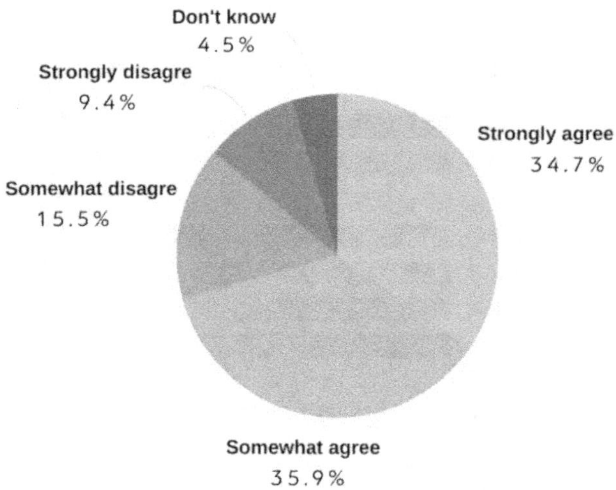

Figure 3. Strongly & somewhat agree that censorship should exist in some form on the Internet.
(Global Internet User Survey 2012). Comparative results for the Internet users in a. the world (global), b. America, c. Europe, d. India/ Middle East/ Africa and e. East Asia.

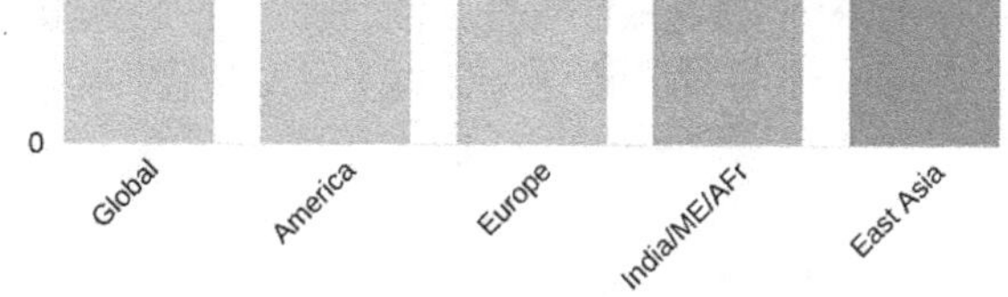

All the above questions can be the topic of a never-ending theoretical debate, without getting anywhere specifically. So, in order to find some answers in practice, an online survey was designed and conducted by the authors in 2007 giving some really interesting initial results. While every effort was made to achieve objectivity, the relatively small sample of the survey means that there is a need for replication on a broader scale.

Below, the authors discuss how transparent CleanFeed actually is, in sections, what the UK based Internet users prefer regarding Internet censorship in the UK, and later, what kind of design improvements the UK based Internet users would like to see in CleanFeed system in order to accept its usage.

CleanFeed: Silent Model Without the Trust?

According to many IT experts (Bright, 2004· Thompson, 2004), CleanFeed system is a silent IRS. In brief, a silent IRS is a system that can regulate content without being noticed by the Internet users (i.e. a system that is transparent for the users). Moreover, in silent IRSs, even in the case where a user finds out that a website is blocked, there are no obvious ways to question the blocking.

In the authors' 2007 survey, an effort was made to measure how silent CleanFeed actually is and to what extent this is reasonable based on the Internet users' trust in the bodies involved in the project.

How Silent Is CleanFeed?

It is quite interesting that, despite the fact that 90.21 percent of survey's respondents spend more than 2 hours per day on the Internet (61.95 percent more than 4 hours per day, see Figure 4), the 81.52 percent of them never heard about CleanFeed before (Figure 5). Among the 18.48 percent of all respondents that were aware of CleanFeed existence before taking part at this survey, 59.26 percent have just heard about it, while 25.93 percent knew some things, and only 14.81 percent were keenly aware of it (Figure 6).

Analysing responses from group 5 (respondents living in the UK for more than 4 years – check Appendix 14 for more details regarding the different groups that were formed for the analysis of the 2007 UK survey's results), the results were slightly different, as was to be expected, but not significant enough to deny the reliability of the results presented above. More specifically, in group 5, only 29.2 percent have ever heard about CleanFeed before (Figure 7), while among them 57.1 percent just heard about it and nothing else, 28.6 percent knew some things and only 14.3 percent were deeply aware of it (Figure 8).

Figure 4. Group 1 - Internet hours per day

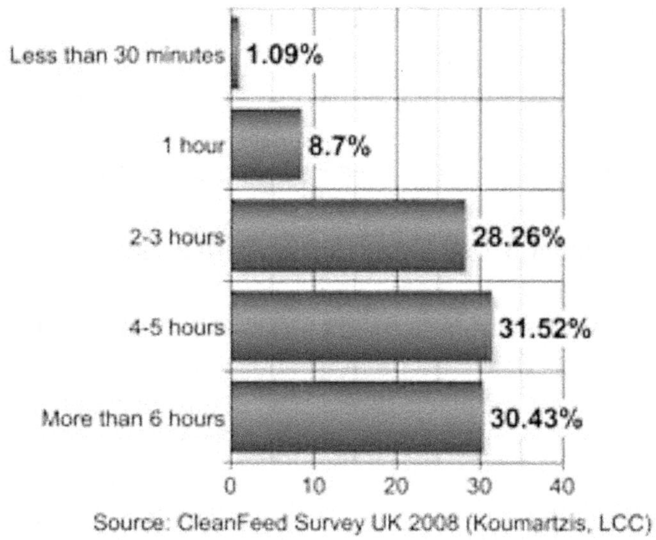

Figure 5. Group 1 - Have you ever faced online censorship?

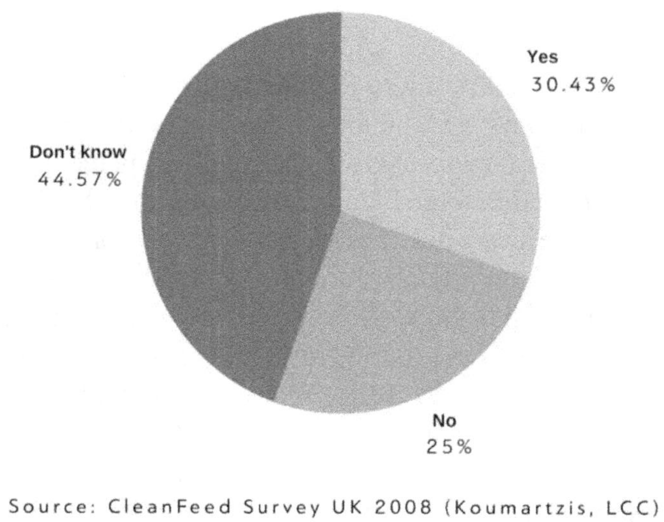

The level of how silent CleanFeed model is exactly can be measured from other issues too, i.e. the means (websites, magazines, books, and so on), and the source of information (BT, the UK government, mass media, and so forth).

The survey showed that of the 18.48 percent of those that have actually heard about CleanFeed software before, 63.2 percent have read it on websites/

Figure 6. Group 1 - Level of Awareness

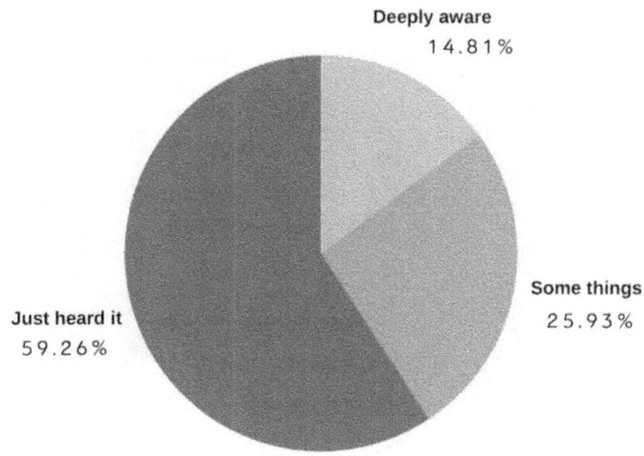

Source: CleanFeed Survey UK 2008 (Koumartzis, LCC)

Figure 7. Group 5 – Have you ever heard about CleanFeed?

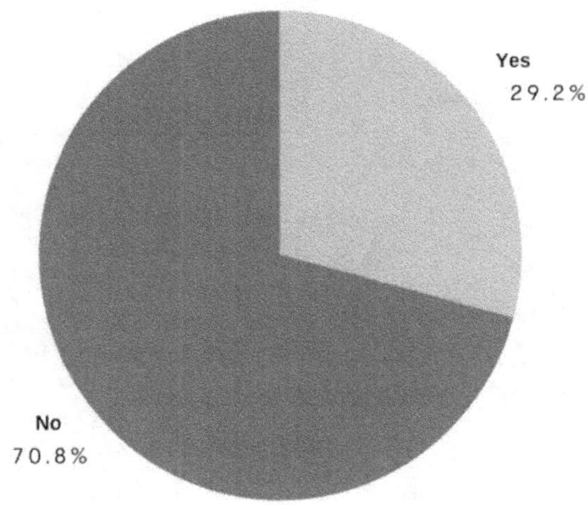

Source: CleanFeed Survey UK 2008 (Koumartzis, LCC)

blogs and others, 31.6 percent have seen something on TV and 10.5 percent have other means of information (see Figure 9). Regarding the source of information, 50 percent of those who knew about CleanFeed software before

Figure 8. Group 5 – CleanFeed: Level of Awareness

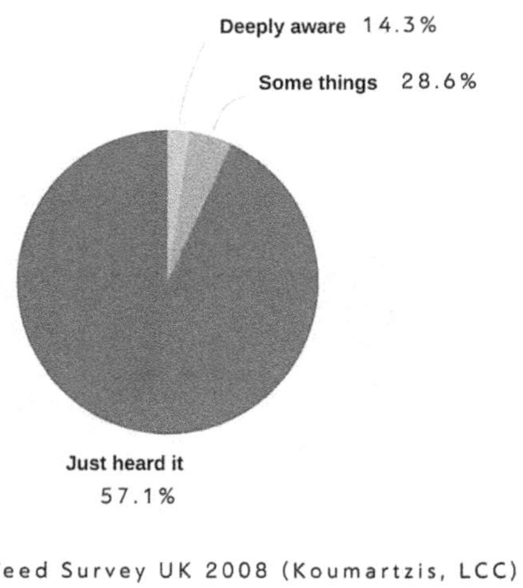

Figure 9. Group 1 - Means of Information

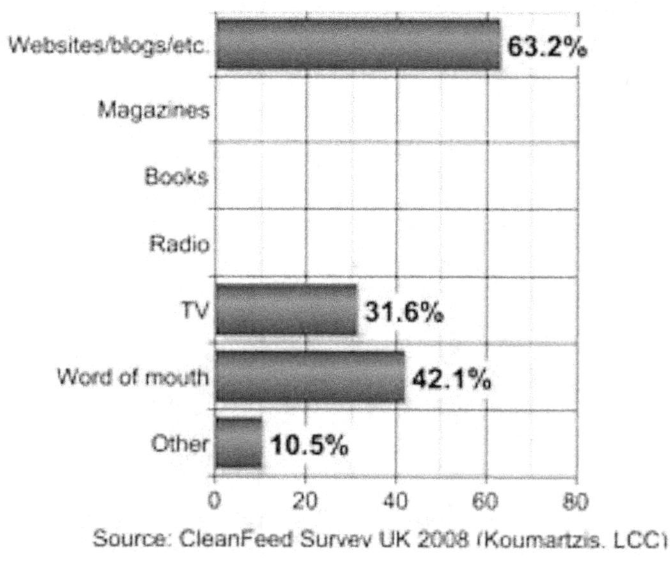

were informed by individuals and 38.9 percent by mass media, while only 11.1 percent was informed by the UK government official statement and 22.2 percent by BT statements (see Figure 10).

Considering the results mentioned above, it is indisputable that CleanFeed is a very effective silent IRS in terms of the UK Internet users' awareness. Furthermore, it is not just designed as a silent IRS in technical terms, but it

Figure 10. Group 1 - Source of Information

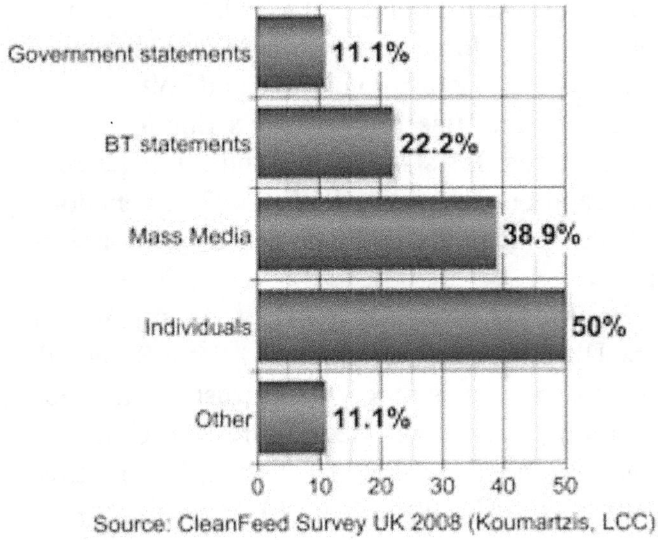

is implemented and maintained as a silent system by every party engaged. So, why did the UK government choose that approach compared to an open IRS? That is a very important question as CleanFeed implementation in the UK soon became a very important precedent among Western democracies worldwide.

A quite possible answer is that, back in 2007, the citizens of any democratic society would probably react passionately against any effort of their government effort to regulate the Internet. This is true in this case as the UK government never asked them and chose to design and implement such a system silently.

Was there a possibility that another, open, IRS could be accepted by the UK Internet users? Is it possible that an open IRS would ever be accepted by the members of any democratic society? The latter is a question of crucial importance and it is thoroughly researched and discussed (in chapters 5 to 11) by the authors of the present book.

A Matter of Trust?

The next question of this survey was *"Is there enough trust on that part of British people in order for the existence of such a silent censorship model to be reasoned?"*. In order for an answer to be found, those entities that are involved in CleanFeed software must be presented. As this book discuss in chapter 2, CleanFeed software was designed by BT in collaboration with the UK Home Office, and the list of banned websites is being provided by IWF.

So, except the UK Home Office that is connected directly to the democratically elected UK government, BT and IWF are closely connected with CleanFeed software. Based on survey's finding, 60.87 percent don't trust/strongly don't trust BT's statements and 39.13 percent trust/strongly trust them (see graph 11). Regarding IWF, 65.22 percent don't trust/strongly don't trust IWF's statements and 34.78 percent trust/strongly don't trust them (see Figure 12).

Again, results based on group 5 respondents only are more reliable as they are keener to be UK citizens or well informed about BT and IWF. Regarding BT, 56.2 percent don't trust/strongly don't trust its statements, while 43.8 percent trust/strongly trust them (see Figure 13). Concerning IWF, 60.4 percent of group 5 respondents don't trust/strongly don't trust it, while 39.6 percent trust/strongly trust it (see Figure 14).

Is There a Need for Internet Regulation in UK?

Regarding the controversy about the need or not for a mandatory blocking content system in the UK targeting child abuse content, the results were quite clear.

Figure 11. Group 1 - Do you trust BT's statement?

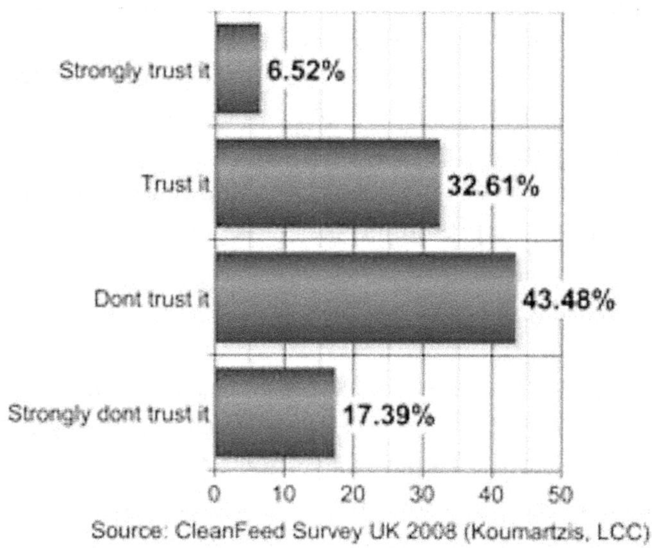

Figure 12. Group 1 - Do you trust IWF?

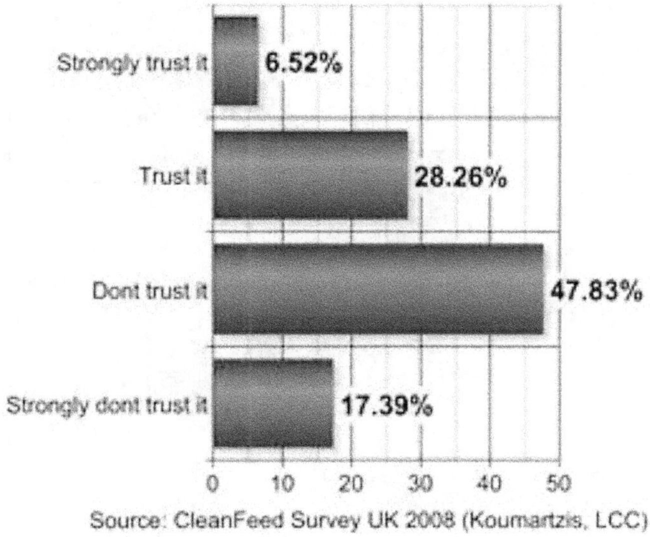

Figure 13.

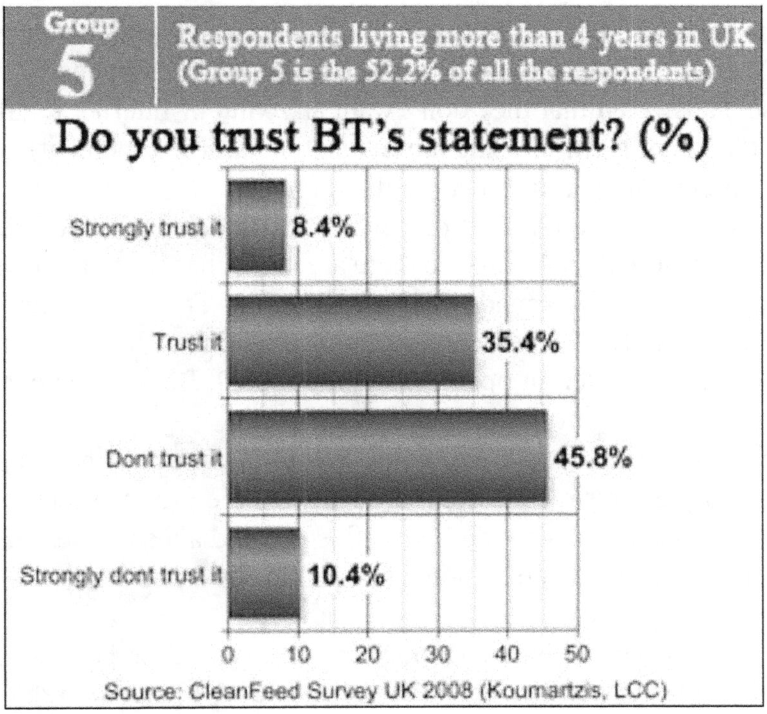

Figure 14.

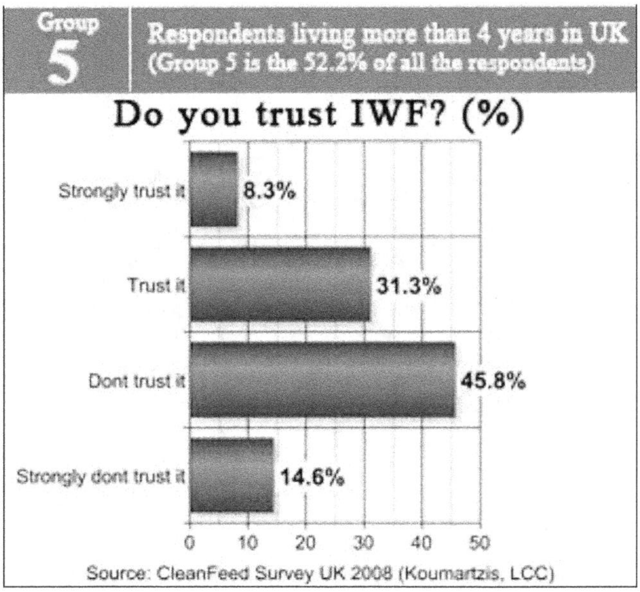

To the question *"What do you prefer?"* (silent censorship/open censorship/none of them/can't say), only 30.43 percent of the total participants (92 verified responses) answered that they don't want any kind of Internet regulation in the UK ("none of them"), while more than the half (58.7 percent) answered that they prefer an open Internet regulation model.

Because of the fact that 52.7 percent of the participants have been living in the UK for more than 4 years, so there are more chances of their being UK citizens, an analysis was made of that sub-group. The results were similar to the above as only 31.3 percent don't want any kind of Internet censorship and 54.1 percent prefer an open censorship model. Below, you can see the relevant graph.

Three other subgroups were made (group 2, group 3 and group 4) in order to analyse their responses. All of those three groups seem to consist of participants keener to be more sensitive to child abuse issues as group 2 is consisted only by female respondents, and group 3 and 4 from parents or/and want-to-be parents.

Regarding group 2 (female respondents), only 22.2 percent do not want any kind of Internet censorship in the UK, while 74.1 percent prefer an open censorship model.

Figure 15. Group 1 - Censorship: What do you prefer?

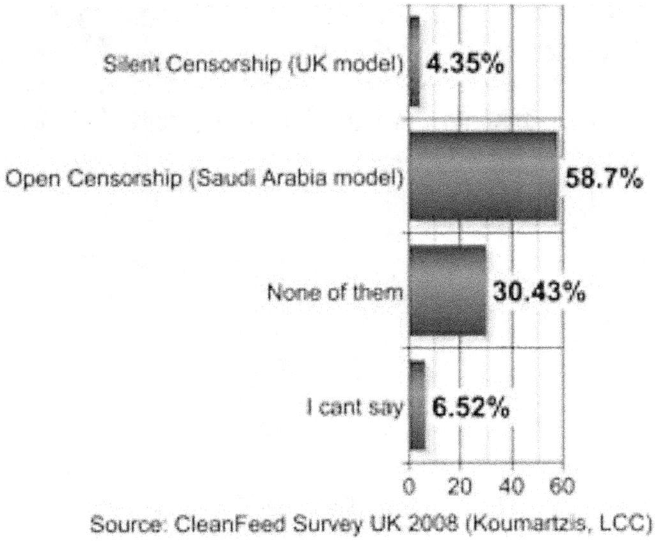

Figure 16.

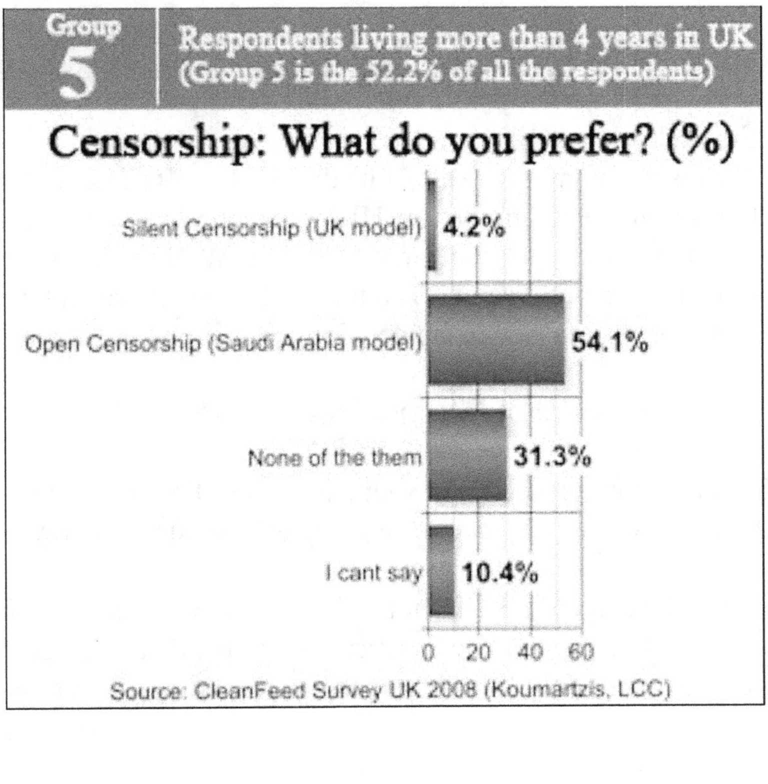

Figure 17.

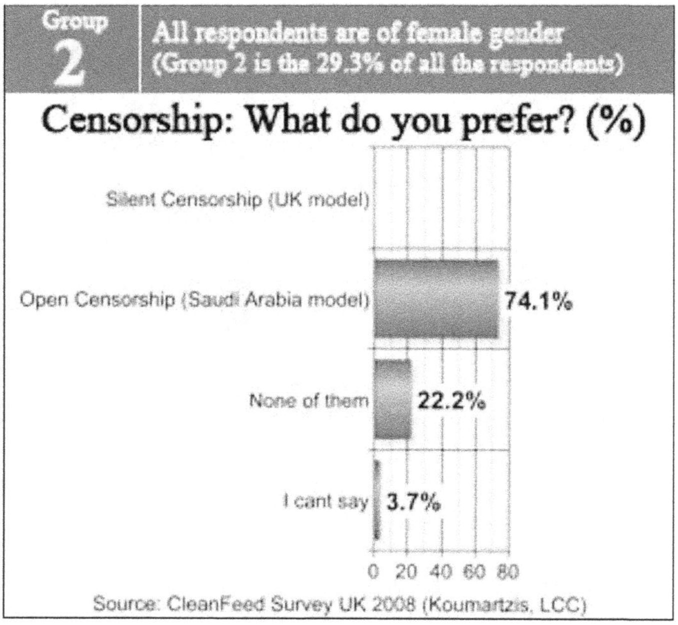

Concerning group 3 (parents or want-to-be parents), 30.7 percent do not want any kind of Internet censorship, while 57.3 percent prefer an open censorship model.

Last, the results of group 4 were quite different as 50 percent do not want any kind of Internet regulation in the UK, while only 33.3 percent prefer an open censorship model, and none prefer the current UK model (silent IRS). Due to the fact that group 4 sample is quite small (just 6.5 percent of the total participants), the results were considered unreliable by the authors.

Silent or Open Model of Internet Regulation?

Regarding the preference between silent and open IRSs, the public opinion was clear. There are actually two different questions in the survey related to that issue.

More specifically, to the question *"Do you agree/disagree with silent censorship?"*, 73.91 percent of all participants responded that they disagree/strongly disagree, and only 16.3 percent that agree/strongly agree (see Figure 20).

Figure 18.

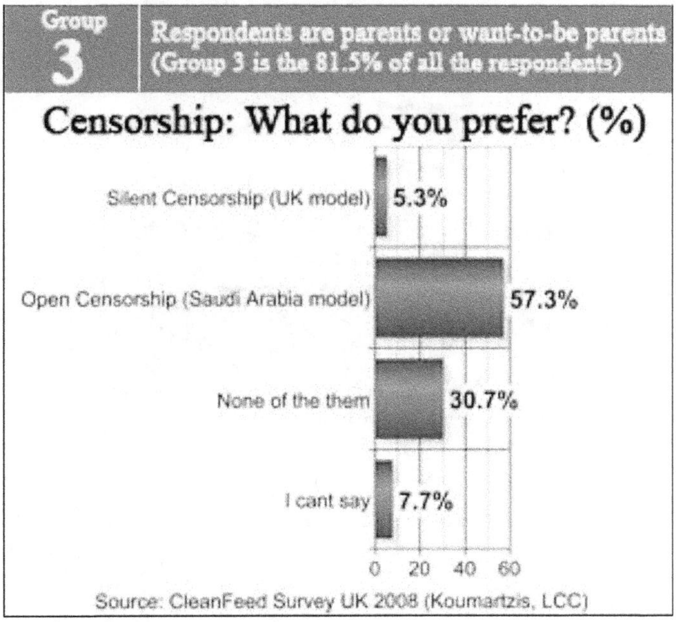

Figure 19.

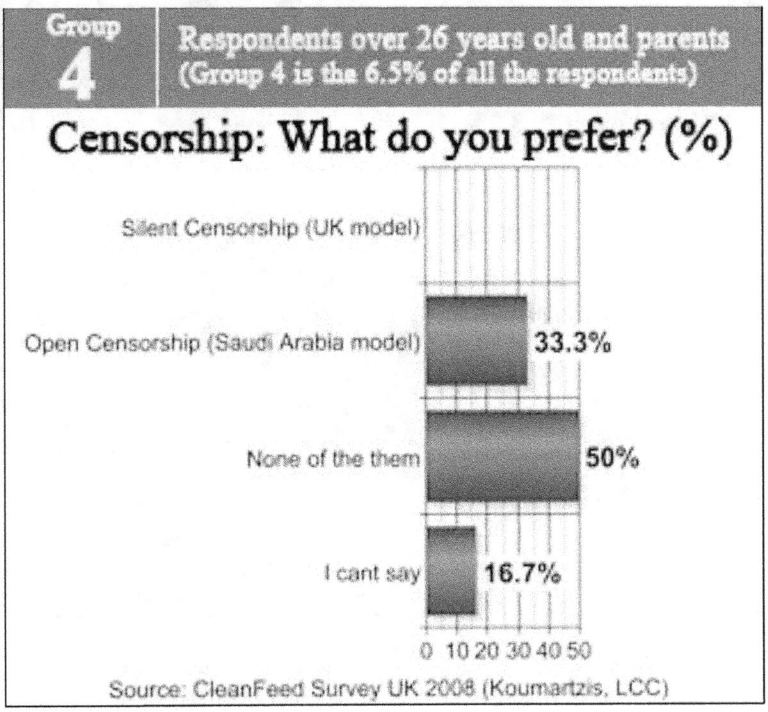

Figure 20. Group 1 - Do you agree/disagree with silent censorship?

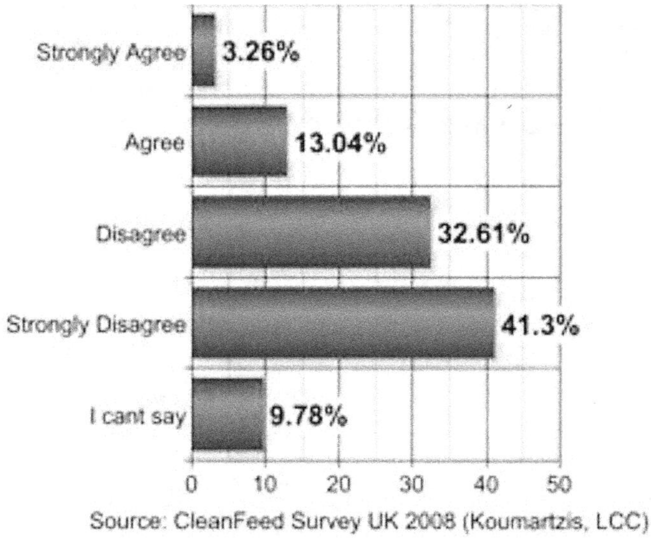

Figure 21.

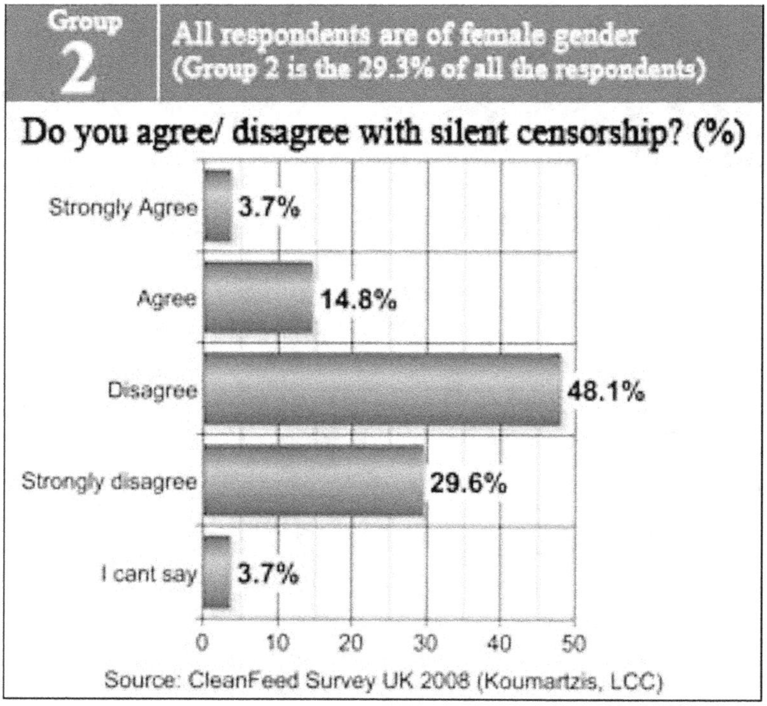

Figure 22.)

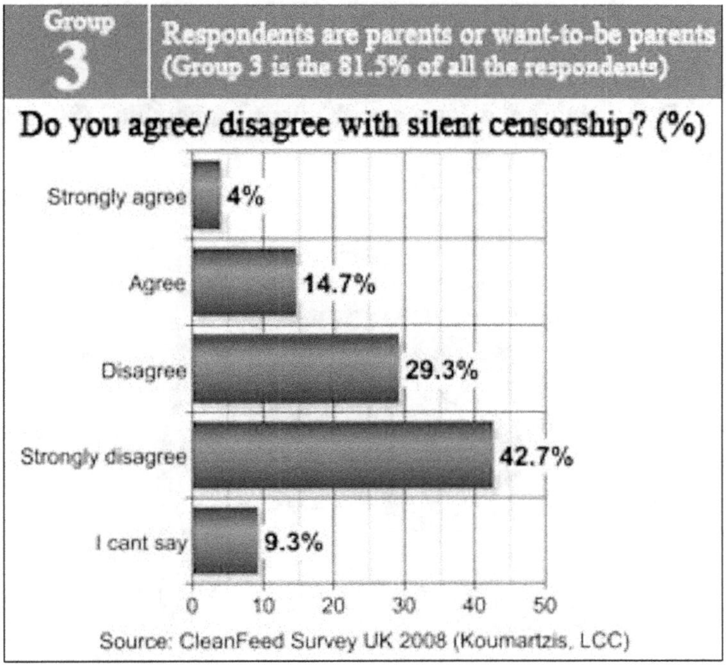

Figure 23.

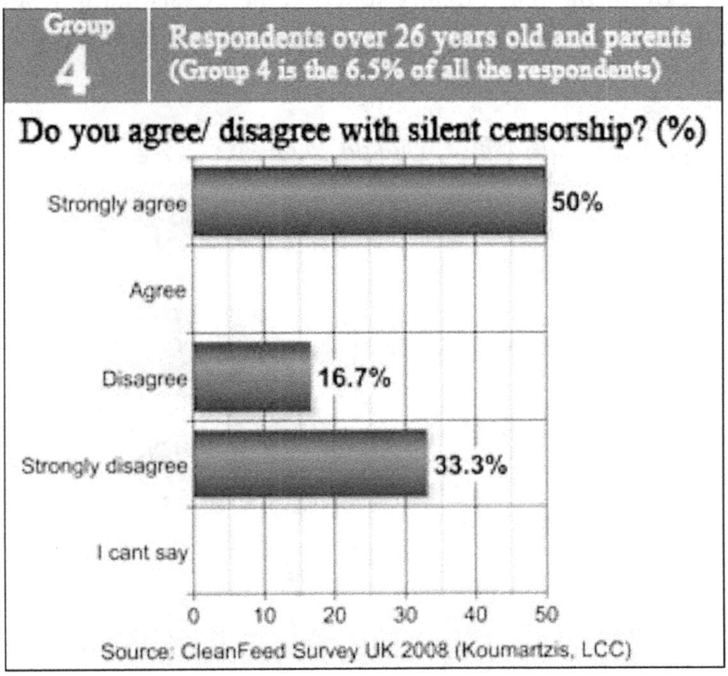

Figure 24.

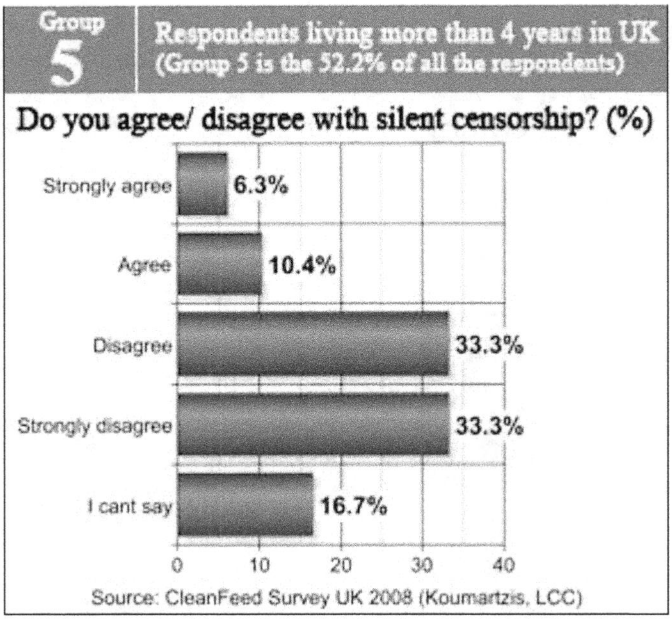

Additionally to question 15, there was a question asking *"What kind of censorship do you prefer?"*. The results of this question were also clear as 58.7 percent of all the participants stated "Open Censorship (Saudi Arabia model)" and only 4.35 percent "Silent Censorship (UK model)".

Figure 25. Group 1 - Censorship: What do you prefer?

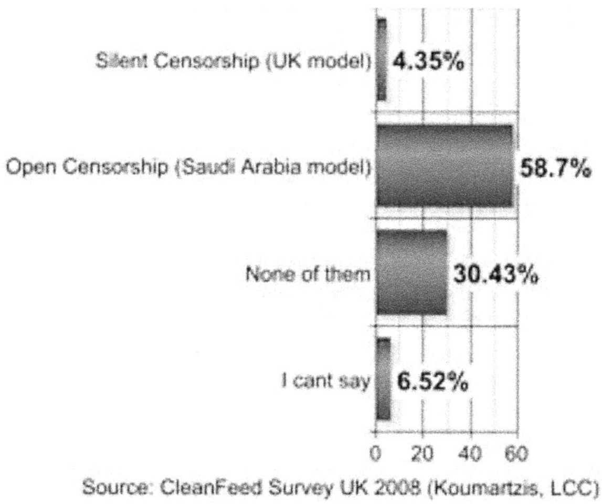

Figure 26.

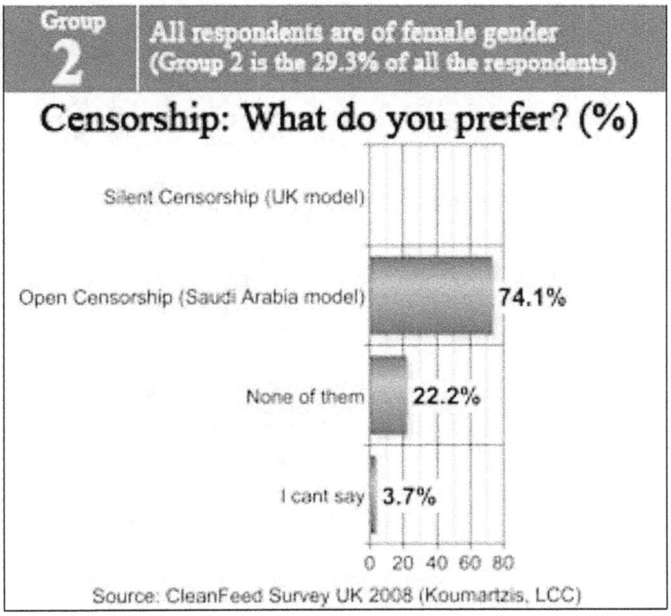

Figure 27.

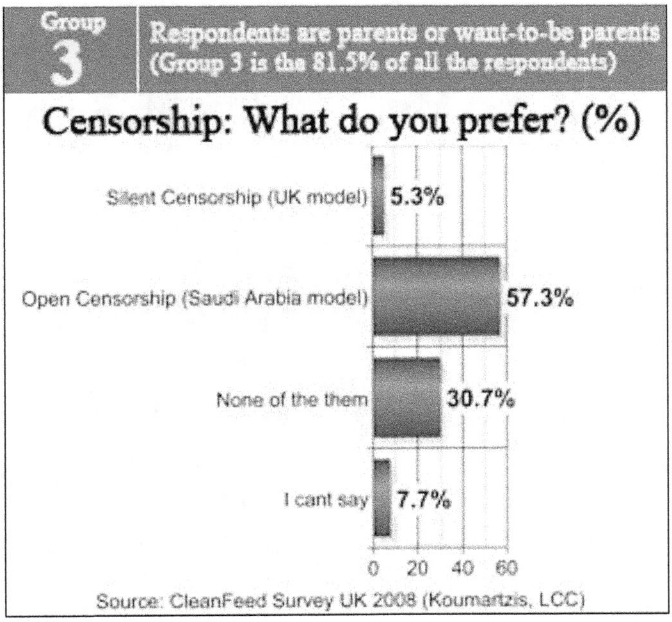

Figure 28.

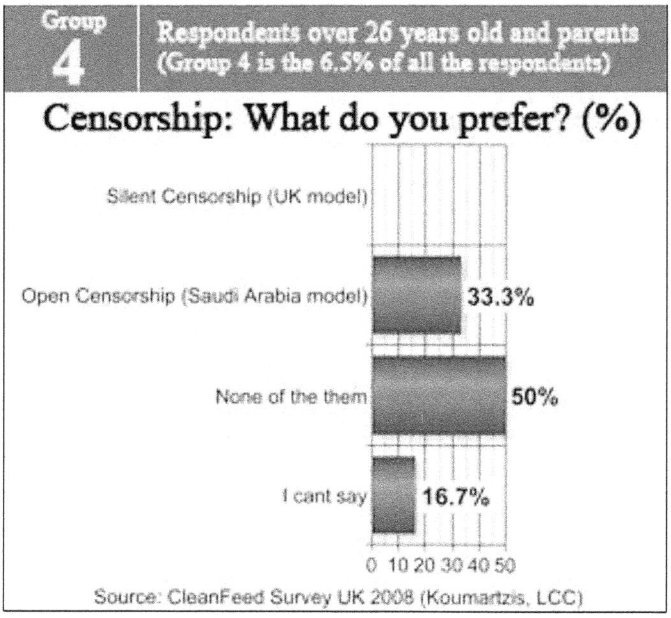

Figure 29.

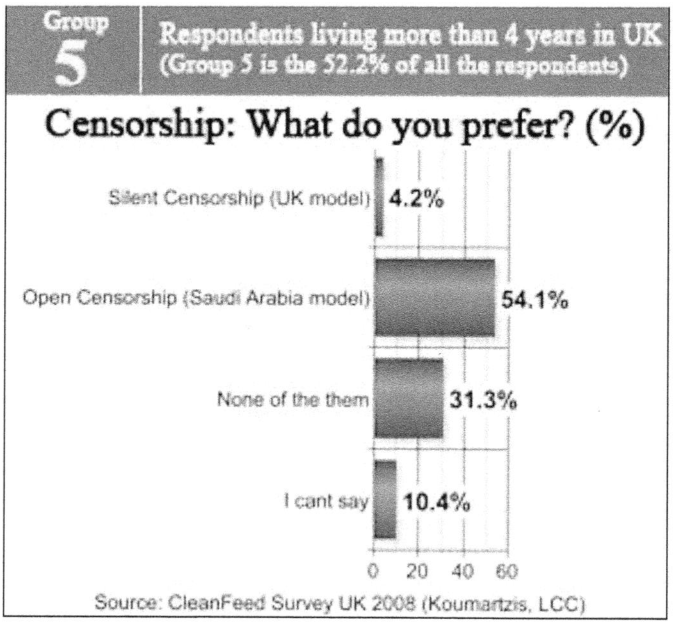

What Design Improvements Can Be Made?

As discussed in the previous section, the UK based Internet users prefer by far an open censorship model to a silent one (58.7 percent compared to 4.35 percent respectively), while they even prefer an open censorship model targeting child abuse content to no censorship at all. But what do they mean by saying that they prefer an "open" model of censorship?

In the survey was included a question regarding what kind of design improvements the UK based Internet users would like to see in CleanFeed software in order to see it as an open censorship model (more than one answers were allowed). Regarding the standard answers to those questions, 65.2 percent of the respondents answered that they would like to see a *"Message stating that the website is blocked,"* 57.3 percent that they would like to have *"Access to a requesting form for unblocking the website,"* and 68.5 percent that they would like to have a *"Better and more frequent informing by BT, IWF and UK government"* (see Figure 30).

Figure 30. Group 1 - Design Improvements for CleanFeed

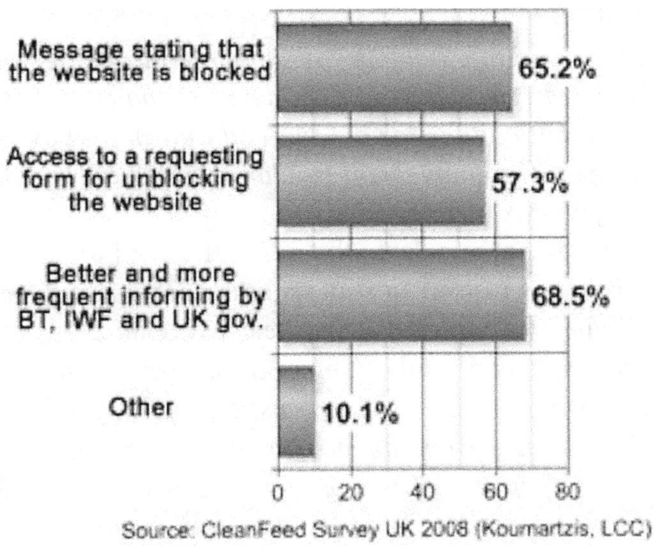

As Figure 15 shows, 10.1 percent of the respondents chose "Other" as an option stating some additional possible improvements. Among them, six respondents proposed that a message be presented stating the reason of the blocking with the message stating that the website is blocked.

Moreover, there were proposals for opening the access for some parts of CleanFeed software to researchers. More specifically, a participant responded *"Awareness amongst the public of the use of CleanFeed should be increased, perhaps through advertising. Independent researchers and bodies should be allowed unlimited access to CleanFeed data and statistics, so that CleanFeed and its users (BT) are continuously monitored to make sure CleanFeed is used ONLY to block child abuse material."*, while another one said, *"If only research is concerned, what BT should do, they should provide special success features on the CleanFeed software. In this case, this thing won't be spreading among society and researchers will also be able to research upon it"* (see appendix 13).

Also, there were some experts in different fields that took part in the survey, but because of the fact that the participants were protected by anonymity, this cannot be verified. For example, a participant with obviously strong legal background stated that *"The use of such software is inappropriate and subject to abuse by government. Existing legal sanctions already exist to target illegal websites through international agreements. Where necessary, hosting companies that host illegal websites can be targeted through the courts (in the UK), or by threatening to block the hosting company at a national level where the host is abroad (by modification of the top-level UK DNS servers, if necessary), hence putting it under pressure to remove offending websites. The use of Cleanfeed-type software at ISP level is a potentially sinister move that could have ramifications far beyond child pornography. ISP's should resist being compelled to implement it. This is the WRONG solution to the problem"* (see appendix 13).

Finally, there was a respondent who stated the need for a broader survey to take place, in order to lead to some more reliable results and force the participating bodies to implement changes to CleanFeed software. More specifically, the respondent said, *"A more transparent method of informing UK citizens concerning any unblocking website. Request forms could probably work in the UK, however I am not sure to what extent they could be taken seriously in order to have an effect on CleanFeed's policy. If broader and formal surveys could be completed, so that they could represent a larger number of UK citizens who are using the Internet on a daily basis and have knowledge on the subject, then I would like to see CleanFeed changing its policy towards a more fair and transparent method of blocking Internet content"* (see appendix 13).

CONCLUSION

In summary, the survey that was conducted has shown that 90.21 percent of all the participants were unaware of the existence of CleanFeed software (this percentage was 61.95 percent for UK based Internet users living in the UK for more than 4 years). From the few that have heard about CleanFeed software before their participation in the survey, only 14.81 percent were deeply aware of it, while few have learnt about it by official statements of the participating bodies (11.1 percent from UK government's statements and 22.2 percent of BT's statements).

What's more, 60.87 percent of the participants do not trust BT and 65.22 percent do not trust IWF either to be responsible for a silent censorship model in the UK. As is discussed in Chapter 12, the majority of the participants prefer an open censorship model targeting child abuse content rather no Internet censorship at all. So, 65.2 percent of all the respondents would like to see a message stating that the website is blocked, 57.3 percent stated they would like to have access to a requesting form for unblocking a website and 68.5 percent that they would like to see a better and more frequent informing by BT, IWF and the UK government.

The Need to Measure Internet Users' Opinion

Data presented prior made it clear that there is no final and universal answer to the question "What kind of IRSs are the Internet users willing to accept?". On the other hand, it is quite clear too that Internet users in many countries and especially in the UK are open, under conditions, to the implementation of an IRS.

All the above contradicts many current common misconceptions, such as "The Internet cannot be regulated thanks to its nature" or "Public opinion is against any kind of Internet regulation."

What's more, the UK initial survey gave a lot of guidelines on how the current BT's IRS can be improved: who UK Internet users trust and who not, what changes must be made to CleanFeed's interface, how important it is for Internet users to be aware of such an IRS implementation, and so on. Additionally, the UK survey can be used as an example for designing and conducting similar surveys in other countries (chapter 4).

Before proceeding with the presentation of the survey's design and results gathered from six countries, the authors discuss how the UK's IRS works.

The following chapter (chapter 3) is really important because BT's CleanFeed is used as a case study later in this book. What's more, it is quite important to know how a current, already implemented, IRS works before designing the right questionnaire to run a survey, and before designing a blueprint for an improved, more user-oriented, version of it.

REFERENCES

Bright, M. (2004). BT puts block on child porn sites. *The Observer*.

Depken, C. A. II. (2016). Who Supports Internet Censorship? *First Monday*, *11*(9). doi:10.5210/fm.v11i9.1390

GlobalScan Incordporated. (2010). *Four in Five Regard Internet Access as a Fundamental Right: Global Poll*. BBC World Service.

Internet Society. (2012). *Global Internet User Survey 2012*. https://www.internetsociety.org/internet/global-internet-user-survey-2012

Koumartzis, N. (2008). *BT's CleanFeed and Online Censorship in UK: Improvements for a More Secure and Ethically Correct Systeym* (Doctoral dissertation). University of the Arts London, London College of Communication, London, UK.

Moses, A. (2009). *Web censorship plan heads towards a dead end*. The Sydney Morning Herald.

Thompson, B. (2004). *Doubts over web filtering plans*. BBC News.

Whirlpool. (2010a). Australian Broadband Survey 2007. *Whirlpool*. https://whirlpool.net.au/survey/2007/

Whirlpool. (2010b). Australian Broadband Survey 2008. *Whirlpool*. https://whirlpool.net.au/survey/2008/

Section 2

How an IRS Works: A Currently and Already Implemented Paradigm

Chapter 3
How an IRS Works:
UK's CleanFeed as a Comparative Model

ABSTRACT

In this chapter, the authors describe in detail the UK's CleanFeed design and the blocking mechanisms that it is using. The description presented is based mainly on two papers by Dr. Clayton of Cambridge Computer Laboratory, while many figures are presented in order for CleanFeed's design to be more understandable to a broader public. The only IT expert (with an academic background) who conducted research on CleanFeed software in technical terms is Dr. Clayton.

INTRODUCTION

Having seen the basic blocking mechanisms used today by ISPs (chapter 1), it is time to describe in detail the UK's CleanFeed design and the blocking mechanisms that it is using. BT has never published CleanFeed's design, nor has it stated such intentions for the future. Moreover, the authors' invitation for an interview with IWF's Chief Executive Peter Robbins (back in 2008) was turned down, stating that *"Regrettably, we do not have the resources to respond to interviews and surveys for research purposes"* (see appendix 11).

On the other hand, the only IT expert (with an academic background) who conducted research on CleanFeed software in technical terms is Dr. Clayton of Cambridge University Computer Laboratory. In his paper *Failures in a Hybrid Content Blocking System* (2008) and his technical report *Anonymity*

DOI: 10.4018/978-1-5225-9973-9.ch003

and Traceability to Cyberspace (2005), the CleanFeed's design is thoroughly discussed. According to him, *"This description is based on several separate accounts and, although it is believed to be substantially correct, it may be inaccurate in some minor details"* and *"Up to a point, BT says that my description is mainly accurate, but not entirely so"* (see appendix 8).

The description presented below is based mainly on the two previously mentioned papers, while many figures are presented in order for CleanFeed's design to be more understandable to a broader public. Clayton's research is the only one focusing on the technical aspects of this IRS to such an extent.

Aims

As it is explained in Chapter 1, the most accurate mechanism for blocking content is the content filtering system, which, however, has a crucial disadvantage: high cost of implementation. On the other hand, there are two other basic mechanisms (packet dropping and DNS poisoning) that are very simple and with low cost of implementation, but at the same time very inaccurate (over-blocking and under-blocking issues, and so forth).

Bearing in mind that CleanFeed software was designed to be implemented in BT's customer network (a vast network with a lot of traffic), it is more than obvious that a purely content filtering system would be too expensive. Studying CleanFeed's design (see the next section), it is easy to understand that BT and the UK Home Office tried to develop an accurate system at a low cost, concluding to a 2-stage system using both packet dropping and content filtering mechanisms.

Design

CleanFeed software is a hybrid content blocking scheme, which means that it consists of two separate stages (see figure 1). In brief, the first stage resembles a packet dropping system except that it does not discard requests, but redirects them to the second stage. In the second stage, a web proxy resembles a content filtering system. DNS poisoning was avoided in both stages in order for CleanFeed software not to affect any protocols (such as email) other than web traffic.

Figure 1. CleanFeed's design
(based on figure 1 in Clayton, 2008)

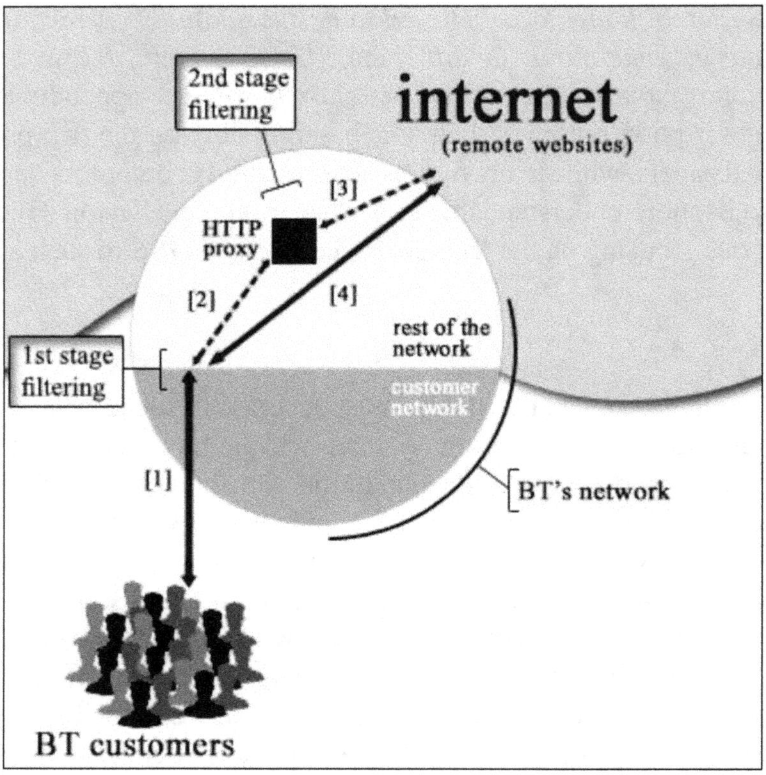

More specifically, the two stages of CleanFeed system are using two different lists in order to decide what to do with the requests. Both of them are extracted from the initial list of banned websites provided by IWF, as mentioned above.

The initial IWF's list is comprised of the URLs of child abuse content (images, video, and so on). This is the list that the 2nd stage is using and to which this paper will refer from now on as List B. The list that the 1st stage is using is extracted from List B and it consists of the IPs of the banned URLs that are included in List B. This is done by taking each URL of IWF's list (List B) and translating the hostnames into an IP address by making a simple *DNS query*[1].

In order to understand the differences between List A and List B, and the reason for the usage of these two lists by CleanFeed system, it is important for the relation between IP and URL to be described. Quite simplified, IP address is actually the numerical name that computers use in order to locate other computers on the Internet (ISI, 2017), while URL is a descriptive name which describes how a computer can "fetch" a resource (text, image, sound, and so forth) on the Internet (Berners-Lee et al., 1994). So, a URL may contain an IP address in order to define in which computer the resource is present. The most important thing to understand is that many URLs can have the same IP and not the opposite. For more details, see the Glossary in Chapter 1.

So, List B consists of a great number of banned URLs that point to online content (images, videos, and so on). List A consists of the IP addresses of List B's URLs, which means that List A is smaller or in a worst case scenario equal to List B. Concerning the fact that a specific website usually consists of a lot of related content, a child abuse website will probably consist of many child abuse images, and so forth. So, many of the banned URLs of List B will have the same IP address. A visual description is given below (figure 2).

Figure 2. List A and B in CleanFeed system (relation between the different lists used by the two stages of CleanFeed system)

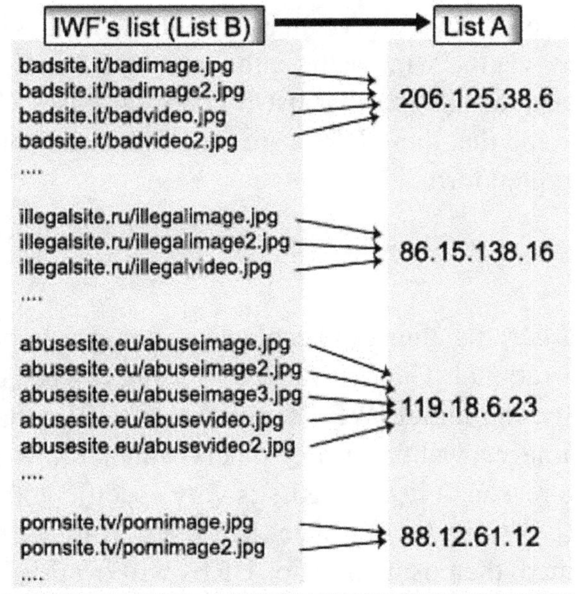

Having explained what kind of lists CleanFeed's two stages are using, we can proceed now by explaining in detail the system's design.

In the first stage, all the traffic coming from the ISP's customers (path 1 in figure 1) is examined, with no exceptions, by a mechanism that decides which requests for content are suspicious and which are not. The examination is made with the IP addresses included in List A. In case a request is made for a suspected website (i.e. requesting content from an IP included in List A), it is redirected to the second stage (path 2 in figure 1). In case the request is for innocuous content (i.e. requesting content from an IP not included in List A), it is redirected straight to the remote website (path 4 in figure 1). By "suspected website" are meant the websites some parts of which may be blocked. The first stage examination mechanism is based on the examination of the destination port number and IP address within the request's packets.

In CleanFeed's second stage, the traffic for suspected websites is examined by a web proxy that can handle HTTP requests. In this stage, the examination is on a URL level and it is made with the URLs included in List B (IWF's list). In case a request is made for accessing a URL in List B, then a "404" response with the message "page unavailable" is returned to the user. When the request is for a website that is not included in List B, then the traffic is redirected to the remote website (path 3 in figure 1) from which the content is sent to the user via the same path (path 3 and path 2 in figure 1).

Finally, because of the fact that list B (IWF list) uses URLs which are human-readable and that these URLs are for child abuse content, this list is held in an "encrypted form."

Outcome

As discussed earlier, the aims of CleanFeed system are to be very accurate and low-cost operational. This is achieved by using two stages and two lists. More specifically, the initial IWF list consists of URLs that point to very specific items (images, webpages, and others) and not to whole websites or servers. For this reason, a list of URLs is very specific and accurate, but it is very long, too. When a lot of traffic (like BT's customer network traffic) has to be examined, then using a list of URLs will overload the network or will raise the need for a really expensive equipment to avoid this.

What CleanFeed does is to make another list (list B), which consists of IP addresses than of URLs. So, list B is not as accurate as the initial IWF's list, or in other words it is not a list of banned websites, but a list of suspected websites; however it is much easier and faster to use when you have to cope with a lot of traffic.

The outcome of the use of an IP list is that CleanFeed can separate the requests of potentially blocked content from those that are definitely for innocuous content. So, the rest of the traffic that has to be examined with the URLs list is much smaller than the initial, and so the procedure is less expensive and much faster. What is the result? As P. Archer stated, *"It takes just 5 servers to run the system for the whole of BT"* (see appendix 9).

Comparing to systems that other countries are using worldwide and the basic mechanisms discussed before, CleanFeed system seems to be the most effective low-cost solution.

The two-stage hybrid system manages to be fast and very accurate in blocking unacceptable content, while keeping the cost low. Yet, the main advantage of this system seems to be its main weakness, too. The two-stage scheme is vulnerable to some extent and can be overpassed by quite simple ways, as this book explains in the next section.

TECHNICAL WEAKNESSES AND CLEANFEED'S EFFECTIVENESS

There is a rich literature discussing in general techniques for circumventing different content blocking schemes (Dornseif, 2003; ONI, 2004; Finkelstein, 2001), and quite a few stating that it is easy to find guidelines and information regarding circumvention techniques (Zimmerman, 1999; Stadler, 2003).

In 2005, a technical report by Clayton (2005) was published presenting many technical weaknesses of CleanFeed system, how a user or content provider can circumvent it, and countermeasures that can be taken in order to make CleanFeed more effective.

Following the publication of this technical paper, BT and IWF spokesmen said that CleanFeed system does not aim to stop determined pedophiles, but only accidental access.

More specifically, IWF's Executive Director Peter Robbins stated that *"We are not there to stop determined paedophiles because they are always going to find a way around it"* (Grossman, 2006), while BT's Director of Internet Operations Mike Galvin stated that: *"We have built a system that will not stop the hardened paedophile [...] CleanFeed' s main aim is to stop accidental access from users following links, such as those in spam email"* (Mathieson, 2005).

Actually, even if at a first glance those statements seem logical and the decision by BT and IWF not to tackle this technical weaknesses sounds reasonable, a closer look proves that this is not the case. By "hardened paedophiles," both IWF and BT spokesmen mean a UK based Internet user with enough determination to find ways to circumvent CleanFeed. But actually, there are many technical weaknesses and circumventing techniques that can be used in order for accidental access to be possible without CleanFeed being able to prevent it (check the next section for more details).

In this section, simple circumventing techniques are being discussed that can be used by a spammer-like user and by a content provider without the need for a determined and/or computer advanced user. In each case, possible countermeasures are being proposed. Regarding techniques discussed in the upcoming sections, the description provided in this paper is based mainly on Clayton's research (2005 & 2008).

Circumventing CleanFeed by a Spammer-Like User

Concerning the hybrid two-stage CleanFeed scheme discussed in detail above it is effective to evade in either stage in order to circumvent it. Actually, in many cases, a user can circumvent CleanFeed without even knowing it by simply clicking on a link provided by spam emails or public forum's posts.

Figure 3. Circumventing techniques for spammer-like users

techniques	no cost	simplicity	determined/ advanced users
(1) Internet Archive Services	✓	✓	✗
(2) Web proxies	✓	✓	✗
(3) URLs variations	✓	✓	✗

Using Internet Archive Services

There is a really simple and with no cost way to circumvent content blocking schemes by using Internet archive services. The most well known is the Internet

Archive (www.archive.org) which allows users to access an older version of a webpage through its *Wayback Machine* service (www.archive.org/web).

After getting in touch with Internet Archive's Office Manager Paul Forrest Hickman (see appendix 10), the authors verified that Internet Archive does not collaborate with IWF in order not to archive the banned websites. In fact, Internet Archive actually captures pages of pornographic nature, which can be removed only after individual notifications by the users and not in collaboration with a special third-body, like IWF. For all the above reasons, the use of Internet Archive as a way to circumvent CleanFeed system is possible and effective.

A minor disadvantage of this technique is that the copy will be some weeks old as every few weeks the new content of each website is archived. The main disadvantage is that the service is not transparent to the user, which means that the user needs to do special actions in order to access each blocked page (Dornseif, 2003).

In theory, this technique can circumvent all types of blocking. In practice, it can only be applied to static websites (no interaction or dynamic content) just offering simple content (images, text, and so on) or to some dynamic pages that render only standard html. In case a dynamic page contains elements (forms, JavaScript, and so forth) that requires interaction with the originating host server, then it cannot be archived fully as it will not contain the original site's functionality (Internet Archive, 2008a). Last, in case a website is password protected (sign-in or register procedures), then it is not archived by Internet Archive (Internet Archive, 2008a).

So, in order for this technique to be used by a spammer, a link can be provided in the main body of an email in order for the user to access an older version of a website with child abuse content. Moreover, because of the fact that users do not usually visit websites via the Internet Archive's *Wayback Machine*, it is more likely that the archived pages are not blocked, even if the actual website is. Finally, there is no need for advanced computer skills by the spammer or any additional cost in order for this technique to be used.

Concerning possible countermeasures, the blocking of the whole Internet Archive website is not obviously an option. According to Paul Forrest Hickman, "[t]he sites are excluded from the Wayback Machine and, depending on how it was excluded, that exclusion is not under our control (robots.txt files and such). Even for manual exclusions, that material is completely inaccessible to everyone (including us)" (see appendix 10).

Figure 4. Using Internet Archive Services (Circumventing techniques for spammer-like users)

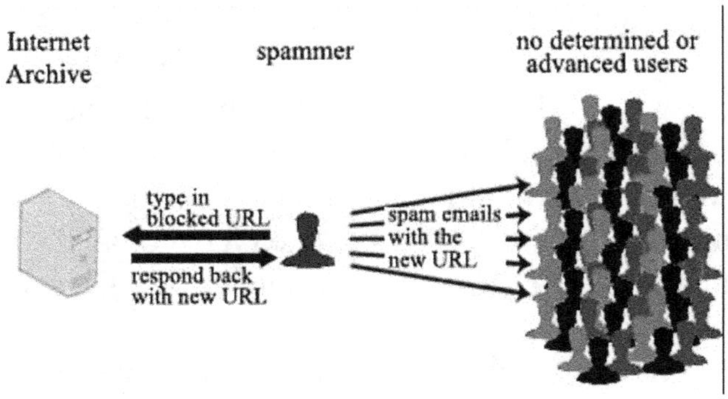

A possible way for IWF to tackle this issue is by manually checking via the Wayback Machine the URLs of its blocked websites. If there are archived webpages of blocked content, then IWF could update its list to include those URLs too.

Web Proxies

It is really simple for a user to configure a browser (Microsoft Internet Explorer, Mozilla Firefox, etc.) to use a web proxy through which all the traffic will be routed. So, every time, the web proxy will connect to the requested website on the browser's behalf. If a user manages to find a web proxy that is not inside BT's customer network, then he will be able to access the blocked content without CleanFeed interfering (Clayton, 2005 & PC Plus, 2011). What an Internet user has to do in order to use that technique is to find a web proxy that is not blocked by CleanFeed system; i.e. probably a web proxy based outside the UK.

The main advantage of this technique is that there are many websites offering lists of publicly accessible proxies (such as http://proxy.org/). Today, there are very large numbers of such proxies, mainly because of the fact that many end-user systems are inadequate configured and so they can be used by anyone who will manage to access them (Clayton, 2005 & Schafer, 2010).

But to configure a browser in order to access a blocked website means that the user consciously intends to access child abuse content. However, there is a way to make a user access such content via a proxy without knowing that he is using this technique. This can be simply done by a spammer using a web-based anonymous proxy service. He can actually type in such a proxy a blocked URL and the proxy will respond back by providing another URL. If then the spammer sends this URL to users via spam emails, the users simply need to click on the URL's link in order to unconsciously access the blocked website via this proxy.

For example, if a spammer wants a link for the website https://www.iwf.org.uk/ through the web-based anonymous proxy service http://mysecretip.info/index.php, he just needs to type in the address on this proxy's website and the latter will respond back with something like that:

http://mysecretip.info/browse.php?u=Oi8vd3d3Lml3Zi5vcmcudWsv&b=61

If IWF's website was blocked by CleanFeed, then the spammer could use the above link in order to send spam emails to users and try to attract them to access child abuse content.

Figure 5. Using web proxies(Circumventing techniques for spammer-like users)

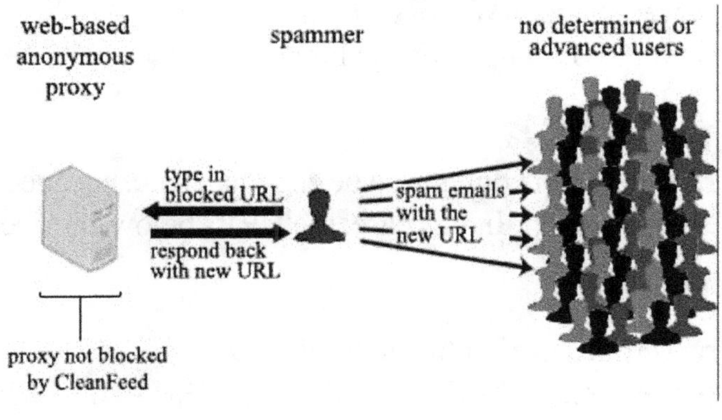

In theory, the best way to countermeasure this technical weakness of CleanFeed is to programme its first stage to send to the second stage not only the requests for "suspected websites," but also any request that is sent to external proxies. The main disadvantage of this proposal is that it will dramatically increase the traffic routed through CleanFeed web proxy, which is really impractical in terms of speed and cost.

Another—not automatic—way to countermeasure this technique is not by improving in technical terms the CleanFeed software, but by expanding IWF's list to include web proxies that are being used for circumventing CleanFeed.

The main disadvantage of this is that it can be done only manually, with the participation of real people.

Last, the possible best way of countermeasuring this technical weakness is by programming CleanFeed to discard all source routed packets, i.e. packets that are trying to access a website via proxies. By implementing this countermeasure, BT will block access to every proxy for its customers.

URLs Variations

This technique is based on the fact that many different URLs can access the same content. For example, there are web servers that do not treat URLs as being case sensitive, which means that all the URLs below can access the same content:

http://www.serverone.com/webpage.html
http://www.SERVERONE.com/webpage.html
http://www.ServerOne.com/webpage.html
http://www.serverone.com/Webpage.Html
http://www.serverONE.com/webpage.html
etc…

Moreover, requests for content can be encoded in i.e. hexadecimal without changing the request itself. In this case, the URLs below can access the same content:

http://www.serverone.com/Webpage.html
http://www.serverone.com/%57%65%62%70%61%67%65%2E%68%74%6D%6C
http://www.serverone.com/%57%65bpage.html
http://www.serverone.com/Webpa%67%65.html
http://www.serverone.com/Webpage%2E%68%74%6D%6C
etc…

What's more, the encoding of the request can be in IP level too, as there are web servers that host only one website and so they can be configured to respond to requests that use the website's IP address and not its hostname. In this case, there are many different URLs that can access the same content as IP addresses can be encoded in many different ways. So, if the www.

serverone.com resolves for examples to 11.12.13.14, then all the URLs below can access the same content:

http://11.12.13.14/Webpage.html
http://1011.1100.1101.1110/Webpage.html (binary)
http://13.14.15.16/Webpage.html (octal)
http://0013.0014.0015.0016/Webpage.html (octal with extra zeroes)
etc…

The main advantage of this technique is that there are really uncountable variations of a URL to choose from, and so unlimited choices to make in order to circumvent CleanFeed system. Moreover, due to the even more common use of IPv6 addresses in the future, which are a wide variety of semantically identical but syntactically differing IPs, there will be even more possible variations (Clayton, 2005 & Graziani, 2012). The most important disadvantage of this technique is that every kind of variation (case-sensitive, encoding, and so on) can be faced automatically in quite a simple way.

This technique can be used without additional cost or effort by the spammer. He just has to add to the main body of the email (a) variation(s) of the blocked URL and then send it as a spam email to users.

Regarding possible countermeasures, the most obvious way to tackle this problem is by CleanFeed software putting all blocked URLs into a canonical form before their encoding. This means that first all the blocked URLs in IWF's list have to be put into a canonical form before the encoding. Then, every URL of every request that comes to the first stage of CleanFeed for examination has to be put into a canonical form before the encoding and the examination itself. This technical improvement can countermeasure the addition of specious characters to URLs (such as extra zeroes) or encoded requests, etc. A detailed description of this countermeasure, full of technical terms and analysis that do not suit the purposes of this book, can be found in Clayton's paper (2005).

Circumventing CleanFeed by a Content Provider

In this section, the paper discusses possible techniques that content providers can use in order CleanFeed not to block their content, even if it is eligible for blocking. In none of the techniques presented below is there the need for a determined and/or computer advanced user. After their implementation

Figure 6. Using URLs variations(Circumventing techniques for spammer-like users)

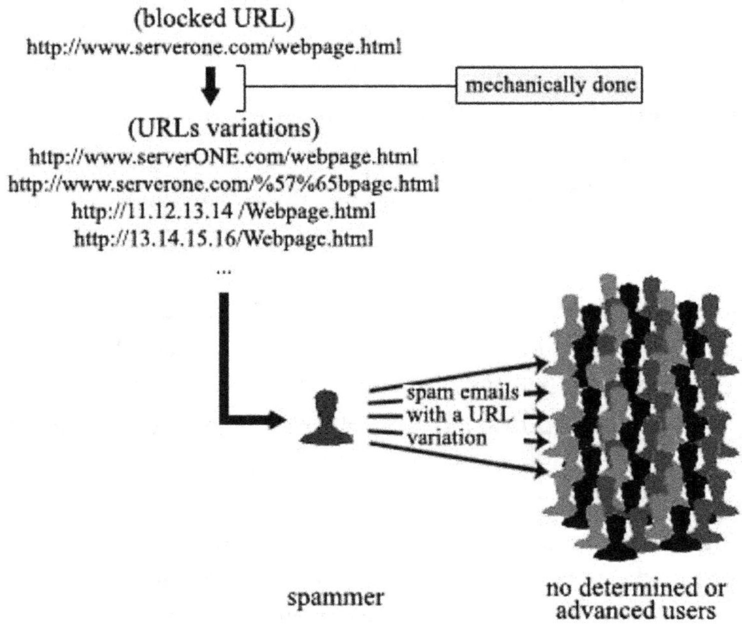

by the content provider, the users can access their illegal material by simply clicking on a link provided to them via a spam or public forum's post.

For each technique presented, proposals are also discussed for countermeasures and technical improvements that CleanFeed system can implement in order to tackle those circumvention issues.

Figure 7. Circumventing techniques for content providers

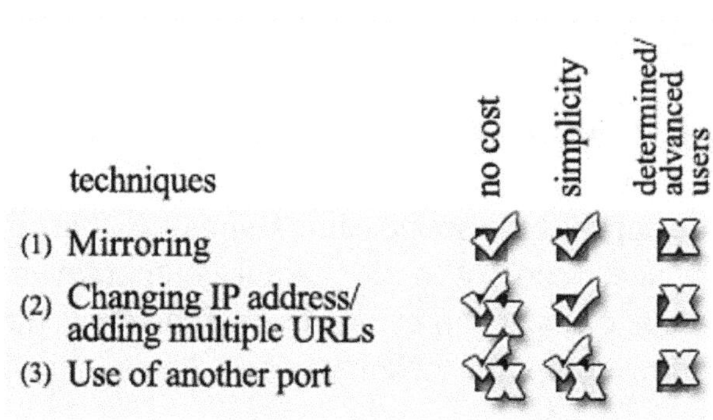

Mirroring

Mirroring is a technique using a host server (mirror) which retrieves the content from the source server and publishes it independently as a website. The retrieving and publishing procedures at mirroring are usually done automatically. Its common use is to reduce traffic in content provider's host servers and maintain the content available, even in cases of over-loading of one host server. Another, not so popular, use is to circumvent blocking schemes by making the same content available via different sources. So, even if a source is blocked, the content can be accessed via other sources. Mirroring technique can be used against IP filtering, DNS poisoning, and filtering HTTP proxies systems.

The main disadvantage of mirroring is—due to its simplicity—that it is only for static websites with no or little interactive elements (forms, JavaScript, and others). Dynamic websites that require procedures like sign-in or register can be mirrored in theory, but in practice this is very difficult and not practical whatsoever. Moreover, among its disadvantages is the fact that it is not transparent to the user, which means that the user has to be informed somehow about the mirror's addresses in order to be able to access them (Dornseif, 2003).

In fact, mirroring technique needs an existing not blocked communication channel in order to be effective, through which users can exchange links. So, the main question is why the users do not use these communications channels to exchange the content too, and not just the links. According to G. Schneider (1999), users of blocked content can exchange addresses of blocked content (domain names, IP addresses, and so forth) very quickly, something that needs further research to be verified (Dornseif, 2003).

Regarding possible countermeasures, the only way is to add the URLs of the mirrors to IWF list in order for CleanFeed system to block them too. Having in mind that the creation of mirrors for static websites is an easy and fast procedure, while the addition of their URLs in the IWF list is time-consuming, this countermeasure is quite impractical.

Changing IP Address/Adding Multiple URLs

This circumventing technique is part of a simple and very easy-to-use technique of moving the content from a blocked location to another unblocked location. The simplest way is by changing the IP address. So, when an IP address is

Figure 8. Mirroring (Circumventing techniques for content providers)

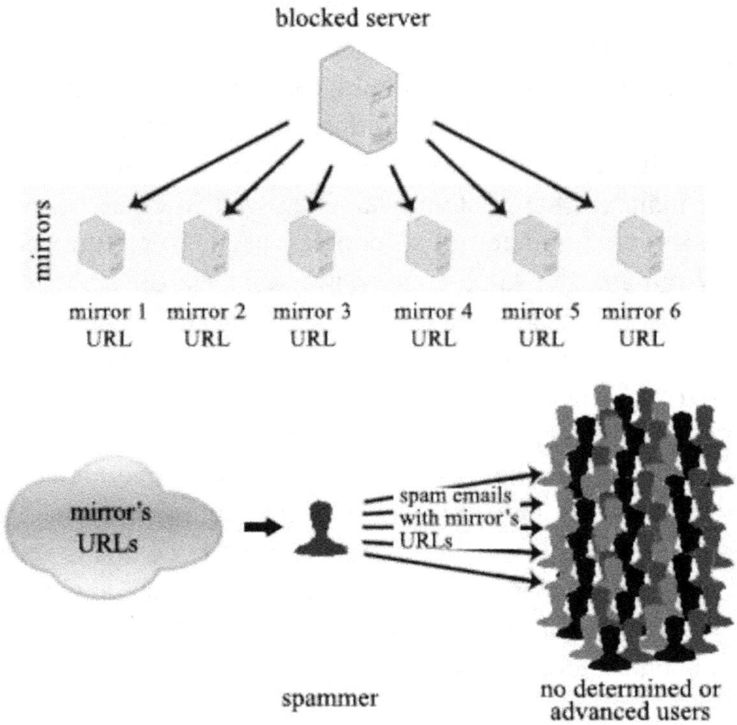

blocked by CleanFeed, then the content provider can move the website to another one; let's say from 10.5.5.0 to 10.5.5.1. Moreover, another way is to simply add URLs that redirect the user to the blocked content, in order for users to be able to access it by typing alternative URLs.

Concerning IP changing, a great advantage of this technique is that, when the content provider owes a whole server, this can be done at no cost and really simply. Moreover, if the IP changing is accompanied with a change to DNS, then this technique is transparent to the user, which means that the user just has to type in his browser the domain name that he already knows. Its most important disadvantage is that in practice IP changing can be done quite fast—even hourly, as in the case of Dutch internet provider xs4all in 1997 (Dornseif, 2003)—, but the DNS changing is not too fast. DNS changing can take even two days, in which case the content provider has to inform users about the new IP address if instant access is important.

Concerning adding multiple URLs, the purchase of a new domain name costs to the content provider, and when multiple URLs are considered, then the cost can be high. The cheapest way to use this technique is by creating sub-domains and using them as URLs for the same content, something that a content provider can do at no cost when it owes a domain name. For example, if CleanFeed blocks the URL www.serverone.com, then the content provider can create sub-domains, such as sub1.serverone.com, sub2.serverone.com, and so on, and connect them to the blocked content's IP address.

Regarding possible countermeasures, there are technical improvements that can be made in order to tackle both IP changing and multiple URLs techniques.

Concerning IP changing, the only way to countermeasure this technique is by updating the IWF's list regularly, adding the new IP addresses to be blocked. This can be done easily by checking logs of DNS activity fast enough, something that will identify that this kind of location movement is occurring (Clayton, 2005 & PC Plus 2011).

Figure 9. Changing IP address (Circumventing techniques for content providers)

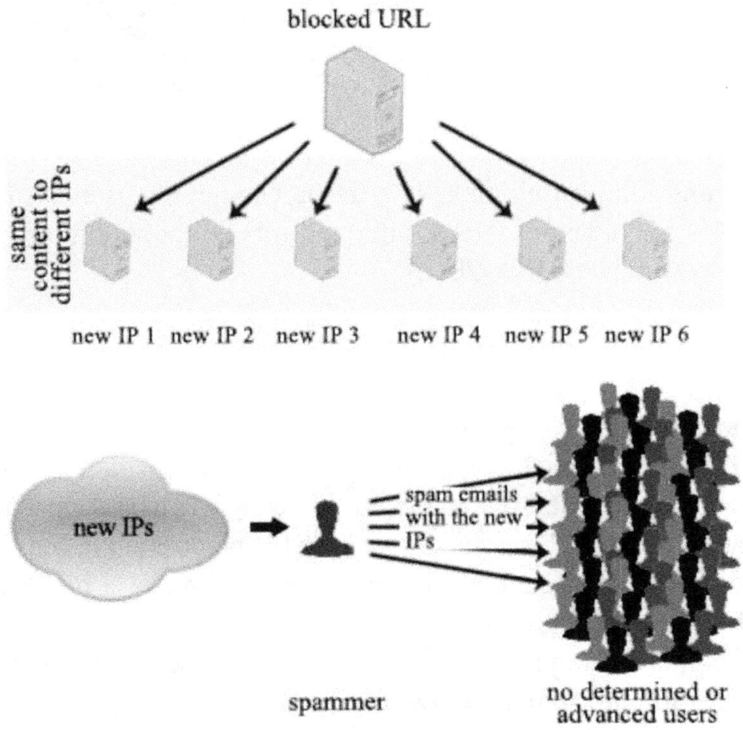

Figure 10. Adding multiple URLs (Circumventing techniques for content providers)

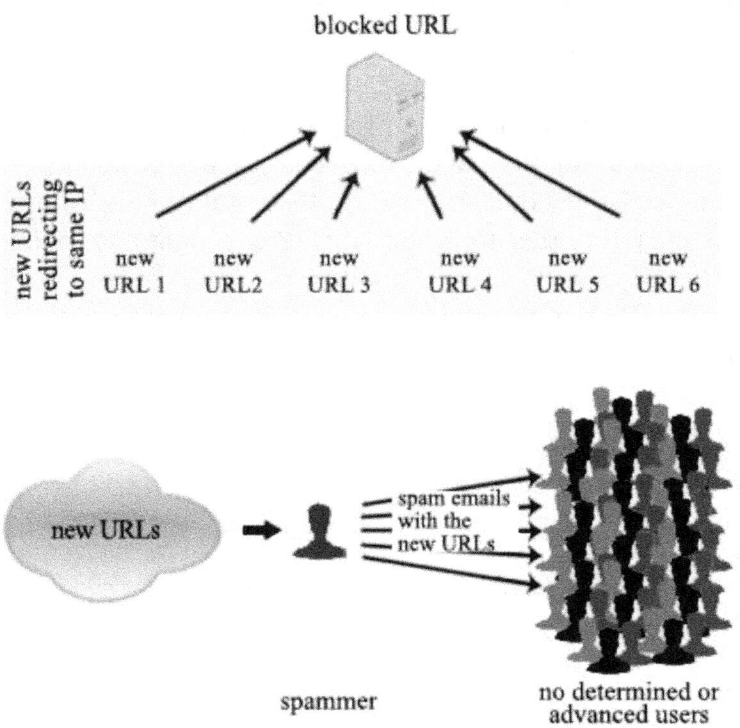

Concerning adding multiple URLs, the best countermeasure is to generate generic rules for blocking URLs, although this is not so simple (Clayton, 2005 & Palo Alto Networks, 2016).

Use Another Port

This technique can be implemented by changing the port number a web server software uses (most common HTTP port is 80) with another port. In the case where a content provider owns a server, this can be done with simple configuration of the web server software and at no cost at all, but this is not the situation when the content provider uses a server of a hosting service company where the cost is high and the procedure can be really complicated. In any case, this technique is not transparent to the user, so content provider needs to inform him, somehow (Dornseif, 2003).

From the spammer-like user point of view, it is really easy to force a user to accidentally access a blocked content by simply providing him via a spam email with a slightly different URL than the blocked one. More specifically, the spammer just has to change the initial URL adding the new port number:

http://www.serverone.com/webpage.html has to change to
http://www.serverone.com:10023/webpage.html

Concerning possible countermeasures, despite the fact that until now CleanFeed blocks only port 80, in technical terms there is no important reason for CleanFeed not to block other ports too. In practice, though, if content providers move massively to another port that is used by another kind of traffic (such as peer-to-peer, and so forth), then over-load issues may arise in the second stage of CleanFeed.

Figure 11. Using another port (Circumventing techniques for content providers)

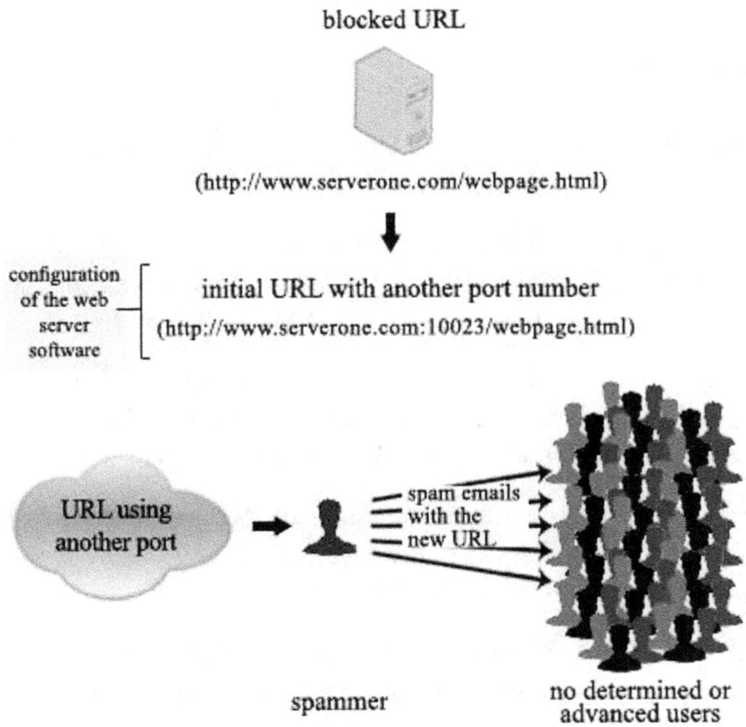

CONCLUSION

Regarding the technical weaknesses of CleanFeed system, the reader can find more details in Clayton's research and his two papers published in the past (2005 & 2008), discussing additionally possible attack techniques for closing down CleanFeed or even a technique to use CleanFeed system as an "oracle" and extract a list of banned websites from it. The general rule, though, is that the more computer literate the user or the content provider is, the wider the variety of circumventing techniques is for him to choose from.

Concerning CleanFeed system and its effectiveness to stop or at least minimise the accidental access of child abuse content from users following links in spam emails or public forum's posts, this is very unlikely to be true. As discussed, many circumventing techniques are available that a. are simple to use and b. can be used at low or even no cost at all. This means that an amateur computer user can actually circumvent CleanFeed.

REFERENCES

Berners-Lee, T. (1994). RFC1738 - Uniform Resource Locators (URL). *Rfc-base.org* http://www.faqs.org/rfcs/rfc1738.html

Clayton, R. (2005). Anonymity and Traceability to Cyberspace (Technical Report UCAM-CL-TR-653). *University of Cambridge, Computer Laboratory.* https://www.cl.cam.ac.uk/techreports/UCAM-CL-TR-653.html

Clayton, R. (2008). Failures of a Hybrid Content Blocking System. In G. Danezis & D. Martin (Eds.), *Privacy Enhancing Technologies, Fifth International Workshop, PET 2005*. Berlin: Springer Verlag.

Dornseif, M. (2003). Government mandated blocking of foreign Web content, Security, E-Learning, EServices. *Proceedings of the 17 DFN-Arbeitstagung uber Kommunikationsnetze*, 617–648.

Finkelstein, S. (2001). *BESS vs The Google Search Engine (Cache, Groups, Images), Censorware Investigations*. http://sethf.com/anticensorware/bess/google.php

Graziani, R. (2012). *IPv6 Fundamentals: A Straightforward Approach to Understanding IPv6*. Cisco Press.

Grossman, W. M. (2006). IWF reforms could pave way for UK net censorship. *The Register*. https://www.theregister.co.uk/2006/12/29/iwf_feature/

ISI. (2017). DOD Standard Internet Protocol. *Information Sciences Institute University of Southern California*. https://www.ietf.org/rfc/rfc0760.txt

Mathieson, S. A. (2005). Back door to the black list. *The Guardian*.

ONI. (2004). Google Search & Cache Filtering Behind China's Great Firewall. *OpenNet Initiative*. https://opennet.net/bulletins/006

Palo Alto Networks (2016). What is URL Filtering? *Info&Insights*.

Plus, P. C. (2011). The United Kingdom's secret firewall. *techradar*. https://www.techradar.com/news/internet/the-united-kingdom-s-secret-firewall-973454/2

Schafer, B. (2010). The UK Cleanfeed system— Lessons for the German debate? *Datenschutz und Datensicherheit*, *34*(8), 535–538. doi:10.100711623-010-0185-1

Schneider, G. (1999). Die Wirksamkkeit der Sperrung von Internet-Zugriffen. *MMR*, 571–577.

Stadler, T. (2003). Anmerkung zu VG Dusseldorf 15 L 4148/20. *MMR*, *2003*, 208–211.

Zimmermann, A. (1999). Polizeiliche Gefahrenabwehr und das Internet. *NJW*, 3145–3152.

Section 3

Measuring Public Opinion Around the World

Chapter 4
The Survey

ABSTRACT

There are very few surveys conducted worldwide regarding internet users' opinions about internet regulation. What's more, the authors have already discussed the importance of measuring public opinion around the world in their endeavour to design and propose a fair IRS that will be accepted by the internet users at a national level. In this chapter, the authors discuss the design of their questionnaire and how it was evolved from the initial 2007 UK questionnaire to the current one that was used for conducting surveys in six different countries. This chapter presents the procedure that was used for collecting responses and what kinds of "safeguard" measures were taken in order to avoid deterioration of the gathered survey data. What's more, the analysis procedure of the gathered data is being presented, and the authors discuss the possibility of biased questionnaires and how the latter can be tackled further in future research.

INTRODUCTION

There are very few surveys conducted worldwide regarding Internet users' opinion about Internet regulation. What's more, the authors have already discussed the importance of measuring public opinion around the world in their endeavor to design and propose a Fair IRS that will be accepted by the Internet users at a national level. After all, the UK paradigm is a great example of what negative public reaction can emerge in any Western democracy if an

DOI: 10.4018/978-1-5225-9973-9.ch004

IRS is going to be implemented "silently" and without consulting Internet users' opinion.

How can someone design and conduct specialized surveys then, in order to help a democratic government to develop a Fair IRS that online citizens will accept at a national level? This is the main question at this point and this chapter provides the appropriate answers.

More specifically, the authors discuss the design of the questionnaire and how it was evolved from the initial 2007 UK questionnaire to the current one that was used for conducting surveys in six different countries. This book presents the procedure that was used for collecting responses and what kinds of "safeguard" measures were taken in order to avoid deterioration of the gathered survey data. What's more, the analysis procedure of the gathered data is being presented, where this book discusses the possibility of biased questionnaires and how the latter can be tackled further in future research. Last, the authors provide a brief summary of this chapter and how it is linked to the next one.

DESIGN OF THE QUESTIONNAIRE

The design of the initial 2007 UK questionnaire was based on previous literature research and media statements in order to gather useful results about what UK based Internet users thought (back then) about Internet regulation in general and BT's CleanFeed specifically (Bright, 2004; Hamade, 2008). Moreover, there were questions about the period they lived in the UK, their religious affiliation, their current parenthood, and their willingness (or not) to have children in the future, and so on (Koumartzis, 2008).

Before conducting the survey, the initial questionnaire was reviewed by two lecturers of London College of Communication (University of the Arts London), Dr. David Penfold (with an academic expertise in research methods) and Keith Martin (with a working expertise in digital technologies). Alterations were made based on the latter's comments. The majority of the collected data proved to be of crucial importance as it helped the authors to make specific and scientifically backed proposals for the improvement of BT's CleanFeed (Koumartzis & Veglis, 2011). On the other hand, the authors identified important issues on specific questions that were then improved in later versions of the questionnaire (see for more details).

In 2010, a questionnaire was designed for surveys in different countries, with the aid and feedback of Dr. Alexandros Baltzis (School of Journalism and Mass Communications, Aristotle University of Thessaloniki). The 2010 questionnaire was an enriched and improved version of the initial one (see appendix 14 for the 2007 UK questionnaire, and appendix 1 for the 2010 Greece Survey's questionnaire).

Regarding the structure of the 2010 questionnaire, there were questions focusing on demographical data related to the participants (part 1), on how often and in what way participants use the Internet (part 2), on what experience and awareness they have regarding Internet regulation worldwide (part 3) and in their countries (part 4), and where they stand regarding the implementation of an IRS in their country and what features the latter had to have in order to accept it (part 5).

The number of questions ranged between 19 and 22 as there were additional ones when related incidents were occurring (as in India Survey, where a question was included regarding 2012 protests against the SOPA/PIPA Internet regulation legislation in USA).

GATHERING PARTICIPANTS FOR THE SURVEYS

The surveys were conducted between 2010 and 2012 in Greece, Germany, Russia, India, Kosovo, and Cyprus (see more details in chapters 5 to 11). What's more, there were surveys conducted in other countries too (such as Turkey, Austria, and Israel) that did not manage to gather the minimum number of participants (i.e. 50) set by the authors to be included in this book.

The role of these surveys was to determine details about its structure, content, average time to complete, focus, and so forth, and use that feedback in case a related mass survey takes place in the specific country (as it was done in the case of Greece).

Each survey was conducted with the aid of a country-based researcher (i.e. academic, university teaching stuff, journalist, and so on). The latter translated the English version of the questionnaire in his language, and helped collect responses from different target groups (i.e. university stuff and students in Germany and Russia, online citizens in India and Cyprus, and so forth).

The surveys were conducted exclusively online for obvious reasons (an IRS implementation will directly and mainly affect online citizens, while questions related to such a scenario needs prior experience surfing through the Internet). For the survey development, publication, and responses' collection, SurveyGizmo.com was used as it is one of the most reliable online services worldwide used by academics and researchers (INC, 2011· Davidson, 2011).

The company kindly offered a professional account for free to the authors for the needs of their research.

Promoting the Use of Surveys Through Webobserver.net

From March 2010 until October 2013 (when the mass survey in Greece took place), the authors constantly promoted the use of surveys as a tool for the design procedure of such systems through WebObserver.net website, welcoming international participation. The website was focusing on presenting the research project to researchers all over the world, providing the needed guidance and tools to run the survey to their country.

It managed to conduct six surveys with limited samples in Greece, Germany, Russia, India, Kosovo, and Cyprus, and another mass survey in Greece (more details in chapters 5 to 11). Furthermore, the questionnaire was translated in Turkish and Modern Hebrew too, and surveys were conducted in Turkey, Israel, and Austria without being able to gather the minimum number of participants (i.e. 50) set by the authors to be included in this research.

Figure 1. Upper part of the first page of WebObserver.net showing the world map of where related surveys took place by the authors or other initiatives.

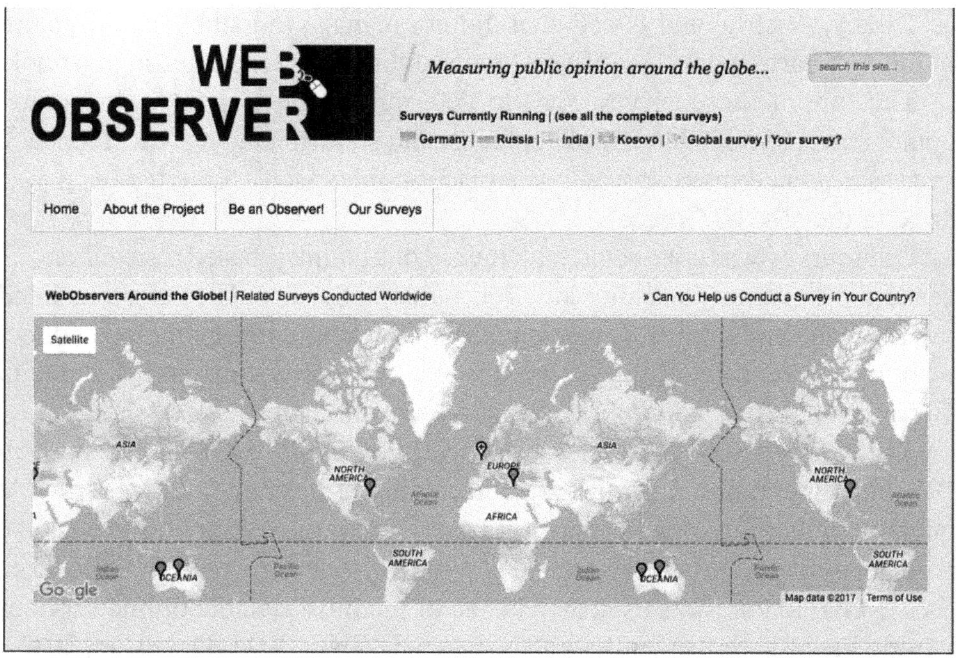

In the about section of the website, there was among others the following text: "WebObserver.net is an international project which aims to measure what Internet users think about the emerging phenomenon of Internet regulation, and at the same time inform citizens around the world for this crucial (for the future of Web) issue.

Our research is based on the surveys conducted in different languages worldwide via cooperation with country-based researchers and university academics. These surveys have many questions in common, enabling us to produce gradually global data regarding Internet regulation, and measure the opinion of users around the globe.

On March 20th 2010, WebObserver.net joined the efforts of academics around the world, in hopes of raising public awareness of a less known but rapidly increasing phenomenon: internet censorship and regulation governance of the web."

Additionally, there was a subpage presenting a priority list and the needs of this initiative, along with explaining what are the tools that the authors provide to other researchers. Among others, there was the following text: "WebObserver.net is looking for participants from many different countries

Figure 2. The lower part of the first page of WebObserver.net inviting researchers around the world to participate in this initiative

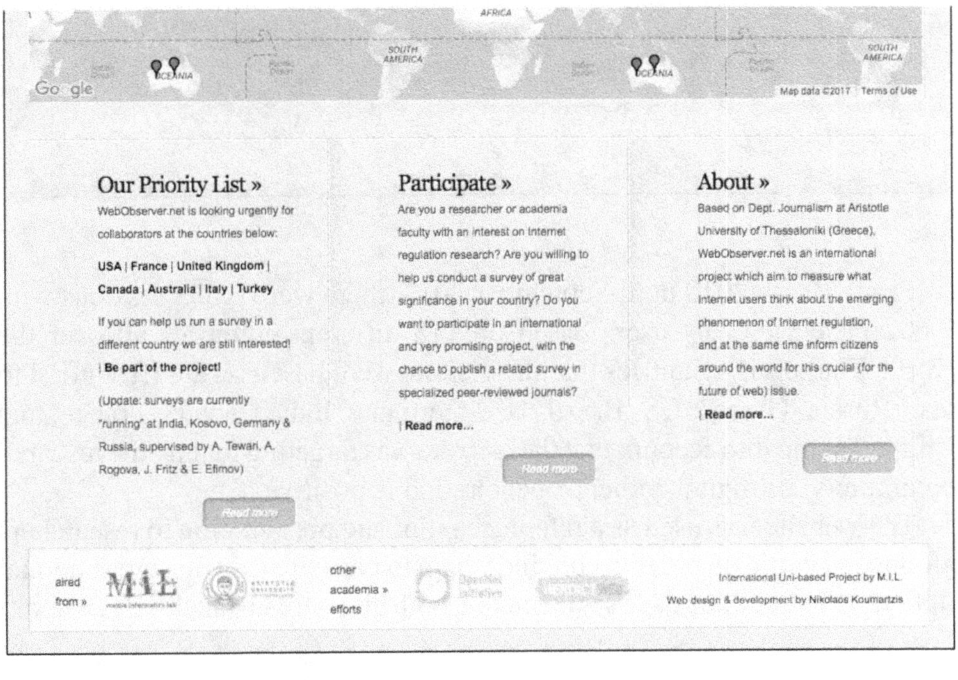

(please see our high-priority list) in order to conduct a survey regarding Internet regulation phenomenon. We provide all the needed questions in English plus all the needed (and technology advanced) tools, and you provide only the translation to your language plus a suggested sample (limited and preferably highly educated)."

Figure 3. The subpage "How to participate?" of WebObserver.net, explaining how a researcher can participate in the initiative and what are the tools provided by the authors

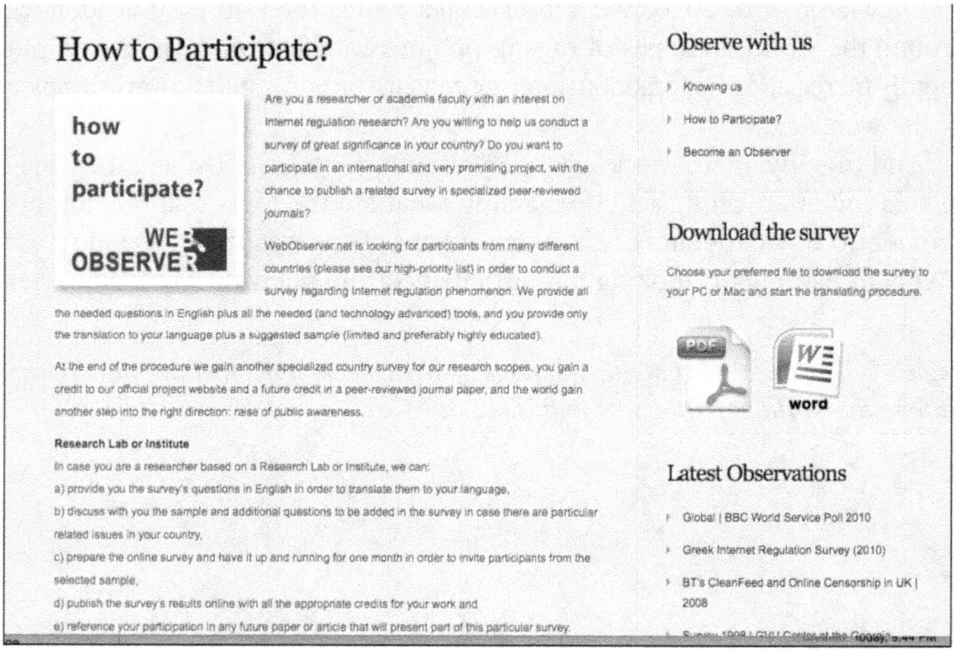

From March 2010 until September 2017, there were 6.533 sessions with 9.602 page views by users based on 118 different countries all over the world. The top 10 countries that the visitors were based on are (from first to last) Russia, Greece, US, Brazil, UK, Germany, Italy, Canada, France, and China. Taking into account that the website was targeting mainly the research community, its digital audience penetration is positive.

The website was used as a reference point and presentation to researchers around the world, in order to convince them to participate in this international initiative. The authors used social media; both mainstream (such as Facebook) and specialised in the academic community (such as Mendeley), in order to get in touch with scientists having conducted research in related fields. What's more, they used direct email communication with suggested liaisons, and promotion at digital and print mainstream media too. The publication of the website was strictly focusing on the academic community and not the general public.

Figure 4. User sessions of WebObserver.net from March 2010 until September 2017 (source: Google Analytics)

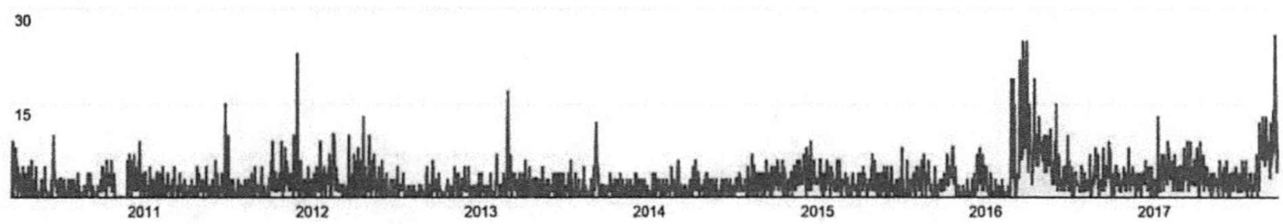

Verifying Survey's Responses

Due to the fact that these surveys were conducted for an extensive period of time (one to three months each) and they were accessible through the Internet from any part of the globe, the authors had to find a way to accept and analyse only verified responses. In this context, there were five simple verification keys:

1. Successful completion of the entire questionnaire.
2. No more than two questionnaires filled by the same IP (there were some exceptions, see below).
3. Time of completion no more than 15 minutes.
4. Time of completion no less than 2 minutes.
5. Country-based IP addresses (with very few exceptions).

The first key was chosen for obvious reasons, as there cannot be data integrity when the participant decides for any reason not to finish the questionnaire. The second key was chosen in order to prevent a respondent from filling in more than one questionnaire. The third key was chosen in order to ensure that no more than one respondent took part in each questionnaire. The fourth key was chosen in order to ensure as much as it is possible that no response was included based on chance answers or automatic algorithms (use of internet

Figure 5. A world map showing the countries that WebObserver.net visitors were based on
(source: Google Analytics)

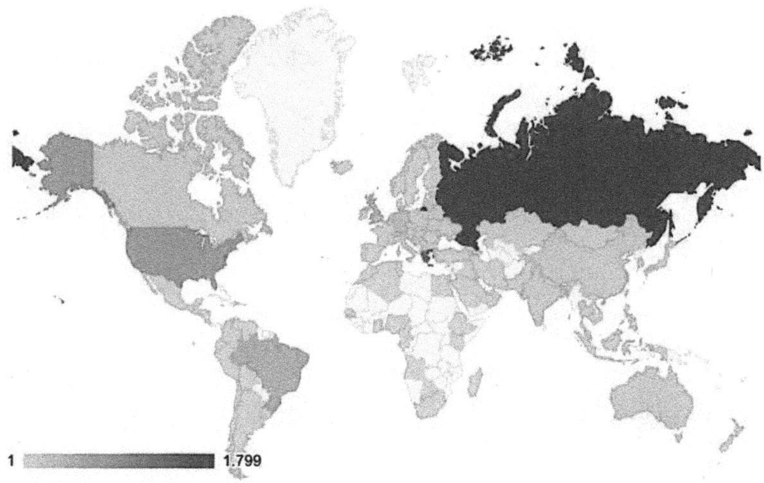

bots, specialised software, and so on). Last, the fifth key was chosen in order to avoid respondents that were not online citizens of the particular country that each survey was focusing on.

Regarding the second verification key, it was mainly used in order to avoid to some extent ballot stuffing (i.e. submission of multiple responses from one person). In every response, the survey software stored the IP of the respondent's computer. In case two or more different responses shared the same IP, all were discarded and only the first response (time variable) was considered during the analysis stage. There were made very few exceptions following prior communication between participants and the researcher, in order for more than 1 participant to fill the questionnaire from computers that share the same IP address (i.e. computers connected to the Internet via the same router, and so forth).

Even if a lot of effort was made to avoid ballot stuffing, it was possible for one person to submit more than one response by simply filling in the questionnaire from computers with a different IP address. Concerning the technology used (i.e. SurveyGizmo.com), every available feature was used in order to achieve data integrity.

DATA REPRESENTATION AND STATISTICAL ANALYSIS

The authors discuss the gathered data both through a. statistical graphics (using pie charts and histograms), and b. statistical analysis (using one by one variable analysis). The statistical graphics (a.) are used in order to visualise the quantitative data of the surveys and communicate the results for some basic straightforward analysis, while statistical analysis (b.) is used to identify trends and associations between different participants' groups in a country or between two or more different countries' Internet users.

Data Representation

Many branches of science use data representation or data visualisation today, as a means of visual communication. The authors consider its usage essential, in order to be able to communicate the gathered survey results to scientists of different fields and to a non-scientific audience.

According to Viegas & Wattenberg (2011), the ideal data representation not only communicates the results clearly, but "stimulates viewer engagement" as well.

According to Few (2016), there are at least eight types of quantitative messages that an audience might attempt to understand from a set of data. The researcher has to find the appropriate graphs to communicate that message in the most efficient way.

In this book, the authors have to communicate survey data a. as categorical subdivisions measured as a ratio to the whole (meaning a percentage out of 100 percent), and b. as frequency distribution (meaning the number of observations of a particular variable for the given interval). According to Few (2016), the best data representation graph for a. is a pie chart, while for b. is a histogram (type of bar chart).

Regarding the analysis' results, the authors discuss each country's survey in separate sections (see chapters 5 to 11) by presenting a great part of the gathered data. For the entirety of the results, please see appendices 15 to 21 at the end of this book.

Non-Parametric Measures for the Statistical Analysis

Concerning the statistical analysis, the non-parametric measures Pearson chi-square (χ^2), Cramer's V coefficient, Goodman - Kruskal's gamma and

Kendall's tau were used. In the following sections, the authors provide a brief introduction for all the latter.

Pearson's Chi-Square and Cramer's V Coefficient

In statistics, Cramér' s V coefficient is a measure of association between two nominal variables (of no intrinsic order) with a value between 0 and +1 (inclusive). Cramer's V is based on Pearson's chi-square (χ^2) and it was initially published by Harald Cramér in 1946 (Cramér, 1946). Cramer's V coefficient answers the question "Is there a relationship between our dependent variable and our independent variable?".

In this book, it is used for questions with nominal data of no intrinsic order. For example, it is used for the survey's question "What kind of content should be regulated if the Indian state decides to implement such a system?", which among others has the answers "Pornographic content," "Hate speech content," "Defamation content," and others.

According to Siardos (2016), "With chi-square and Cramer's V, we compare the observed frequencies in the cells of a contingency table with what we would expect to see if the two variables are independent. Chi-square says that there is a significant relationship between variables, but it does not say just how significant and important this is." The authors use Pearson's chi-square and Cramer's V in order to answer the question "How strong does the association appear to be?" between two nominal variables. More specifically, there is no association between the variables when Cramér's V is 0, and there is complete association when it is 1 (Acock & Stavig, 1979).

Goodman-Kruskal's Gamma

In statistics, Goodman-Kruskal's gamma is an ordinal measure of association. The authors use it to measure the strength of association of the cross tabulated data when both variables are measured at the ordinal level.

According to Siardos (2016), "It is suitable for use with ordinal variables or with dichotomous nominal variables. It is based on values of paired observations compared in terms of their relative rankings on the independent and dependent variables."

Goodman-Kruskal's gamma values range from −1 (100% negative association, or perfect inversion) to +1 (100% positive association, or perfect agreement), while a value of 0 indicates no association at all (Goodman & Kruskal, 1972).

It is worth mentioning that gamma statistic is preferable to Kendall's Tau, when the data contain many tied observations (Siardos, 2016).

Kendall's Tau

The Kendall tau coefficient is a statistic used to measure the ordinal association between two measured quantities (Agresti, 2010). Tau-b is used for square tables (numbers of rows and columns are equal), while tau-c is used for rectangular tables.

According to Siardos (2016), "It ranges from -1.0 (all pairs disagree) to 1.0 (all pairs agree). [...] Tau will only reach 1.0 when all of the cases in a table are on the major diagonal of the table, while gamma can reach 1.0 with cases off the major diagonal."

Regarding the statistical analysis of the present book, an example of the use of Kendall's tau-c is the following. If Kendall's tau-c for the gender/IRS level is -0.160 (participants' gender in correlation with their willingness to accept the implementation of an Internet regulation system), the data indicates that gender is negatively associated with Internet regulation system level.

As Siardos (2016) points out, "Tau is just the same as gamma coefficient. However, it is a statistic that is more 'conservative' (typically lower in value) than gamma."

POSSIBILITY OF BIASED QUESTIONNAIRE AND PROPOSALS FOR FUTURE SURVEYS

Before proceeding to the tackling of the objectives stated in the introduction of the current chapter, it is very important to discuss the possibility of the questionnaire used being biased and based on those conclusions to propose specific improvements for future related surveys.

How Biased Was the Questionnaire Used?

Regarding the former, different actions, measures were taken to avoid such a scenario. First of all, the questionnaire was evaluated by three academics from two different universities (University of the Arts, London and Aristotle University of Thessaloniki), and changes were made based on their feedback.

What's more, the initial questionnaire was designed in 2007 and, until today, many improvements were implemented based on participants' and academics' feedback. Also, part of the survey's results were presented in peer-reviewed journals and conferences in English, generating even further evaluation by academics and researchers around the world (Koumartzis, 2008· Koumartzis & Veglis, 2011a, 2011b, 2011c, 2012, 2014 and 2015). Last, there was a final evaluation stage of the questionnaire by the regional liaison, during its translation to the language of each country.

On all occasions, the survey was welcomed without any negative opinions expressed, except few exceptions. These exceptions were then evaluated separately by the authors and academic staff in order to determine if it can lead to further improvements. An example of such an exception was documented during the 2007 UK Survey, where one particular participant reacted quite passionately, claiming that the text used in the invitation was biased. After researcher's inquiry to London College of Communication to evaluate the issue, two academics were informed and conclude that there is no such an issue.

At this point, it is important to state that, at the end of the survey, researcher's email was always provided in order for anyone who would like to comment to get in touch with him. Again, there were no further negative opinions expressed about the questionnaire or the survey procedure in general.

Concerns and Solutions During the Survey's Design and Execution

Bias in questionnaires is a serious problem and, in order for accurate data to be gathered, researchers have to avoid or at least minimise bias in the design of their questionnaires. According to Choi & Pak (2008), there are three categories of main sources of bias: *"the way a question is designed, the way the questionnaire as a whole is designed, and how the questionnaire is administered."* A careful study of this paper was made in order to avoid common and obvious faults.

Comparing the questionnaires used with the points stated in the aforementioned paper, some particular proposals for improvements can be made. This kind of improvements were implemented during the surveys' stage, and in the latter stage of the mass survey in Greece. Some examples are discussed below.

Regarding the design of the questions, Choi & Pak state that a researcher must try to use neutral words wherever is needed. For example, the use of "censorship system" (used in questions 16 & 17 of the initial 2007 UK Survey, see Appendix 13) must be avoided and the use of "content blocking system" or "content filtering system" may be preferred (as it was done in all surveys).

Moreover, long questions must be avoided; something though that cannot be done in some cases where, in order for the participants to be able to answer, they must be informed first to some extent. A possible solution is this kind of questions not to be answered at all by those participants who do not know enough and need further information, but only by those respondents that already have all the information needed via sources not connected to the researcher. This can be done by automatically enabling or disabling the access to those questions based on the participants' answer(s) to some initial questions. The 2010 and on surveys implemented that solution to an extent.

Regarding the administration of the questionnaire and more specifically the invitations sent to possible respondents, again researchers must try to use neutral words wherever is needed and, if it is possible, not to describe at all the problem that is researched. Concerning the latter, it can be easily done when the participants needed are ensured, but when this is not the case an invitation without an interesting description has far fewer possibilities to attract the respondents needed.

So, the obvious solution to that problem is for the survey to be promoted or even run by a body capable of attracting the desired number of participants. A practical solution will be to include related questions to an annual broadband survey run by UK ISPs, something like the *Australian Broadband Survey for 2007* (Whirlpool, 2010a).

CONCLUSION

In this chapter, the authors explain how the initial questionnaire was designed and later improved, how the participants' responses were collected and verified, and how the results are going to be presented and analysed. What's more, they discuss the possibility of bias questions in the questionnaire, and how this can be tackled for future research.

Having discussed all the above, it is time this book to proceed with presenting all the gathered data from different countries' surveys that were conducted from 2010 and onwards. This is the topic of the next chapters, where the authors present and analyse survey's data gathered from Greece, Germany, Russia, India, Kosovo, and Cyprus.

REFERENCES

Acock, A., & Stavig, G. (1979). A Measure of Association for Nonparametric Statistics. *Social Forces, 57*(4), 1381–1386. doi:10.2307/2577276

Agresti, A. (2010). *Analysis of Ordinal Categorical Data* (2nd ed.). New York: John Wiley & Sons. doi:10.1002/9780470594001

Bright, M. (2004, June 6). BT puts block on child porn sites. *The Observer.*

Choi, B., & Pak, A. (2008). A Catalog of Biases in Questionnaires. *PubMed Central Journal List.* http://www.pubmedcentral.nih.gov/articlerender.fcgi?artid=1323316

Cramér, H. (1946). *Mathematical Methods of Statistics.* Princeton University Press.

Davidson, M. (2011). Survey Gizmo responds to online polling growth. *Boulder County Business Report.*

Few, S. (2016). Selecting the Right Graph for Your Message. *Perceptual Edge.* http://www.perceptualedge.com/articles/ie/the_right_graph.pdf

Goodman, L. A., & Kruskal, W. H. (1972). Measures of Association for Cross Classifications, IV: Simplification of Asymptotic Variances. *Journal of the American Statistical Association, 67*(338), 415–421. doi:10.1080/01621459.1972.10482401

Hamade, S. N. (2008). Internet Filtering and Censorship. In *Fifth International Conference on Information Technology: New Generations.* New York: IEEE Computer Society.

INC. (2011). *Top Software Companies on the 2011 Inc. 5000. INC Magazine.*

Koumartzis, N. (2008). *BT's CleanFeed and Online Censorship in UK: Improvements for a More Secure and Ethically Correct Systeym* (Doctoral dissertation). University of the Arts London, London College of Communication, London, UK.

Koumartzis, N., & Veglis, A. (2011a). Internet Regulation: The Need for More Transparent Internet Filtering Systems and improved measurement of public opinion on Internet Filtering. *First Monday, 16*(10). https://firstmonday.org/ojs/index.php/fm/article/view/3266/3071

Koumartzis, N., & Veglis, A. (2011b). On the Pursue for a Fair Internet Regulation system. *Sixteenth IEEE Symposium on Computers and Communications (ISCC11).*

Koumartzis, N., & Veglis, A. (2011c). The Future of Internet Regulation: Current Trends, a Dangerous Precedent and the Role of Internet Users. *Euro-NF International Workshop on Traffic and Congestion Control for the Future Internet.*

Koumartzis, N., & Veglis, A. (2012). Internet Regulation: A New Approach: Outline of a system formed to be controlled by the Internet Users. *Computer Technology and Application, 3*(1), 16–23.

Koumartzis, N., & Veglis, A. (2014). Internet Regulation and Online Censorship. *International Journal of E-Politics, 5*(4), 65–80. doi:10.4018/ijep.2014100104

Koumartzis, N., & Veglis, A. (2015). Internet Regulation and Online Censorship. *The First International Congress on the Internet, Trolling and Addiction (ITA15).*

Siardos, G. (2016). Non parametric measures. *Appendix 12.*

Viegas, F., & Wattenberg, M. (2011). How To Make Data Look Sexy. *CNN.* http://edition.cnn.com/2011/OPINION/04/19/sexy.data/

Whirlpool. (2010a). Australian Broadband Survey 2007. *Whirlpool.* https://whirlpool.net.au/survey/2007/

Chapter 5
Research in Greece

ABSTRACT

This chapter presents data gathered by Greece related to an initial survey that was conducted by the authors during June 2010 at the Aristotle University of Thessaloniki. This survey was based on a limited but highly educated sample consisting mainly of MA and PhD students, along with teaching staff of the Department of Journalism and Mass Communications. The authors present statistical graphics in order to visualise the quantitative data.

INTRODUCTION

Chapters 1 and 2 present many examples of why a Fair IRS must be highly adaptable to each country's special political needs in order to be accepted by the general public. This is why the authors strongly believe that surveys can play a key role in designing the right FIRS for each country and implementing it with high percentages of acceptance by the general public.

The following chapters present valuable data gathered by six related surveys that were conducted by the authors in different countries worldwide. This chapter focus on the survey conducted in Greece.

In the sections below, the authors present statistical graphics in order to visualise the quantitative data gathered in surveys conducted in Greece, Germany, Russia, India, Kosovo, and Cyprus. Additionally to the latter, statistical analysis is being conducted (using one by one variable analysis) in order to identify trends and associations between different groups in the same country and between Internet users in different countries.

DOI: 10.4018/978-1-5225-9973-9.ch005

GREECE SURVEY

The presentation of the surveys' data starts with Greece Survey that was conducted during June 2010 at the Aristotle University of Thessaloniki (Koumartzis 2014). This survey was based on a limited but highly educated sample consisting mainly of MA and PhD students, along with teaching staff of the Department of Journalism and Mass Communications. These participants were chosen because of the fact that they were quite familiar with web technologies and well informed about the issue of Internet regulation. The survey managed to gather responses from 60 participants.

The authors begin by presenting some of the survey's results that are related to their research topic, and end with their conclusions. The rest of the survey's results can be found in Appendix 15. The statistical graphs below are in the original language, with an explanation in English for each one of them.

GREEK INTERNET USERS AND INTERNET REGULATION POLICIES

Below, the authors present a series of related inquiries regarding their research topic.

A question of major significance was "Are you informed regarding the global phenomenon of Internet regulation?", to which respondents stated that they were informed to some extent at an overall rate of 85 percent. More

Figure 1. Are you aware of the global phenomenon of Internet regulation? (Greece Survey)

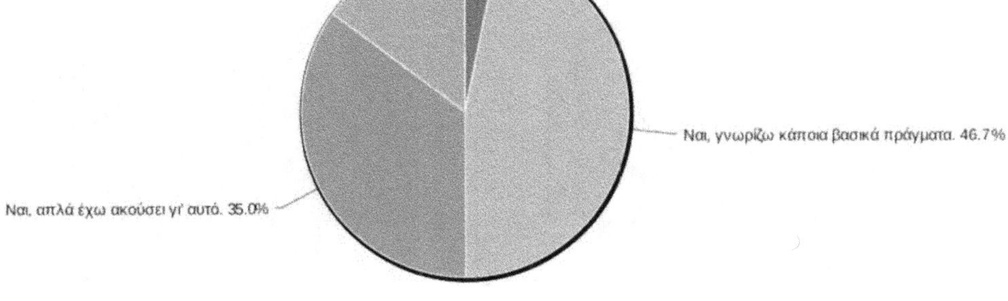

specifically, 3.3 percent of the participants stated well-informed, 46.7 percent that they just knew the basics, 35 percent that they just heard about it, and only 15 percent stated that they knew nothing at all.

Figure 2. What were the means of your information? (Greece Survey)

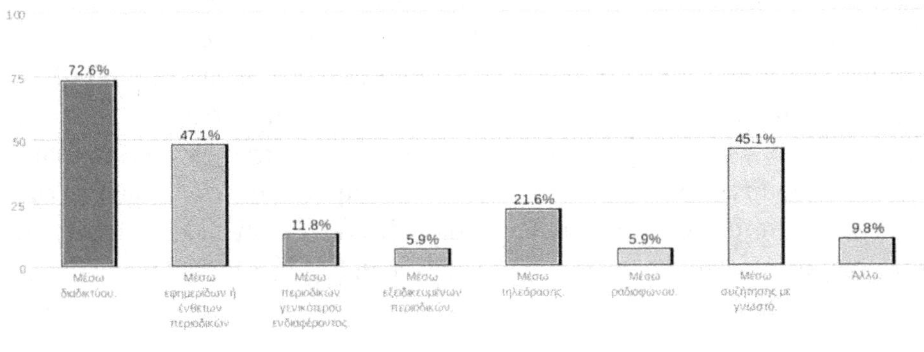

Regarding the means of their information, it is worth mentioning that 72.6 percent read about it online, 47.1 percent via newspapers, and 45.1 percent through private conversation.

Concerning the source of information, 62.5 percent of the respondents stated that it was mass media, and 52.1 percent that they were specialised researchers and related scientists. Only 4.2 percent stated that it was through government briefing or statements, and 47.9 percent that their source were individuals they knew personally.

Figure 3. Who was the source of your information? (Greece Survey)

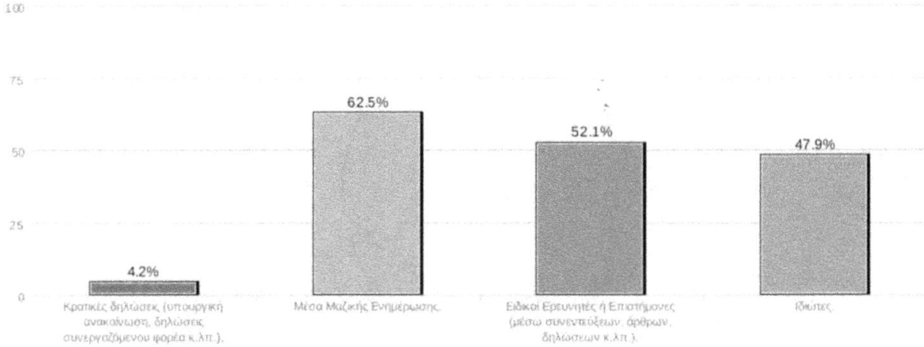

Another interesting question was "Have you ever experienced any kind of Internet censorship as a user?". 16.7 percent of the respondents stated "Yes, at least once," 38.3 percent stated "No, never," while a 45 percent stated that they actually do not know.

Figure 4. Have you ever faced online censorship in the past? (Greece Survey)

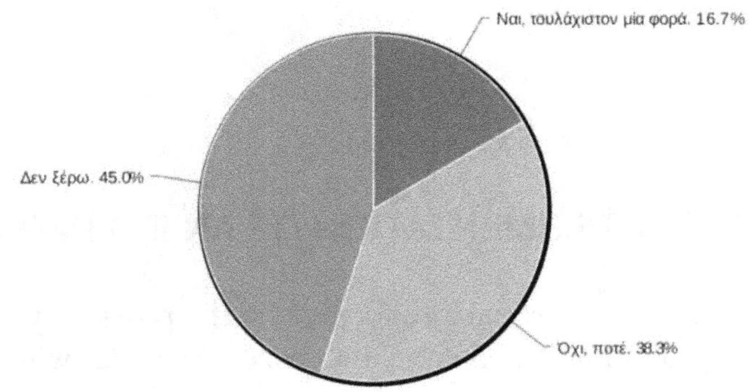

From those who answered "Yes, at least once" to the previous question, 41.7 percent stated that they were using the Internet in Greece and they were trying to visit a foreign website, while 33.3 percent stated that they were trying to visit a Greek website.

Figure 5. Were you using the Internet from Greece? (Greece Survey)

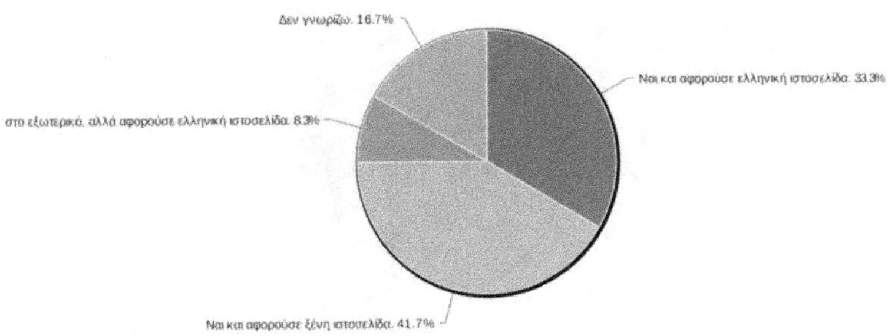

What's more, there was a question asking "Have you ever heard about Internet censorship incidents that took place abroad?", to which 55.9 percent answered positively and 44.1 percent negatively.

Figure 6. Have you ever heard of censorship incidents outside Greece? (Greece Survey)

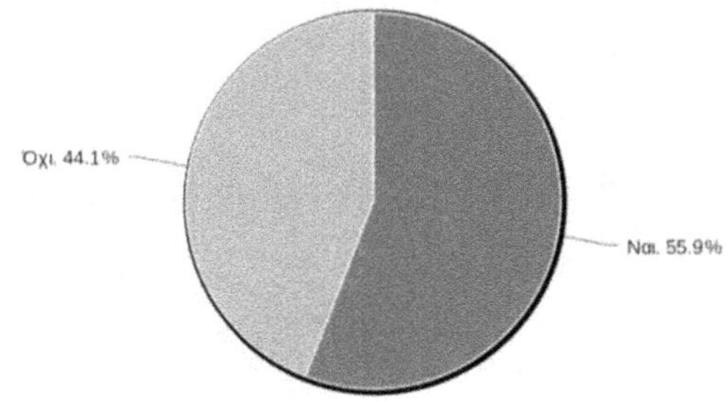

ABOUT THE IMPLEMENTATION OF AN IRS IN GREECE

The last part of this questionnaire focuses on the possibility of an Internet Regulation System implementation in Greece, and under which conditions.

To the question "Do you agree with the implementation (by the state) of an IRS focusing on the regulation of highly sensitive online content, such as child pornography, hate speech, or pro-terrorism websites and so on," 49.2 percent answered "Yes," 30.5 percent "Yes, under condition," and only 20.3 percent answered "No."

Figure 7. Do you agree with the implementation of an Internet regulation system by the state focusing on illegal content? (Greece Survey)

Regarding the type of online content that a Greek IRS should regulate, 61 percent stated "hate-speech websites," 61 percent "pornographic websites," 25.4 percent "defamatory content," and only 13.6 percent stated "online piracy websites (movies, music, books, and so forth)."

Figure 8. What kind of content should be regulated if your country's state decides to implement such a system? (Greece Survey)

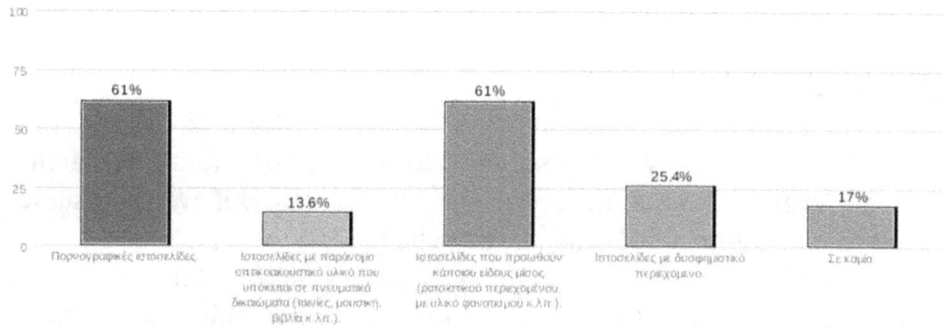

Last, concerning the entity that they prefer to be in control of such an IRS, 59.3 percent of the respondents stated "Research or Educational Institutes inside universities," 32.2 percent "Related non-governmental organisations (such as *Reporters without borders,* and so on)," and only 20.3 percent stated that they prefer a "State service in the related Ministry" or "Research institutes not related to universities."

Figure 9. In case an Internet regulation system is implemented in Greece, from whom do you believe it must be operated in order to function with justice and to be accepted by the majority of [you country] citizens? (Greece Survey)

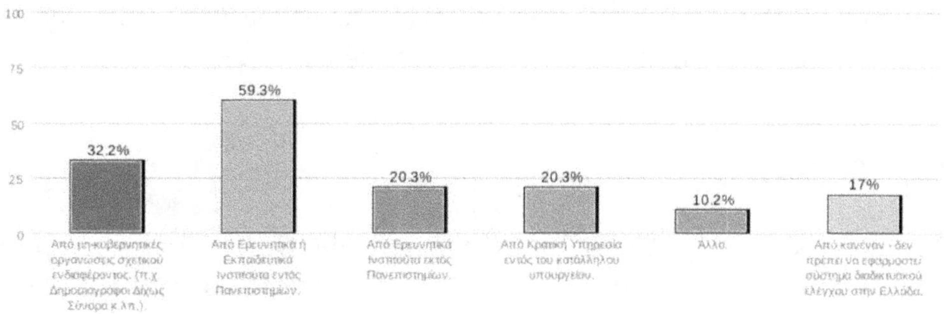

Unfortunately, a statistical analysis of the aforementioned data (gathered through SurveyGizmo Internet service) was not feasible. This was due to a crucial bug that SurveyGizmo faced during the time period when this survey took place, leading to the loss of raw data (among which was the authors'

initial survey in Greece). Fortunately, survey's graphs and figures were still available giving the authors the chance to present and discuss the results.

CONCLUSION

This survey was mainly used as a pilot for the authors' future research in Greece, Germany, Russia, India, Kosovo, and Cyprus. But even as a survey, there are some quite interesting points to be made.

First of all, it is quite impressive that the great majority of the participants were aware of the global phenomenon of Internet regulation, while half of them stated that they were well informed. Despite these high rates, almost none of them were informed through official statements of current IRS's participating bodies.

So, what opinion has such a well informed and highly educated sample regarding the implementation of an IRS in Greece? The participants are without a question positive concerning this matter, with most of them trusting a university-based institute to function such an IRS. The latter detail is very important, but cannot be generalised for the Greek society as this sample consisted only of university students and teaching staff. The authors actually verified that detail in a later mass survey in Greece in 2013.

Furthermore, the sample was much more positive about such an IRS targeting hate-speech and pornographic content, rather than online defamation and copyright infringement cases. This detail shows that, even if Greek society is open to the implementation of an IRS, at the same time it is very concerned and protective regarding freedom of speech and free access to data.

REFERENCES

Koumartzis, N. (2008). *BT's CleanFeed and Online Censorship in UK: Improvements for a More Secure and Ethically Correct Systeym* (Doctoral dissertation). University of the Arts London, London College of Communication, London, UK.

Koumartzis, N., & Veglis, A. (2011a). Internet Regulation: The Need for More Transparent Internet Filtering Systems and improved measurement of public opinion on Internet Filtering. *First Monday, 16*(10). https://firstmonday.org/ojs/index.php/fm/article/view/3266/3071

Koumartzis, N., & Veglis, A. (2011b). On the Pursue for a Fair Internet Regulation system. *Sixteenth IEEE Symposium on Computers and Communications (ISCC11).*

Koumartzis, N., & Veglis, A. (2011c). The Future of Internet Regulation: Current Trends, a Dangerous Precedent and the Role of Internet Users. *Euro-NF International Workshop on Traffic and Congestion Control for the Future Internet.*

Koumartzis, N., & Veglis, A. (2012). Internet Regulation: A New Approach: Outline of a system formed to be controlled by the Internet Users. *Computer Technology and Application, 3*(1), 16–23.

Koumartzis, N., & Veglis, A. (2014). Internet Regulation and Online Censorship. *International Journal of E-Politics, 5*(4), 65–80. doi:10.4018/ijep.2014100104

Koumartzis, N., & Veglis, A. (2015). Internet Regulation and Online Censorship. *The First International Congress on the Internet, Trolling and Addiction (ITA15).*

Chapter 6
Research in Germany

ABSTRACT

This chapter presents data gathered by a Germany-related survey that was conducted by the authors between 29th of November and 18th of December 2011, with the aid of Johannes Fritz (Research Assistant at Friedrich-Alexander Universität Erlangen-Nürnberg). The sample was limited but highly educated, consisting mainly of students and teaching staff of the Friedrich-Alexander Universität Erlangen-Nürnberg. The authors present statistical graphics in order to visualise the quantitative data. Additionally, statistical analysis is being conducted (using one by one variable analysis) in order to identify trends and associations between different groups in the same country.

INTRODUCTION

A related survey was conducted in Germany between 29th of November and 18th of December 2011, with the aid of Johannes Fritz (Research Assistant at Friedrich-Alexander Universität Erlangen-Nürnberg). The sample was once again limited but highly educated, consisting mainly of students and teaching staff of the Friedrich-Alexander Universität Erlangen-Nürnberg. This survey managed to gather responses from 72 participants.

The authors begin by presenting some of the survey's results that are related to their research topic, continue with statistical analysis to find trends and associations, and end with their conclusions. The rest of the survey's results can be found in Appendix 16. The statistical graphs that are shown are in the original language, with an explanation in English for each image.

DOI: 10.4018/978-1-5225-9973-9.ch006

GERMAN INTERNET USERS AND INTERNET REGULATION POLICIES

Below, the authors include a series of related inquiries regarding their research topic.

Figure 1. Are you aware of the global phenomenon of Internet regulation? (Germany Survey)

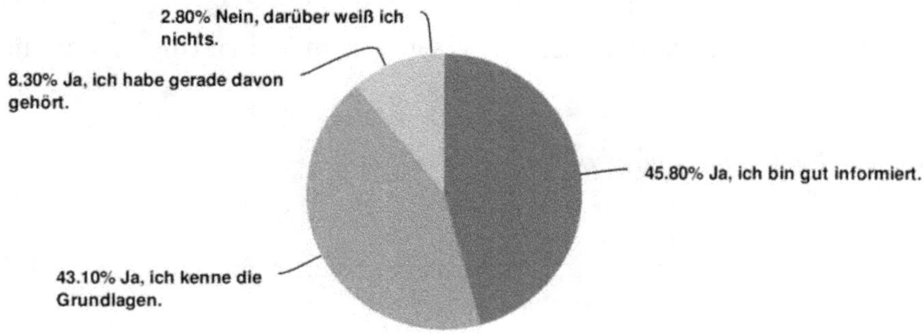

A question of major significance was "Are you informed regarding the global phenomenon of Internet regulation?", to which respondents (in their

Figure 2. What were the means of your information? (Germany Survey)

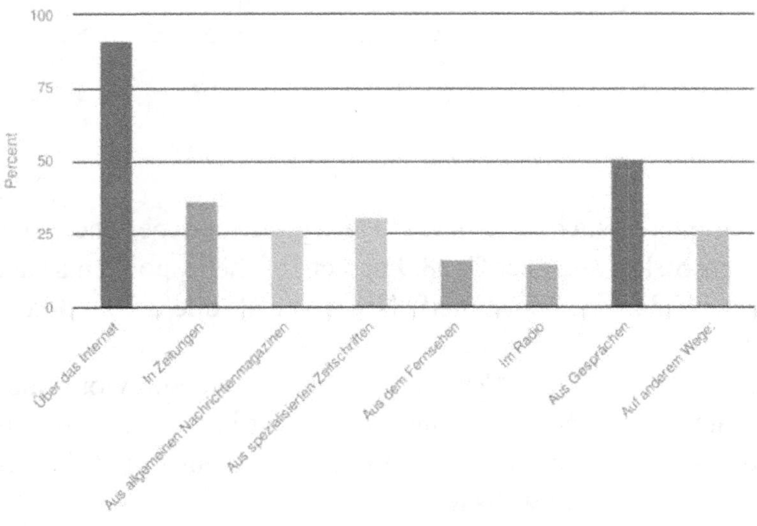

great majority) stated that they were informed to some extent at an overall rate of 97.2 percent. More specifically, 45.8 percent of the participants stated well-informed, 43.1 percent that they just knew the basics, 8.3 percent that they just heard about it, and only 2.8 percent stated that they knew nothing at all.

Regarding the means of their information, it is worth mentioning that 91.3 percent read about it online, 50.7 percent through private conversations, 36.2 percent via newspapers, and 30.4 percent via specialised magazines.

Concerning the source of information, 74.3 percent of the respondents stated that it was mass media, 68.6 percent that their source were individuals they knew personally, 64.3 percent that they were specialised researchers and related scientists, and 20 percent via government briefing or statements.

Figure 3. Who was the source of your information?
(Germany Survey)

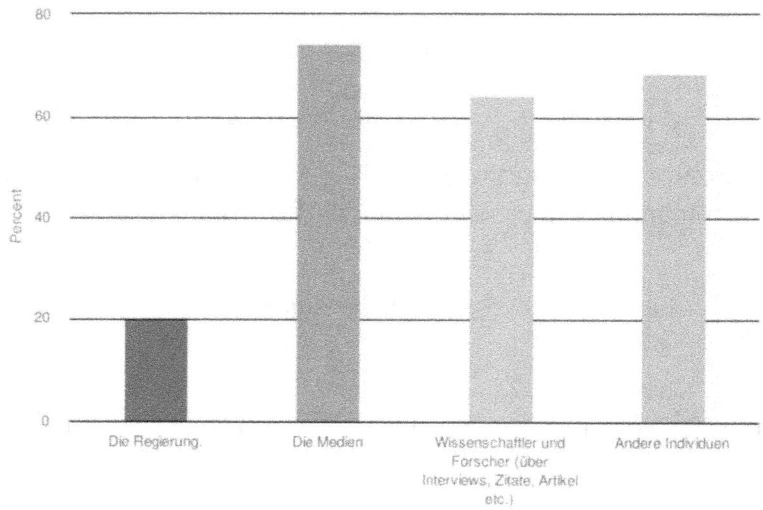

Another interesting question was "Have you ever experienced any kind of Internet censorship as a user?". 38.9 percent of the respondents stated "Yes, at least once," 34.7 percent stated "No, never," while a 26.4 percent stated that they actually do not know.

Of those who answered "Yes, at least once" to the previous question, 50 percent stated that they were using the Internet in Germany and they were trying to visit a foreign website, while 34.4 percent stated that they were trying to visit a German website.

Figure 4. Have you ever faced online censorship in the past?
(Germany Survey)

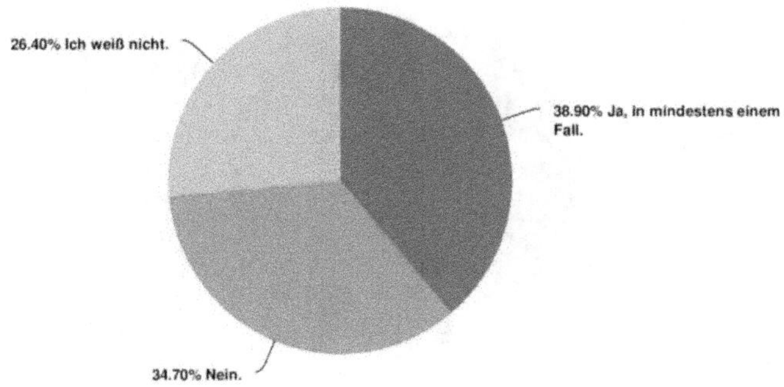

Figure 5. Was the censorship based in Germany?
(Germany Survey)

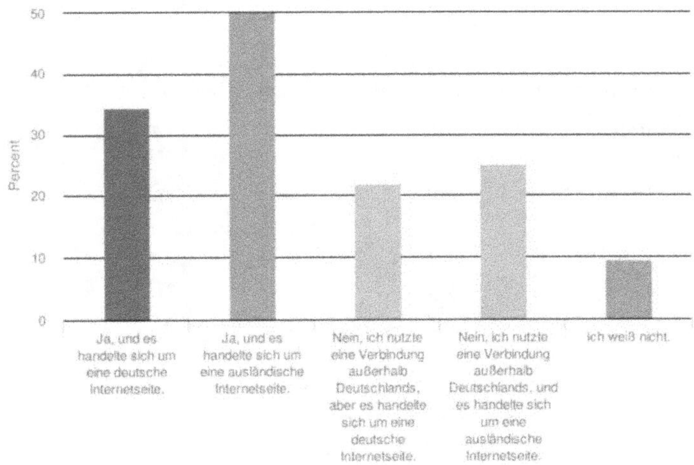

What's more, there was a question asking "Have you ever heard about Internet censorship incidents that took place abroad?", to which a staggering 94.4 percent answered positively.

ABOUT THE IMPLEMENTATION OF AN IRS IN GERMANY

The last part of this questionnaire focused on the possibility of an Internet Regulation System implementation in Germany, and under which conditions.

Figure 6. Have you ever heard of censorship incidents outside Germany?
(Germany Survey)

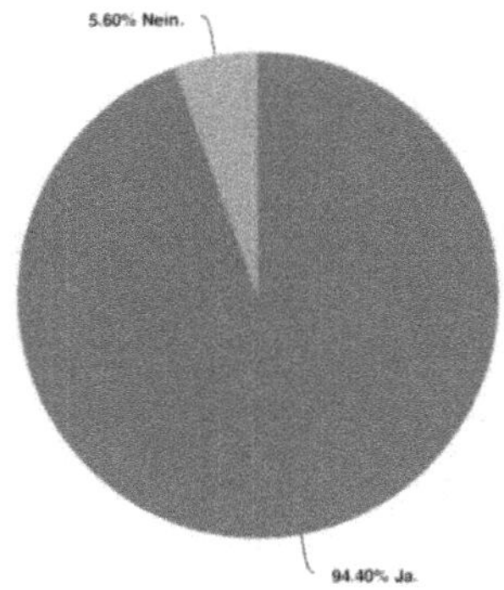

To the question "Do you agree with the implementation (by the state) of an IRS focusing on illegal online content?", 69.6 percent answered "No," 23.2 percent "Yes, under condition," and only 7.2 percent "Yes."

Figure 7. Do you agree with the implementation of an Internet regulation system by the state focusing on illegal content?
(Germany Survey)

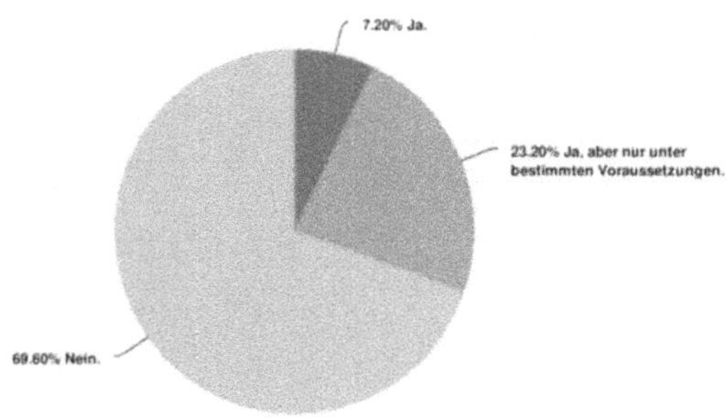

Regarding the type of online content that a German IRS should regulate, 52.9 percent stated "child pornography," 27.9 percent "hate-speech websites," 11.8 percent "defamatory content," 10.3 percent "pornographic websites," and only 7.4 percent stated "online piracy websites for copyright content (movies, music, books, and so on)." An interesting 48.5 percent stated that they do not want any kind of online content to be regulated.

Last, concerning the entity that they prefer to be in control of such an IRS, 64.7 percent stated "No one. An IRS can never be implemented in Germany."

Figure 8. What kind of content should be regulated if your country's state decide to implement such a system?
(Germany Survey)

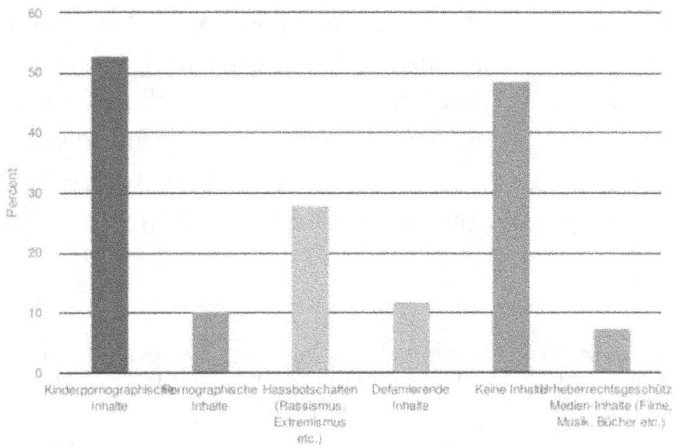

Figure 9. In case an Internet regulation system is implemented in Germany, from whom do you believe it must be operated in order to function with justice and to be accepted by the majority of [you country] citizens?
(Germany Survey)

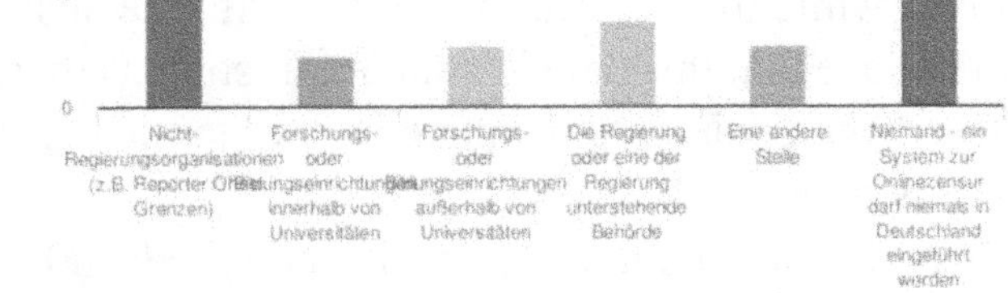

Among the other options, 19.1 percent answered "Related non-governmental organisations (such as *Reporters without borders,* and others)," and 14.7 percent "The government or a governmental service."

TRENDS AND ASSOCIATIONS WITH THE AID OF STATISTICAL ANALYSIS

In a questionnaire with so many questions, an exhausting statistical analysis can prove rather time-consuming without providing really necessary data. It is not in the scope of this book to present all the existing associations between groups and different answers, but only to focus on some of them that (according to the authors) can play a key role in the future design of a mass survey in the country and the development of a FIRS that can be accepted by the German Internet users.

Table 1. Agreement on the implementation of an IRS & age group (Pearson chi-square)

		Age Group					Total
		Under 18	**18-24**	**25-34**	**35-54**	**55+**	
Do you agree an IRS to be implemented in a national level?	Yes	1	1	3	0	0	5
	Yes, under conditions	0	9	4	1	2	16
	No	0	12	18	16	2	48
Total		1	22	25	17	4	69

χ^2= 24.723, df= 0, α= 0.02

Pearson chi-square statistical analysis showed (χ^2=24.723) a significant association (a=0.02) between age group and agreement on the question set. Adjusted standardised residuals indicate that the age group "under 18" is associated with answer "Yes," the age group "18-24" with the answer "Yes, under conditions," while the age group "35-54" with the answer "No."

The authors believe that this data is quite interesting as there is an almost smooth transition from positive to negative answer to the question set as the participants' age increases.

Pearson chi-square statistical analysis showed (χ^2=17.008) a significant association (a=0.000) between religious belief and agreement on the question set. Adjusted standardised residuals indicate that religious people are associated with the answer "Yes, under conditions," while non-religious people are associated with the answer "No." According to the authors, this may be an expected (to some extent) trend, but quite important as it is not present in all countries that were surveyed.

Table 2. Agreement on the implementation of an IRS & religious beliefs (Pearson chi-square)

		Do You Consider Yourself Religious?		Total
		Yes	No	
Do you agree an IRS to be implemented in a national level?	Yes	3	2	5
	Yes, under conditions	7	9	16
	No	3	45	48
Total		13	56	69

χ^2= 17.008, df= 2, α= 0.000

On the other hand, there is no association between agreement on the question set and neither gender, education level, parenthood, prior knowledge of the global phenomenon of Internet regulation, source of information, and so forth.

CONCLUSION

Regarding the German sample, the results showed that almost everyone was aware of the global phenomenon of Internet regulation, while almost half of the participants stated that they were well informed. So, it is quite safe to say that the German Internet users are among the most informed regarding this phenomenon.

These scores are quite similar to the ones gathered from the Greek survey, but there is a significant difference. While in Greece almost none of the participants were informed through official statements, in Germany this is not true. A quite important part of the German society (one out of five) stated that they were informed, among others, through official statements. In conclusion, the discussion of Internet regulation is an important aspect of the current political life in Germany, where similar cases date back to 1996 (Wired, 1997) and more modern related cases being well documented as well (Efroni, 2008).

This might be one of the reasons why the majority of the sample was negative to the implementation of an IRS in Germany, where only a small part of the society (three out of ten) is open to such a development. Another reason is definitely the fact that the majority of the German Internet users do not trust anyone to function such an IRS.

In addition, this reluctance to accept the implementation of an IRS is obvious from the fact that only a marginal majority agreed that child pornography websites should be one of the targets. Neither hate-speech websites nor defamation content managed to score high rates.

Concerning the statistical analysis of the results, it is quite important that there is no association between education level or parenthood and the willingness to accept Internet regulation. On the other hand, as the participant's age increases, there is an almost smooth transition from answer "Yes" to the answer "No": younger participants are keener to accept without conditions the implementation of an iRS, while older ones are absolutely negative to such a development. This can be explained by the fact that older citizens have experienced an authoritarian regime that was restricting free speech (RMVP, 1936).

Religious beliefs are playing an important role too to the German Internet users as religious Internet users proved to be positive, while non-religious Internet users were negative to the implementation of an IRS. These findings verify the general opinion of media analysts that religion and free speech have a long history of conflict (Biddle, 2006; IoC, 2013).

REFERENCES

Biddle, C. (2006). Religion vs. Free Speech. *The Objective Standard, 1*(2).

Efroni, Z. (2008). German Court Orders to Block Wikipedia.de Due to Offending Article. *Center for Internet and Society Blog, Stanford University Law School.* http://cyberlaw.stanford.edu/blog/2008/11/german-court-orders-block-wikipediade-due-offending-article

IoC. (2013). Religion and free speech: it's complicated. *Index on Censorship.* https://www.indexoncensorship.org/2013/03/free-expression-and-religion-overview/

RMVP. (1938). *Liste des schädlichen und unerwünschten Schrifttums* [List of harmful and unwanted literature]. Reichsministerium für Volksaufklärung und Propaganda.

Wired. (1997). Germany gets Radikal about extremists on web. *Wired Magazine.* https://www.wired.com/1997/01/germany-gets-radikal-about-extremists-on-web/

Chapter 7
Research in Russia

ABSTRACT

This chapter presents data gathered by a Russia-related survey that was conducted by the authors with the aid of Evgeniy Efimov (head teacher at the Volgograd State Technical University) between 11th of November and 24th of December 2011. Once again, the sample was limited but highly educated, consisting mainly of students and teaching staff of the Volgograd State Technical University. The authors present statistical graphics in order to visualise the quantitative data. Additionally, statistical analysis is being conducted (using one by one variable analysis) in order to identify trends and associations between different groups in the same country.

INTRODUCTION

The authors have conducted a related survey in Russia, with the aid of Evgeniy Efimov (head teacher at the Volgograd State Technical University) between 11th of November and 24th of December 2011. Once again, the sample was limited but highly educated, consisting mainly of students and teaching staff of the Volgograd State Technical University. In this survey, 53 respondents have participated.

The authors begin by presenting some of the survey's results that are related to their research topic, continue with statistical analysis to find trends and associations, and end with their conclusions. The rest of the survey's results can be found in Appendix 17. The statistical graphs that are shown are in the original language, with an explanation in English for each image.

DOI: 10.4018/978-1-5225-9973-9.ch007

RUSSIAN INTERNET USERS AND INTERNET REGULATION POLICIES

Below, the authors include a series of related inquiries regarding their research topic.

Figure 1. Are you aware of the global phenomenon of Internet regulation? (Russia Survey)

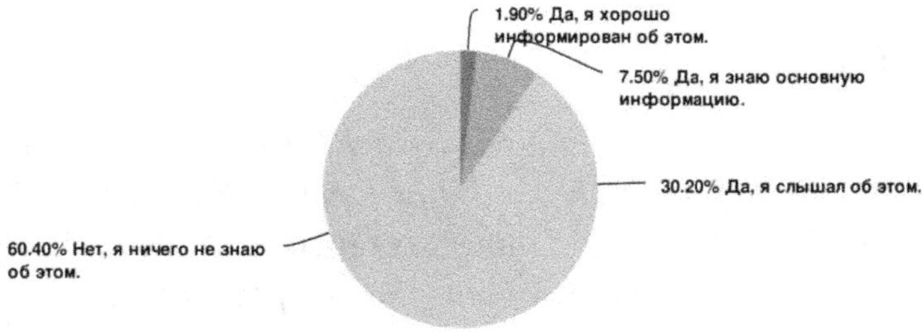

A question of major significance was "Are you informed regarding the global phenomenon of Internet regulation?", to which the respondents stated that they do not know anything (60.4 percent) or have just heard about it (30.2 percent). Only 1.9 percent said that they are well-informed, and 7.5 percent that they knew the basics.

Figure 2. What were the means of your information? (Russia Survey)

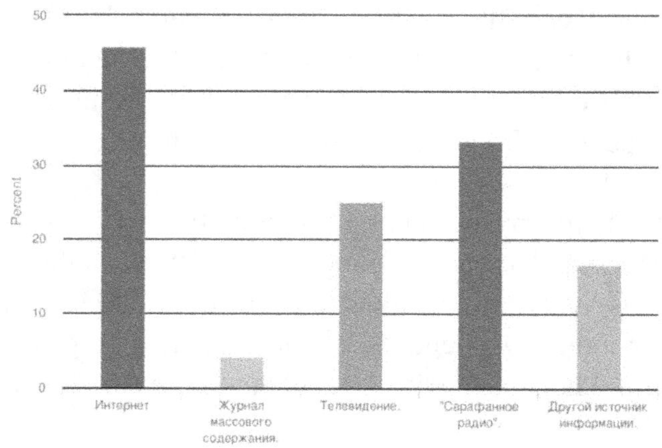

Regarding the means of their information, it is worth mentioning that 45.8 percent read about it online, 33.3 percent "by word of mouth," and 25 percent via television broadcasts.

Concerning the source of information, 72 percent of the respondents stated that they were individuals they knew, 32 percent stated mass media, and 12 percent that they were specialised researchers and related scientists.

Figure 3. Who was the source of your information? (Russia Survey)

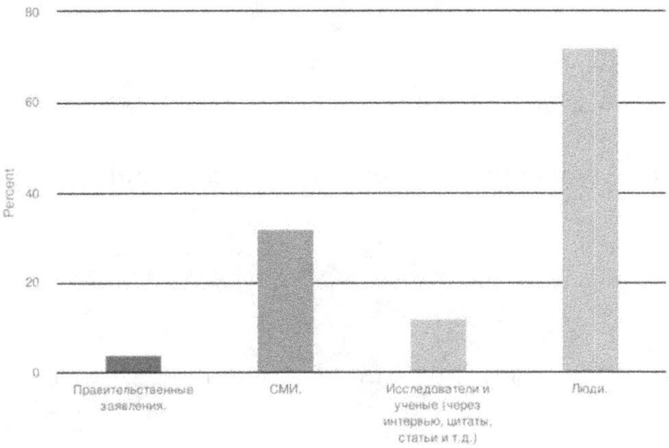

Another interesting question was "Have you ever experienced any kind of Internet censorship as a user?". 52.9 percent stated "No," 21.6 percent "Yes, at least once," and 25.5 percent "I do not know."

Of those who answered "Yes, at least once" to the previous question, 22.6 percent stated that they were using the Internet in Russia and they were trying to visit a Russian website, while 71 percent stated "I do not know."

ABOUT THE IMPLEMENTATION OF AN IRS IN RUSSIA

The last part of this questionnaire focused on the possibility of an Internet Regulation System implementation in Russia, and under which conditions.

To the question "Do you agree with the implementation (by the state) of an IRS focusing on illegal online content?," 46.8 percent answered "Yes," 34 percent "Yes, under condition," and only 19.1 percent "No."

Figure 4. Have you ever faced online censorship in the past? (Russia Survey)

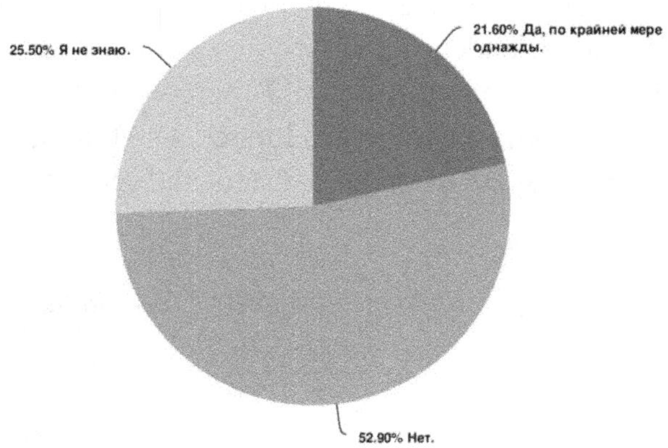

Figure 5. Was the censorship based in Russia? (Russia Survey)

Figure 6. Do you agree with the implementation of an Internet regulation system by the state focusing on illegal content? (Russia Survey)

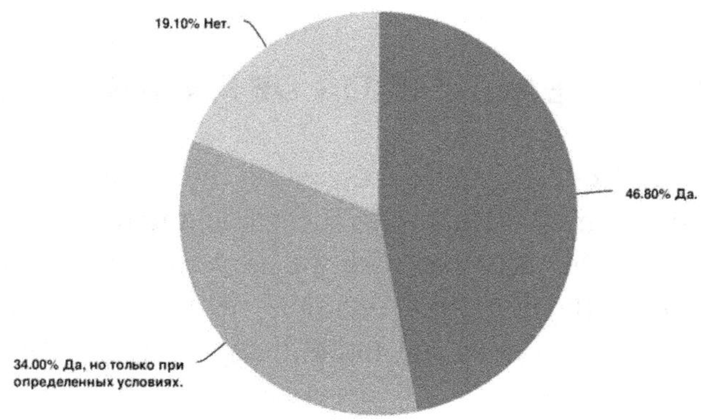

Figure 7. What kind of content should be regulated if your country's state decide to implement such a system? (Russia Survey)

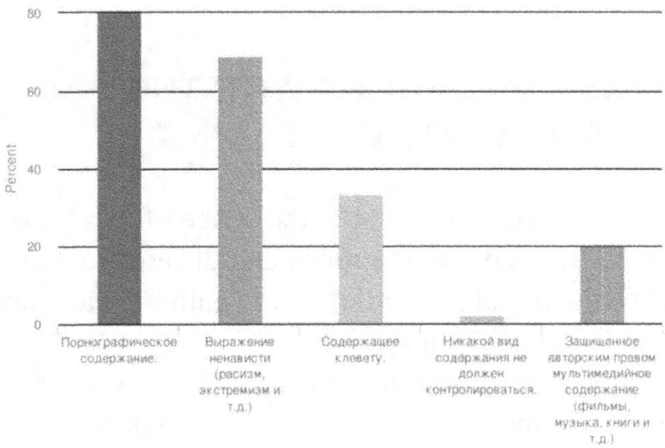

Regarding the type of online content that a Russian IRS should regulate, 80 percent stated "pornographic content," 68.9 percent "hate-speech websites," and 33.3 percent "defamatory content."

Last, concerning the entity that they prefer to be in control of such an IRS, 35.6 percent stated "The related Ministry," 26.7 percent stated "No-government organisation (such as Reporters Without Borders, and others)," 26.7 percent

Figure 8. In case an Internet regulation system is implemented in Russia, from whom do you believe it must be operated in order to function with justice and to be accepted by the majority of [you country] citizens? (Russia Survey)

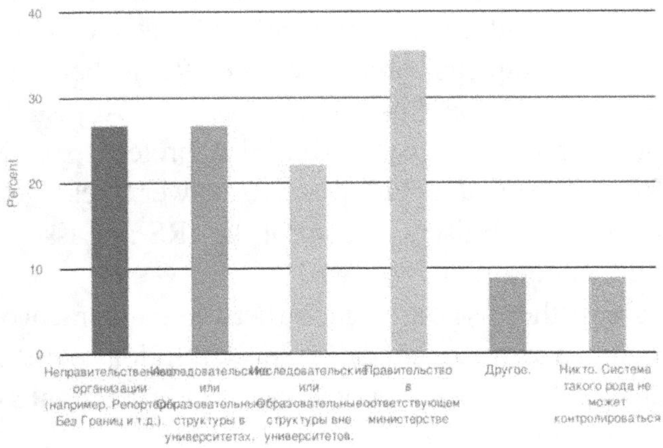

"Research institutions inside state universities," and 22.2 percent "Research institutions outside state universities."

TRENDS AND ASSOCIATIONS WITH THE AID OF STATISTICAL ANALYSIS

As it was mentioned above, it is not in the scope of this book to present all the existing associations between groups and different answers, but only to focus on some of them that (according to the authors) can play a key role in the future research in this country.

It is quite impressive that only one significant association was found between different groups and agreement on the implementation of an IRS.

Table 1. Agreement on the implementation of an IRS and willingness the IRS to be controlled by the government's appropriate Ministry (Pearson chi-square)

		Government Appropriate Ministry (IRS to Be Controlled by Whom?)		**Total**
		Unchecked	**Checked**	
Do you agree an IRS to be implemented in a national level?	Yes	11	11	22
	Yes, under conditions	16	0	16
	No	4	5	9
Total		31	16	47

χ^2= 12.608, df= 2, α= 0.002

More specifically, Pearson chi-square statistical analysis showed (χ^2=12.608) a significant association (a=0.002) between agreement on the question set and participants' preference the IRS to be controlled by the appropriate Ministry of the Russian government. Adjusted standardised residuals indicate that those participants that prefer a state's Ministry to control the IRS are associated with positive answer "Yes," while those that do not prefer a state's Ministry to control the IRS are associated with the answer "Yes, under condition."

Except the above, there is no association between agreement on the question and neither gender, age group, education level, religious beliefs, parenthood, prior knowledge of the global phenomenon of Internet regulation, source of information, and so on.

CONCLUSION

In conclusion, the survey showed that the majority of the Russian participants did not know anything regarding the global phenomenon of Internet regulation, while almost none of them stated that they were well informed.

This is expected to some extent as almost none of the participants stated that they heard about it through official statements. The latter, combined with the fact that traditional media scored very low as a means of information, shows that the hesitation of the Russian government to inform their citizens is closely related to the hesitation of the traditional media to discuss the issue openly.

Despite all the above, the majority of the sample preferred the implementation of an IRS in Russia rather than no Internet regulation at all. This is quite impressive if we consider that similar results were produced in both Greece and the UK so far, i.e. societies which are considered undeniably and widely democratic in contrast with Russia that it is considered by many Western specialised political scientists an authoritarian or semi-authoritarian regime (Evans, 2011; Ottaway, 2003).

Opposed to the latter, more than one-third of the sample trusts the Russian government to implement such an IRS, a score that is higher compared to any other option. This might seem incomprehensible from a Westerner point of view, but shows how different the majority of the Russian society thinks in political terms. After all, it is a society where the liberal intelligentsia is still a quite small minority and liberal ideas have not managed to win widespread support so far (Markwick & Gill, 2000; Rose, Munro & Mishler, 2004).

In case of an IRS implementation, the great majority of the sample is positive in targeting generic pornographic and hate-speech content. On the other hand, the scores are quite low regarding defamation and copyright infringement cases. Similar results were also recorded in Greece, so it is quite safe to lead to the same conclusion: even if Russian society is open to the implementation of an IRS, at the same time it is very concerned and protective regarding freedom of speech and free access to data.

Last, statistical analysis of the Russian survey led the authors to the finding of an important statistical association. More specifically, the Russian citizens that are unconditionally positive to the implementation of an IRS are, at the same time, the ones that trust the government to function such an IRS. On the other hand, the Russian citizens that do not trust the government to function the IRS are the ones that are positive towards an IRS implementation, but only under conditions.

REFERENCES

Evans, A. B. (2011, January). The failure of democratization in Russia: A comparative perspective. *Journal of Eurasian Studies*, *2*(1), 40–51. doi:10.1016/j.euras.2010.10.001

Ottaway, M. (2003). *Democracy challenged: The rise of semi-authoritarianism*. Washington, DC: Carnegie Endowment for International Peace.

Chapter 8
Research in India

ABSTRACT

This chapter presents data gathered by an India-related survey that was conducted by the authors with the aid of Anshul Tewari and Astik Sinha, both professional journalists. The survey ran between 3rd of February and 20th of April 2012. The sample was limited, with 57 respondents, coming from different social and educational backgrounds. The authors present statistical graphics in order to visualise the quantitative data. Additionally, statistical analysis is being conducted (using one by one variable analysis) in order to identify trends and associations between different groups in the same country.

INTRODUCTION

Another survey was conducted in India, with the aid of Anshul Tewari and Astik Sinha, both professional journalists. The survey ran between 3rd of February and 20th of April 2012. The sample was limited, with 57 respondents, coming from different social and educational backgrounds (the participants were gathered thanks to coverage by media that the aforementioned journalists work for).

The authors begin by presenting some of the survey's results that are related to their research topic, continue with statistical analysis to find trends and associations, and end with their conclusions. The rest of the survey's results can be found in Appendix 18. The statistical graphs that are shown are in the original language, with an explanation in English for each image.

DOI: 10.4018/978-1-5225-9973-9.ch008

INDIAN INTERNET USERS AND INTERNET REGULATION POLICIES

Below, the authors include a series of related inquiries regarding their research topic.

Figure 1. Are you aware of the global phenomenon of Internet regulation? (India Survey)

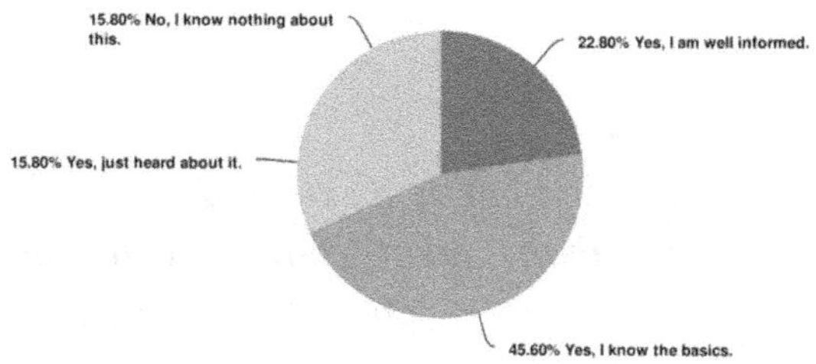

A question of major significance was "Are you aware of the global phenomenon of Internet regulation?", to which most of the respondents stated that they know the basics (45.6 percent) or they are well-informed (22.8 percent). Only 15.8 percent stated they just heard about it, and another 15.8 percent that they do not know anything.

Regarding the means of their information, it is worth mentioning that 83.7 percent read about it online, 63.3 percent through "Newspapers," 40.8 percent "by word of mouth," and 38.8 percent via television broadcasts.

Figure 2. What were the means of your information? (India Survey)

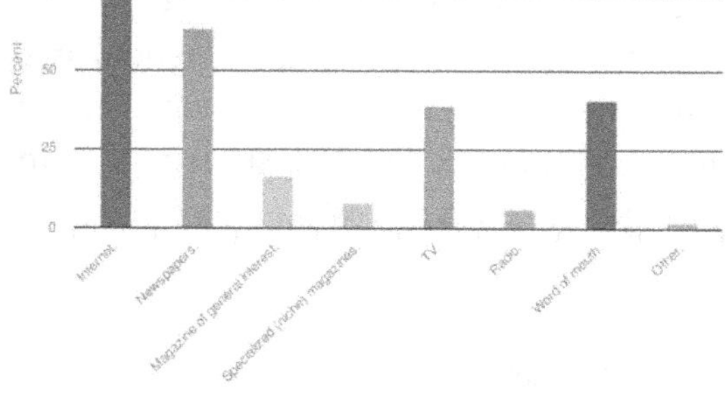

Concerning the source of information, 87.8 percent of the respondents stated mass media, 46.9 percent stated "Individuals," 36.7 percent "Researchers and scientists," and only 22.4 percent that they were informed thanks to "Government statements."

Figure 3. Who was the source of your information? (India Survey)

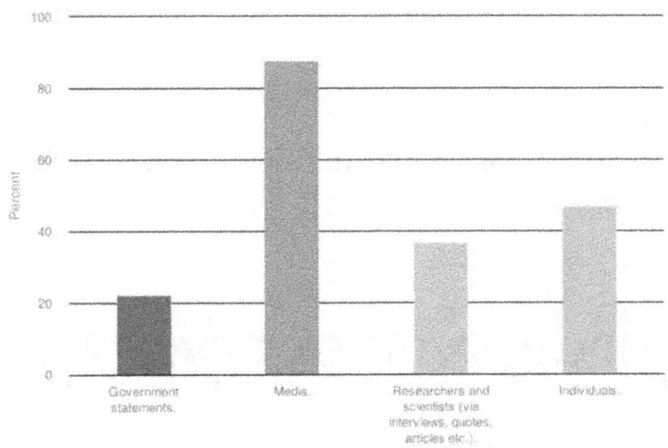

Another interesting question was "Have you ever faced online censorship in the past?". 54 percent stated "No," 24 percent "Yes, at least once," and 22 percent "I do not know."

Figure 4. Have you ever faced online censorship in the past? (India Survey)

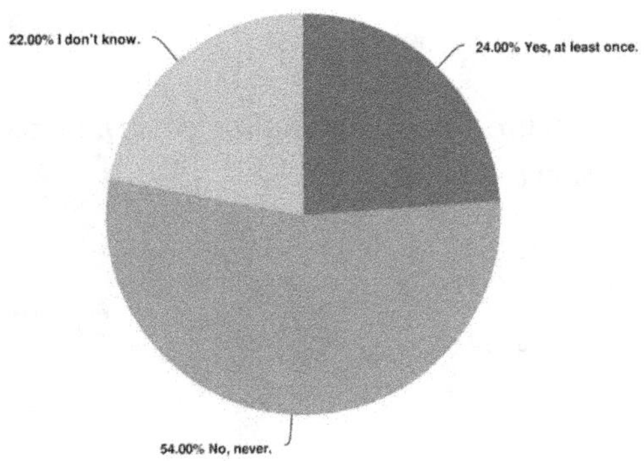

Of those who answered "Yes, at least once" to the previous question, 24.1 percent stated that they were using the Internet in India and they were

Figure 5. Were you using the Internet from India? (India Survey)

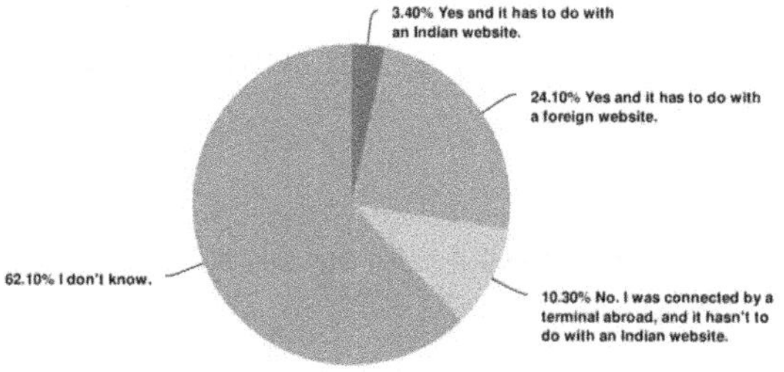

trying to visit a foreign website, while the majority of the respondents (62.1 percent) stated "I do not know."

ABOUT THE IMPLEMENTATION OF AN IRS IN INDIA

The last part of this questionnaire focused on the possibility of an Internet Regulation System implementation in India, and under which conditions.

To the question "Do you agree with the recent Indian governments attempt to regulate content online?," only 6.3 percent stated "Yes, I totally agree," and 16.7 percent stated "Yes, there should be some regulation with clear guidelines." The majority of the respondents were negative, though, as 39.6 percent stated "No, as the government is attempting to silence dissenting voices," and 37.5 percent stated "No, as I am against any form of Internet regulation."

Figure 6. Do you agree with the recent Indian governments attempt to regulate content online? (India Survey)

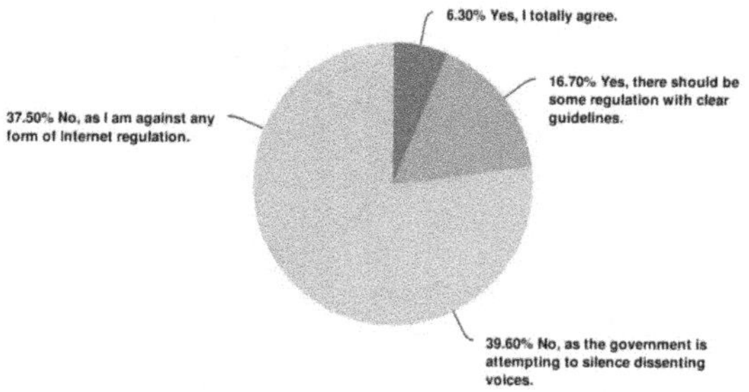

Figure 7. Did the massive protest against SOPA/IPA (internet regulation legislation in USA) affect you? (i.e. Wikipedia blackout, reddit blackout, Google became "black" for a day etc.) (India Survey)

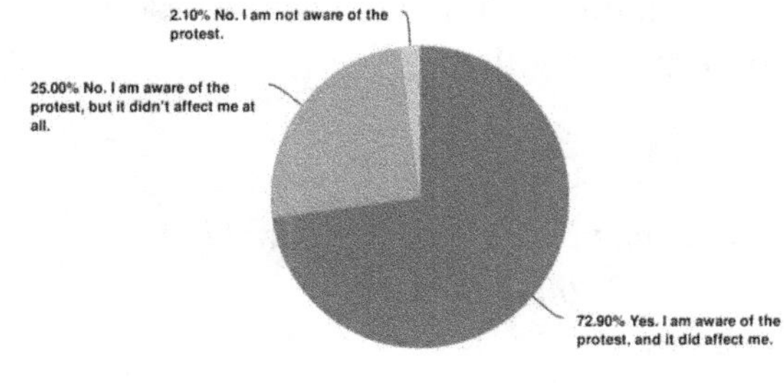

Due to the massive protest against SOPA/PIPA that took place near the survey's conduction, another question was included: "Did the massive protest against SOPA/PIPA (Internet regulation legislation in the USA) affect you? (i.e. Wikipedia blackout, reddit blackout, Google became "black" for a day, and so forth." 72.9 percent of the respondents stated "Yes. I am aware of the protest, and it did affect me," and 25 percent stated "No. I am aware of the protest, but it did not affect me at all."

The next question was the main one of this survey: "Do you agree with the implementation of an Internet regulation system by the state focusing on illegal content?." 58 percent of the participants were positive (14 percent stated "Yes," 44 percent stated "Yes, but only under conditions," while 42 percent were negative (stating "No").

Figure 8. Do you agree with the implementation of an Internet regulation system by the state focusing on illegal content? (India Survey)

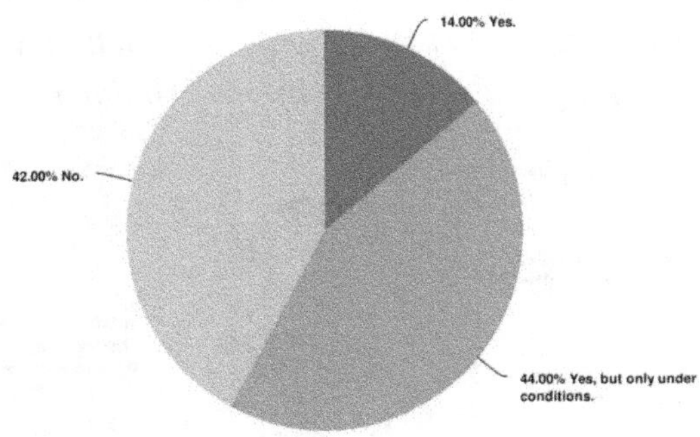

Regarding the type of online content that an India IRS should regulate, 49 percent stated "hate speech content," 38.8 percent "pornographic content," 24.5 percent "defamation content," and 24.5 percent "copyrighted multimedia content." On the other hand, 24.5 percent of the respondents stated that "no kind of content" should be regulated.

Figure 9. What kind of content should be regulated if your country's state decides to implement such a system? (India Survey)

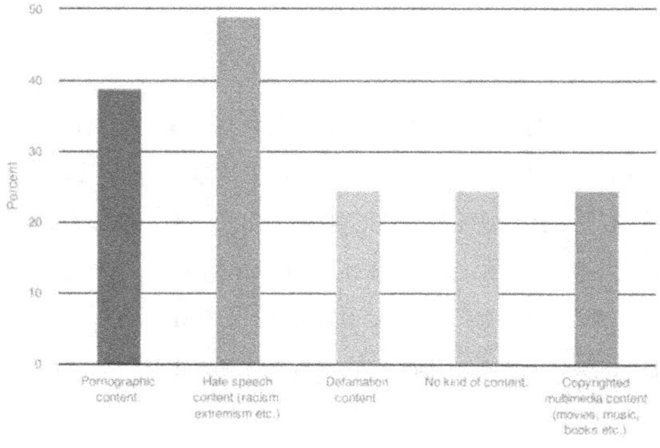

Last, concerning the entity that they prefer to be in control of such an IRS, 48 percent stated "No-government organisation (such as Reporters Without Borders, and others)," 16 percent "Research institutions inside state universities," 14 percent "Research institutions outside state universities,"

Figure 10. In case an Internet regulation system is implemented in India, from whom do you believe it must be operated in order to function with justice and to be accepted by the majority of [you country] citizens? (India Survey)

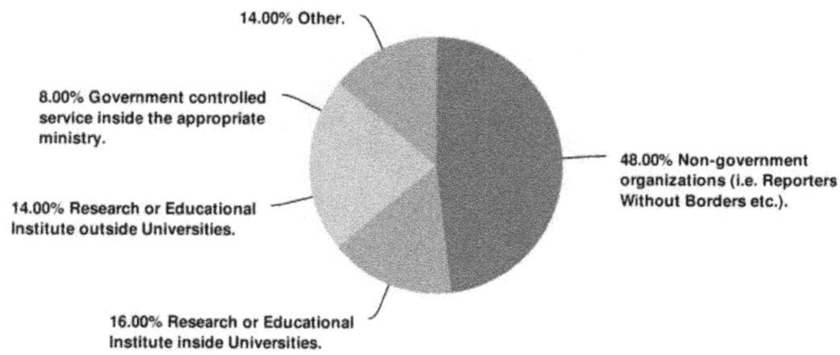

and only 8 percent "Government controlled service inside the appropriate ministry."

TRENDS AND ASSOCIATIONS WITH THE AID OF STATISTICAL ANALYSIS

As mentioned before, it is not in the scope of this book to present all the existing associations between groups and different answers, but only to focus on some of them that are considered of crucial value by the authors.

As in Russian Survey, in India's data too it was quite difficult to find any trend or association. More specifically, there is no association between agreement on the question set and neither gender, education level, religious beliefs, parenthood, prior knowledge of the global phenomenon of Internet regulation, source of information, means of information, and so forth.

Table 1. Agreement on the implementation of an IRS & hate-speech online content (Pearson chi-square).

		Hate-Speech Content (What Content an IRS Should Target)		Total
		Unchecked	Checked	
Do you agree an IRS to be implemented in a national level?	Yes	0	7	7
	Yes, under conditions	12	10	22
	No	14	7	21
Total		26	24	50

χ^2= 9.450, df= 2, α= 0.009

On the other hand, Pearson chi-square statistical analysis showed (χ^2=9.450) a significant association (a=0.009) between agreement on the question set and preference of this IRS to target hate-speech online content. Adjusted standardised residuals indicate that participants who want an IRS to target hate-speech content are associated with positive answer (answer "Yes") to the question set, while participants who do not are associated with the answers "No." According to the authors, this association has to be further researched in a future mass survey in India.

CONCLUSION

In conclusion, the results showed that the great majority was aware of the global phenomenon of Internet regulation, while a significant part of the society (two out of ten) was well informed. With a high level of awareness of the global phenomenon, it is even more important that the majority of the participants were positive to the implementation of an IRS in India.

So, which is the reason behind this documented need of the Indian society for Internet regulation? The highest score regarding the targeted content was recorded with the option "hate-speech websites"; almost half of the participants were positive in regulating this kind of content.

This connection was furthermore verified during the statistical analysis of the results; the only significant statistical association that was found was between agreement on regulation of the Internet and IRS targeting hate-speech content. This is perfectly understandable if we take into account that there are quite many hate-speech laws in the Constitution of India focusing on preventing discord among its many ethnic and religious communities (Bhandari & Bhatt, 2012). The problem is so intense and the need to find a solution so pressing that the Law Commission of India released a report quite recently (Daniyal, 2017) proposing even more laws in order to further restrain hate-speech among the different communities.

In that sense, India survey is a great example of how a survey can reveal valuable data regarding the design and implementation of an IRS based on each society's needs.

REFERENCES

Bhandari, M. K., & Bhatt, M. N. (2012). Hate Speech and Freedom of Expression: Balancing Social Good and Individual Liberty. *The Practical Lawyer*. http://www.supremecourtcases.com/index2.php?option=com_content&itemid=5&do_pdf=1&id=22819

Daniyal, S. (2017). Does India need stronger hate speech laws? The Law Commission seems to think so. *Scroll.in*. https://scroll.in/article/832978/does-india-need-stronger-hate-speech-laws-the-law-commission-seems-to-thinks-so

Chapter 9
Research in Kosovo

ABSTRACT

This chapter presents data gathered by a Kosovo-related survey that was conducted by the authors with the aid of Artan Rogova, Research Fellow at the EU's Group for Legal and Political Studies. The survey was conducted between 17th of March and 16th of May 2012 and managed to gather 70 responses. All the participants were employees of the aforementioned EU's group, and therefore having university education. The authors present statistical graphics in order to visualise the quantitative data. Additionally, statistical analysis is being conducted (using one by one variable analysis) in order to identify trends and associations between different groups in the same country.

INTRODUCTION

A survey was conducted in Kosovo too, with the aid of Artan Rogova, Research Fellow at the EU's Group for Legal and Political Studies. The survey was conducted between 17th of March and 16th of May 2012 and managed to gather 70 responses. All the participants were employees of the aforementioned EU's group, and therefore having university education.

The authors begin by presenting some of the survey's results that are related to their research topic, continue with statistical analysis to find trends and associations, and end with their conclusions. The rest of the survey's results can be found in Appendix 19. The statistical graphs that are shown are in the original language, with an explanation in English for each image.

DOI: 10.4018/978-1-5225-9973-9.ch009

KOSOVO INTERNET USERS AND INTERNET REGULATION POLICIES

Below, the authors include a series of related inquiries regarding their research topic.

Figure 1. Are you aware of the global phenomenon of Internet regulation? (Kosovo Survey)

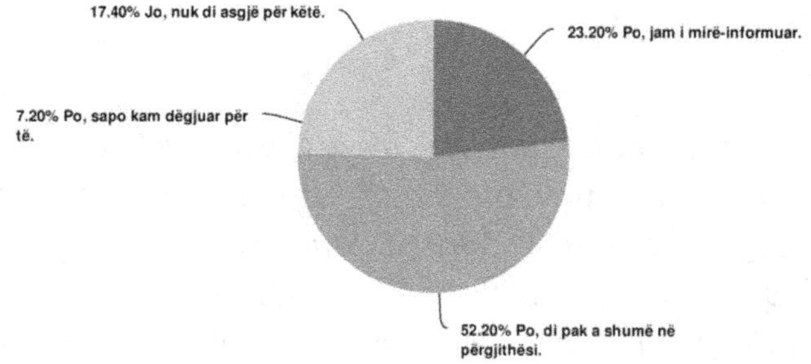

A question of major significance was "Are you aware of the global phenomenon of Internet regulation?," to which most of the respondents stated that they know the basics (52.2 percent), 23.2 percent that they are well-informed. Only 7.2 percent stated they just heard about it, and another 17.4 percent that they do not know anything.

Figure 2. What were the means of your information? (Kosovo Survey)

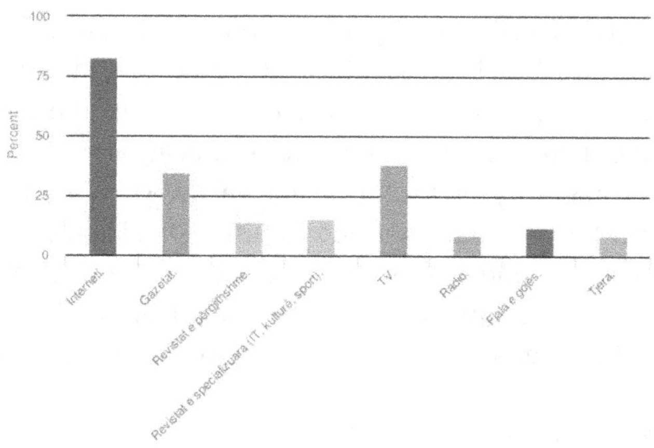

Regarding the means of their information, it is worth-mentioning that 82.8 percent read about it online, 37.9 percent via television broadcasts, and 34.5 percent through "Newspapers."

Concerning the source of information, 74.1 percent of the respondents stated mass media, 43.1 percent "Researchers and scientists," 22.4 percent "Individuals, and only 1.7 percent that they were informed thanks to "Government statements."

Figure 3. Who was the source of your information? (Kosovo Survey)

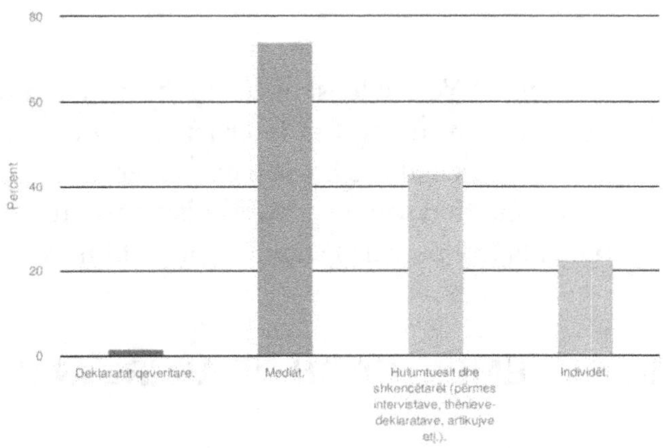

Another interesting question was "Have you ever faced online censorship in the past?." 39.1 percent stated "Yes, at least once," 40.6 percent "No," and 20.3 percent "I do not know."

Figure 4. Have you ever faced online censorship in the past? (Kosovo Survey)

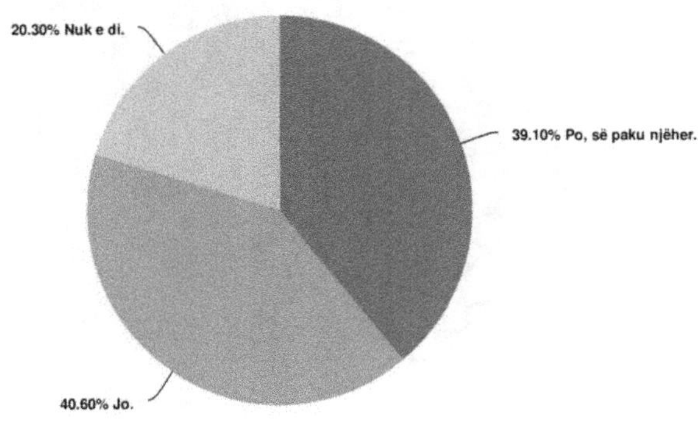

Figure 5. Were you using the Internet from Kosovo? (Kosovo Survey)

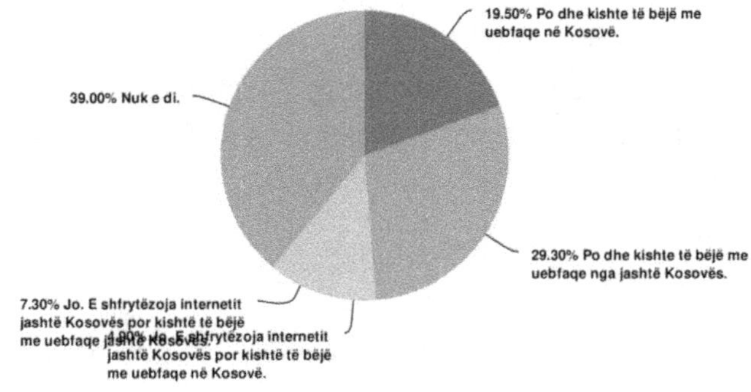

Of those who answered "Yes, at least once" to the previous question, 19.5 percent stated that they were using the Internet in Kosovo and they were trying to visit a Kosovo's website, 29.3 percent stated that they were using the Internet in Kosovo and they were trying to visit a foreign website, while many of the respondents (39 percent) stated "I do not know."

ABOUT THE IMPLEMENTATION OF AN IRS IN KOSOVO

The last part of this questionnaire focused on the possibility of an Internet Regulation System implementation in Kosovo, and under which conditions.

Figure 6. Do you agree with the implementation of an Internet regulation system by the state focusing on illegal content? (Kosovo Survey)

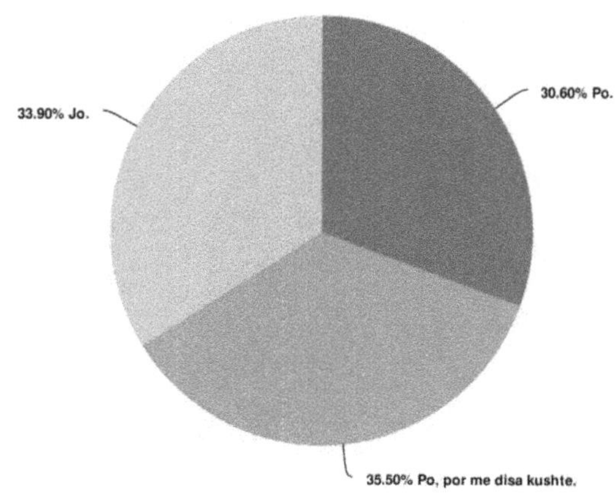

This question was the main one of this survey: "Do you agree with the implementation of an Internet regulation system by the state focusing on illegal content?." 65.6 percent of the participants were positive (30.6 percent stated "Yes," 35.5 percent stated "Yes, but only under conditions," while 33.9 percent were negative (stating "No").

Figure 7. What kind of content should be regulated if your country's state decides to implement such a system? (Kosovo Survey)

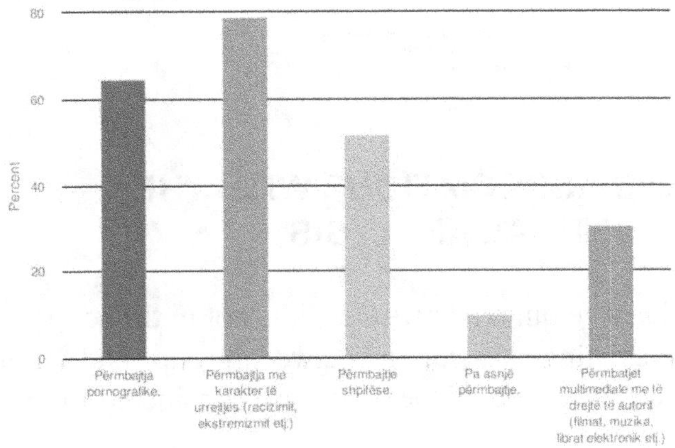

Regarding the type of online content that a Kosovo IRS should regulate, 79 percent stated "hate speech content," 64.5 percent "pornographic content," 51.6 percent "defamatory content," and 30.6 percent "copyrighted multimedia content." On the other hand, only 9.7 percent of the respondents stated that "no kind of content" should be regulated.

Last, concerning the entity that they prefer to be in control of such an IRS, 29 percent stated "Government controlled service inside the appropriate ministry," 24.2 percent "No-government organisation (such as Reporters Without Borders etc.)," 11.3 percent "Research institutions inside state universities," 22.6 percent "Research institutions inside state universities," and 12.9 percent "Research institutions outside state universities."

Figure 8. In case an Internet regulation system is implemented in Kosovo, from whom do you believe it must be operated in order to function with justice and to be accepted by the majority of [you country] citizens? (Kosovo Survey)

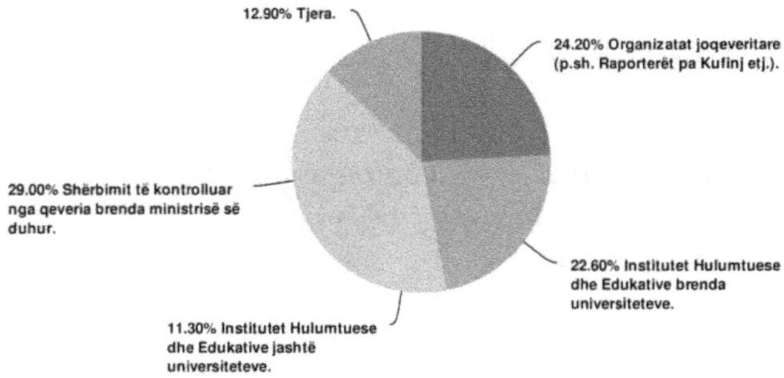

TRENDS AND ASSOCIATIONS WITH THE AID OF STATISTICAL ANALYSIS

As mentioned before quite a few times, it is not in the scope of this book to present all the existing associations between groups and different answers, but only to focus on some of them that are considered of crucial value by the authors.

Pearson chi-square statistical analysis showed (χ^2=7.033) a significant association (a=0.030) between religious belief and agreement on the question set. Adjusted standardised residuals indicate that religious people are associated with positive answer (answer "Yes"), while non-religious people are associated with the answer "Yes, conditioned."

Table 1. Agreement on the implementation of an IRS & religious belief (Pearson chi-square).

		Do You Consider Yourself Religious?		**Total**
		Yes	**No**	
Do you agree an IRS to be implemented in a national level?	Yes	14	5	19
	Yes, under conditions	8	14	22
	No	8	13	21
Total		30	32	62

χ^2= 7.033, df= 2, α= 0.030

Pearson chi-square statistical analysis showed (χ^2=13.185) a significant association (a=0.040) between awareness of the Internet regulation phenomenon and agreement on the question set. Adjusted standardised residuals indicate that well-informed people are associated with the answer "Yes, conditioned," while people who know nothing about are associated with the answer "Yes."

Table 2. Agreement on the implementation of an IRS & level of awareness of the global phenomenon of Internet regulation (Pearson chi-square).

		Are You Aware of the Internet Regulation Phenomenon?				Total
		Yes, I Am Well-Informed	**Yes, I Know the Basics**	**Yes, Just Heard About It**	**No, I Don't Know Nothing**	
Do you agree an IRS to be implemented in a national level?	Yes	2	9	1	7	19
	Yes, under conditions	9	11	2	0	22
	No	3	12	1	5	21
Total		14	32	4	12	62

χ^2= 13.185, df= 6, α= 0.040

Pearson chi-square statistical analysis showed (χ^2=6.680) a significant association (a=0.035) between agreement on the question set and preference this IRS to target pornographic content. Adjusted standardised residuals indicate that participants who want an IRS to target pornographic content are associated with positive answer (answer "Yes") to the question set, while participants who do not are associated with the answers "No."

Table 3. Agreement on the implementation of an IRS & pornographic online content (Pearson chi-square)

		Pornographic Content (What Content an IRS Should Target)		Total
		Unchecked	**Checked**	
Do you agree an IRS to be implemented in a national level?	Yes	4	15	19
	Yes, under conditions	6	16	22
	No	12	9	21
Total		22	40	62

χ^2= 6.680, df= 2, α= 0.035

On the other hand, there is no association between agreement on the question set and neither gender, age, education level, parenthood, source or means of information, and so forth.

CONCLUSION

Summarising, the results showed that the great majority was aware of the global phenomenon of Internet regulation, while a great part of the participants (two out of ten) were well informed. So, it is quite safe to say that the Kosovar Internet users are among the most informed regarding this phenomenon.

What's more, the great majority of the Kosovars agrees with the implementation of an IRS, while there are many options that recorded quite high rates concerning the content that should be targeted: hate-speech websites, pornographic content, and defamation content.

These findings can be comprehended to some extent if we take into account that the Kosovars' daily lives are highly interconnected with the online content. More specifically, the Internet penetration across the country is comparable to global norms (Stikk, 2013) and the Kosovars are the keenest Internet users in the Balkans (Marusic, 2014). This is true in even rural areas, where the percent of Internet users are even higher than in urban regions (Ahmeti, 2014).

Last, significant associations were found between agreement on the implementation of an IRS and religious belief, level of awareness of the global phenomenon of Internet regulation, and willingness an IRS to target pornographic online content. Focusing on the former, even if it is expected that religious people are keener to accept online content regulation (Biddle, 2006; IoC, 2013), it is quite impressive that even non-religious are keen to accept such a development "under conditions."

In that sense, the Kosovar survey is a great example of how a survey can collect valuable data that can lead to the recognition of social groups traditionally opposed to limiting speech but which, in the right context, positively favour such a development.

REFERENCES

Ahmeti, B. (2014). Internet Usage in Kosovo. *Digital Spoiler*. https://digitalspoiler.com/internet-usage-kosovo/

Biddle, C. (2006). Religion vs. Free Speech. *The Objective Standard, 1*(2).

IoC. (2013). Religion and free speech: it's complicated. *Index on Censorship*. https://www.indexoncensorship.org/2013/03/free-expression-and-religion-overview/

Marusic, S. J. (2014). Kosovo Leads Balkans in Internet Addiction. *Balkan Insight*. http://www.balkaninsight.com/en/article/kosovars-lead-balkans-internet-usage-chart

Stikk. (2013). Internet penetration and usage in Kosovo. *Kossovo Association of Information and Communication Technology (STIKK)*. http://www.mfa-ks.net/repository/docs/STIKK_raport_eng_2013_short_web.pdf

Chapter 10
Research in Cyprus

ABSTRACT

This chapter presents data gathered by a Cyprus-related survey that was conducted by the authors with the aid of many professional Cypriot journalists. The survey was conducted between 6th of September and 13th of November 2012 and managed to gather 62 responses. The participants came from a different social and educational background as they were gathered thanks to online media coverage. The authors present statistical graphics in order to visualise the quantitative data. Additionally, statistical analysis is being conducted (using one by one variable analysis) in order to identify trends and associations between different groups in the same country.

INTRODUCTION

A survey was conducted in Cyprus with the aid of many professional Cypriot journalists. The survey was conducted between 6th of September and 13th of November 2012 and managed to gather 62 responses. The participants came from a different social and educational background as they were gathered thanks to online media coverage.

The authors begin by presenting some of the survey's results that are related to their research topic, continue with statistical analysis to find trends and associations, and end with their conclusions. The rest of the survey's results can be found in Appendix 20. The statistical graphs that are shown are in the original language, with an explanation in English for each image.

DOI: 10.4018/978-1-5225-9973-9.ch010

CYPRIOT INTERNET USERS AND INTERNET REGULATION POLICIES

Below, the authors include a series of related inquiries regarding their research topic.

Figure 1. Are you aware of the global phenomenon of Internet regulation? (Cyprus Survey)

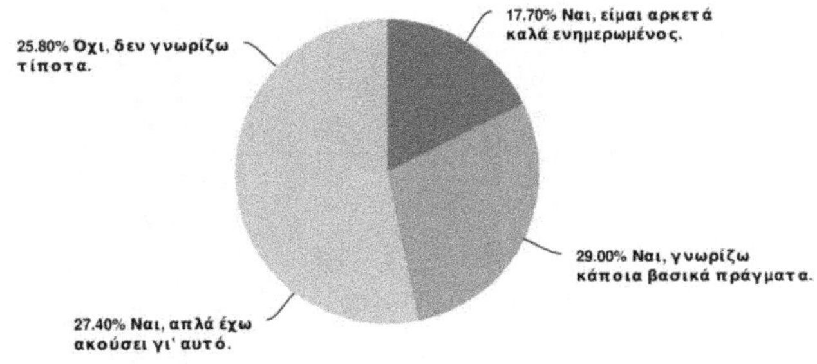

A question of major significance was "Are you aware of the global phenomenon of Internet regulation?," to which most of the respondents stated that they know the basics (29 percent), 17.7 percent that they are well-informed. Only 27.4 percent stated they just heard about it, and another 25.8 percent that they do not know anything.

Figure 2. What were the means of your information? (Cyprus Survey)

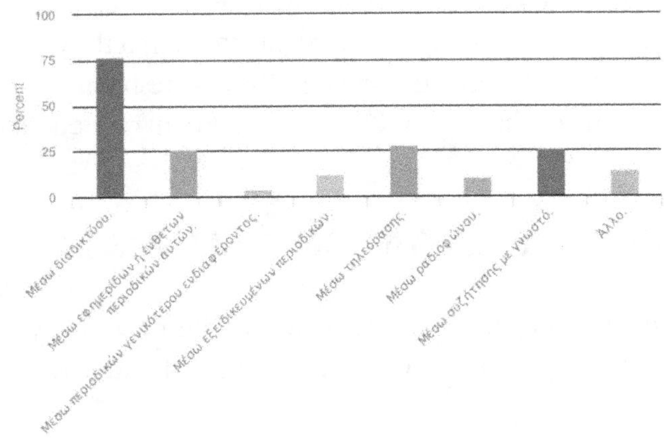

Regarding the means of their information, it is worth mentioning that 76.5 percent read about it online, 27.5 percent via television broadcasts, 25.5 percent through "Newspapers," and 25.5 "by word of mouth."

Concerning the source of information, 75 percent of the respondents stated mass media, 35.4 percent "Researchers and scientists," 16.7 percent "Individuals," and only 2.1 percent that they were informed thanks to "Government statements."

Figure 3. Who was the source of your information? (Cyprus Survey)

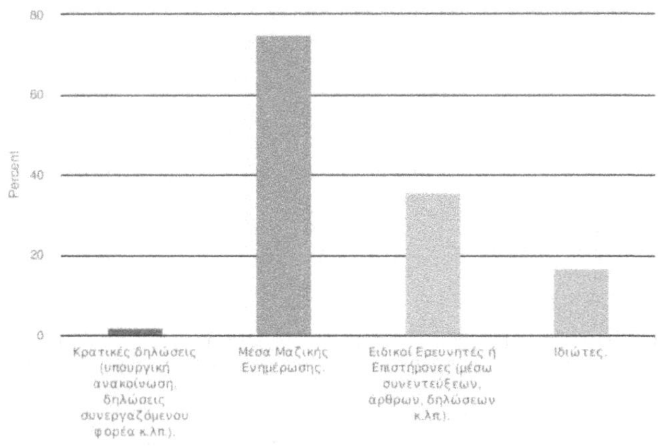

Another interesting question was "Have you ever faced online censorship in the past?." 11.7 percent stated "Yes, at least once," 60 percent "No," and 28.3 percent "I do not know."

From those who answered "Yes, at least once" to the previous question, 20.8 percent stated that they were using the Internet in Cyprus and they were trying to visit a foreign website, 12.5 percent stated that they were connecting to the Internet from a foreign country and they were trying to visit a foreign website, while many of the respondents (66.7 percent) stated "I do not know."

ABOUT THE IMPLEMENTATION OF AN IRS IN CYPRUS

The last part of this questionnaire focused on the possibility of an Internet Regulation System implementation in Kosovo, and under which conditions.

Figure 4. Have you ever faced online censorship in the past? (Cyprus Survey)

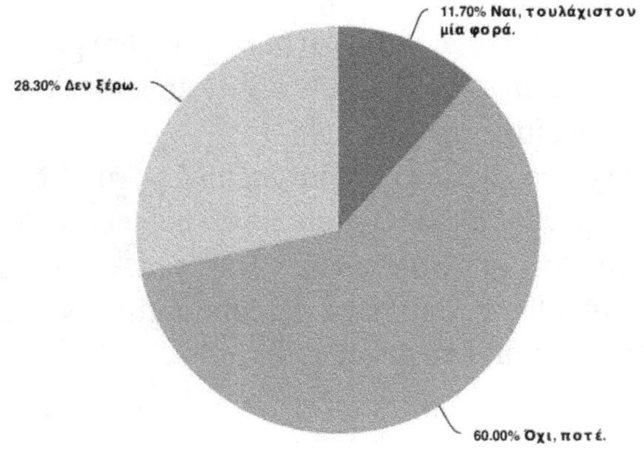

Figure 5. Were you using the Internet from Cyprus? (Cyprus Survey)

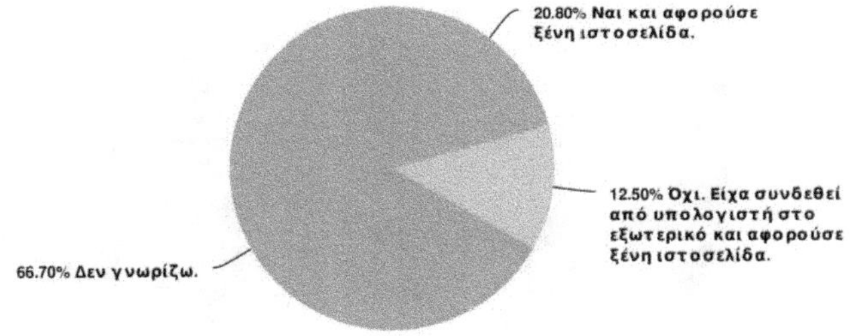

Figure 6. Do you agree with the implementation of an Internet regulation system by the state focusing on illegal content? (Cyprus Survey)

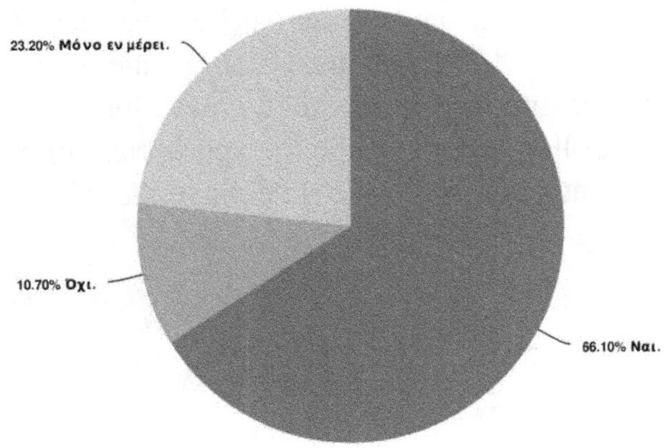

This question was the main one of this survey: "Do you agree with the implementation of an Internet regulation system by the state focusing on illegal content?." 89.3 percent of the participants were positive (66.1 percent stated "Yes," 23.2 percent stated "Yes, but only under conditions," while only 10.7 percent were negative (stating "No").

Regarding the type of online content that a Cyprus IRS should regulate, 67.9 percent stated "pornographic content," 64.3 percent "hate speech content," 26.8 percent "defamatory content," and 23.2 percent "copyrighted multimedia content." On the other hand, only 19.6 percent of the respondents stated that "no kind of content" should be regulated.

Figure 7. What kind of content should be regulated if your country's state decide to implement such a system? (Cyprus Survey)

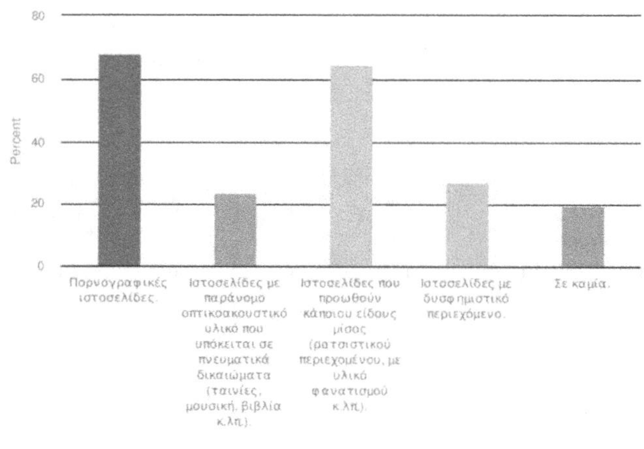

Last, concerning the entity that they prefer to be in control of such an IRS, 42.9 percent "No-government organisation (such as Reporters Without Borders, and so on)," 39.3 percent "Research institutions inside state universities," 25 percent "Research institutions inside state universities," 25 percent stated "Government controlled service inside the appropriate ministry," and 17.9 percent "Research institutions outside state universities."

Figure 8. In case an Internet regulation system is implemented in Cyprus, from whom do you believe it must be operated in order to function with justice and to be accepted by the majority of [you country] citizens? (Cyprus Survey)

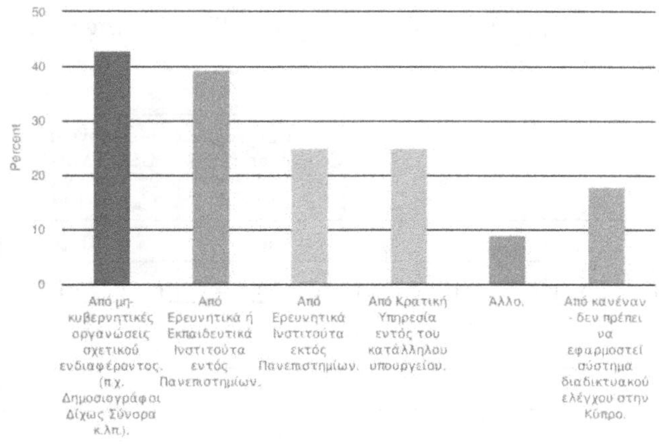

TRENDS AND ASSOCIATIONS WITH THE AID OF STATISTICAL ANALYSIS

As mentioned before quite a few times, it is not in the scope of this book to present all the existing associations between groups and different answers, but only to focus on some of them that are considered of crucial value by the authors.

Pearson chi-square statistical analysis showed (χ^2=9.705) a significant association (a=0.008) between religious belief and agreement on the question set. Adjusted standardised residuals indicate that religious people are associated

Table 1. Agreement on the implementation of an IRS & religious beliefs (Pearson chi-square).

		Do You Consider Yourself Religious?		Total
		Yes	No	
Do you agree an IRS to be implemented in a national level?	Yes	21	16	37
	No	2	4	6
	Yes, under conditions	1	12	13
Total		24	32	56

χ^2= 9.705, df= 2, α= 0.008

with positive answer (answer "Yes"), while non-religious people are associated with the answer "Yes, conditioned."

Table 2. Agreement on the implementation of an IRS & pornographic online content (Pearson chi-square)

		Pornographic Content (What Content an IRS SHOULD TARGET)		Total
		Unchecked	Checked	
Do you agree an IRS to be implemented in a national level?	Yes	6	31	37
	No	5	1	6
	Yes, under conditions	7	6	13
Total		18	38	56

χ^2= 14.319, df= 2, α= 0.001

Pearson chi-square statistical analysis showed (χ^2=14.319) a significant association (a=0.001) between agreement on the question set and preference this IRS to target pornographic content. Adjusted standardised residuals indicate that participants who want an IRS to target pornographic content are associated with positive answer (answer "Yes") to the question set, while participants who do not are associated with the answer "Yes, under conditions."

Pearson chi-square statistical analysis showed (χ^2=9.480) a significant association (a=0.009) between agreement on the question set and preference this IRS to target hate-speech content. Adjusted standardised residuals indicate that participants who want an IRS to target hate-speech content are associated

Table 3. Agreement on the implementation of an IRS & hate-speech online content (Pearson chi-square)

		Hate-Speech Content (What Content an IRS Should Target)		Total
		Unchecked	Checked	
Do you agree an IRS to be implemented in a national level?	Yes	8	29	37
	No	4	2	6
	Yes, under conditions	8	5	13
Total		20	36	56

χ^2= 9.480, df= 2, α= 0.009

with positive answer (answer "Yes") to the question set, while participants who do not are associated with the answer "Yes, under conditions."

On the other hand, there is no association between agreement on the question set and neither gender, age, education level, parenthood, level of awareness of the global phenomenon of Internet regulation, source or means of information, and so forth.

CONCLUSION

Summarising the survey's results in Cyprus, the vast majority was aware of the global phenomenon of Internet regulation. Once again, this leads to the conclusion that Cypriot Internet users constitute a sample with high awareness of this topic.

The vast majority of this sample (nine out of ten) was positive to the implementation of an IRS in their country, targeting illegal content. Concerning the content that should be targeted, the highest rates were recorded in hate-speech and pornographic content. The same exact preferences were recorded during the Greek survey too, verifying the general notion that the Cypriot and Greek societies share many similarities (Psaltis & Cakal, 2014).

Last, significant associations were found during the statistical analysis of the gathered data. More specifically, there is association between acceptance of an IRS implementation and religious belief, along with association between acceptance of an IRS implementation and willingness the latter to target pornographic and hate-speech content.

Taking into account the hate-speech issues in Cyprus since the country and Nicosia partition in 1974 (Anastasiou, 2017; Smith, 2017), the association between hate-speech content and willingness to accept an IRS implementation is quite expected. This is even more comprehensible due to the rise in online hate-speech targeting particularly migrants and ethnic communities, thanks to the recent economic suffering (Solomou et al., 2013). In that sense, Cyprus is a valuable example of how such a survey can verify general notions in specific countries, i.e. how the rise in hate-speech is deeply interconnected with the financial suffering of a modern society.

REFERENCES

Anastasiou, A. (2017). UN wants Cyprus to prosecute more hate speech. *Cyprusail Online*. http://cyprus-mail.com/2017/05/13/un-wants-cyprus-prosecute-hate-speech/

Psaltis, C., & Cakal, H. (2014). Social Identity in a Divided Cyprus. In S. McKeown, R. Haji, & N. Ferguson (Eds.), *Understanding peace and conflict through social identity theory: Contemporary and world-wide perspectives* (pp. 229–244). Springer.

Smith, H. (2007). *Internet Law and Regulation*. London: Sweet & Maxwell.

Solomou, A., Athinodorou, I., Patsalidou, A., & Tsekouras, C. (2013). Report of the Republic of Cyprus. *International Legal Research Group on Online Hate Speech, ELSA International*. https://www.academia.edu/7836525/Online_Hate_Speech_in_Cyprus

Chapter 11
Sum Up:
Statistical Analysis and General Conclusions

ABSTRACT

This chapter presents the trends and associations between the surveys they conducted in different countries, thanks to a series of statistical analyses that lead to valuable conclusions. Among others, the authors used Pearson chi-square analysis, Kruskal-Wallis H, and Mann-Whitney U tests.

AGGREGATED STATISTICAL ANALYSIS AND CONCLUSIONS OF THE SURVEYS

Regarding the trends and associations between the aforementioned surveys in different countries, a series of statistical analysis was conducted leading to valuable conclusions.

Firstly, a Pearson Chi-square analysis was carried out for the question "Do you agree with the implementation of an Internet Regulation System focusing on highly sensitive online content?" and the origin of the participants. It showed (χ^2=128.207) a significant association (a=0.000) between country of origin and agreement on the question set. What's more, the aforementioned association is confirmed using the non-parametrical methods of Kruskal-Wallis H and Mann-Whitney U tests.

DOI: 10.4018/978-1-5225-9973-9.ch011

More specifically, Kruskal-Wallis H test (see table below) indicates that Greek and Cypriot Internet users are associated with the answer "Yes," the German Internet users are associated with the answer "No," while the rest (Russian, Indian and Kosovar Internet users) are associated with the answer "Yes, under conditions." Taking into account that "Yes" value was 1, "Yes, under conditions" value was 2, and "No" value was 3, Greece's and Cyprus's low mean ranks and Germany's high mean rank can be understood.

Table 1. Ranks. All countries.

	Country	N	Mean Rank
(18) Do you agree with the implementation of an Internet regulation system by the state focusing on illegal content?	Greece	409	299.30
	Germany	69	531.97
	Russia	47	340.86
	India	50	465.79
	Kossovo	62	408.54
	Cyprus	56	298.46
	Total	693	

χ^2= 128.207, df= 5, α= 0.000

Further statistical analysis using Mann-Whitney U test was conducted for one-by-one analysis between two countries each time. Significant associations were found between Internet users of Greece-Germany, Greece-India, Greece-Kosovo, Germany-Russia, Germany-India, Germany-Kosovo, Russia-India, India-Cyprus and Kosovo-Cyprus (see tables below).

Further statistical analysis for the pairs mentioned above is out of the scope of this book as it will provide with numerous data and tables more appropriate for a book on the scientific field of Statistics. Conversely, in-depth statistical analysis was conducted between different groups in the same country (as presented in previous chapters) in the authors' effort to find associations and

Table 2. Ranks. Greece – Germany comparison

	Country	N	Mean Rank	Sum of Ranks
(18) Do you agree with the implementation of an Internet regulation system by the state focusing on illegal content?	Greece	409	216.77	88659.50
	Germany	69	374.22	25821.50
	Total	478		

U= 4814.5, α= 0.000

Table 3. Ranks. Greece – India comparison

	Country	N	Mean Rank	Sum of Ranks
(18) Do you agree with the implementation of an Internet regulation system by the state focusing on illegal content?	Greece	409	217.64	89015.50
	India	50	331.09	16554.50
	Total	459		

U= 5170.5, α= 0.000

Table 4. Ranks. Greece – Kossovo comparison.

	Country	N	Mean Rank	Sum of Ranks
(18) Do you agree with the implementation of an Internet regulation system by the state focusing on illegal content?	Greece	409	225.99	92429.50
	Kossovo	62	302.04	18726.50
	Total	471		

U= 8584.5, α= 0.000

Table 5. Ranks. Germany – Russia comparison.

	Country	N	Mean Rank	Sum of Ranks
(18) Do you agree with the implementation of an Internet regulation system by the state focusing on illegal content?	Germany	69	72.32	4990.00
	Russia	47	38.21	1796.00
	Total	116		

U= 668.0, α= 0.000

Table 6. Ranks. Germany – India comparison

	Country	N	Mean Rank	Sum of Ranks
(18) Do you agree with the implementation of an Internet regulation system by the state focusing on illegal content?	Germany	69	66.91	4616.50
	India	50	50.47	2523.50
	Total	119		

U= 1248.5, α= 0.003

Table 7. Ranks. Germany – Kossovo comparison

	Country	N	Mean Rank	Sum of Ranks
(18) Do you agree with the implementation of an Internet regulation system by the state focusing on illegal content?	Germany	69	78.47	5414.50
	Kossovo	62	52.12	3231.50
	Total	131		

U= 1278.5, α= 0.000

Table 8. Ranks. Germany – Cyprus comparison

	Country	N	Mean Rank	Sum of Ranks
(18) Do you agree with the implementation of an Internet regulation system by the state focusing on illegal content?	Germany	69	80.05	5523.50
	Cyprus	56	41.99	2351.50
	Total	125		

U= 755.5, α= 0.000

Table 9. Ranks. Russia – India comparison

	Country	N	Mean Rank	Sum of Ranks
(18) Do you agree with the implementation of an Internet regulation system by the state focusing on illegal content?	Russia	47	39.33	1848.50
	India	50	58.09	2904.50
	Total	97		

U= 720.5, α= 0.000

trends that will prove valuable for the design of mass surveys and the final development of a Fair IRS for each country.

There are quite a few important similarities and differences to be noted among the six countries where the surveys took place.

First of all, the majority of the Internet users in all the countries except Russia were aware of the global phenomenon of Internet regulation, with

Table 10. Ranks. India – Cyprus comparison

	Country	N	Mean Rank	Sum of Ranks
(18) Do you agree with the implementation of an Internet regulation system by the state focusing on illegal content?	India	50	66.48	3324.00
	Cyprus	56	41.91	2347.00
	Total	106		

U= 751.0, α= 0.000

Table 11. Ranks. Kossovo – Cyprus comparison

	Country	N	Mean Rank	Sum of Ranks
(18) Do you agree with the implementation of an Internet regulation system by the state focusing on illegal content?	Kossovo	62	68.13	4224.00
	Cyprus	56	49.95	2797.00
	Total	118		

U= 1201.0, α= 0.002

Germany and Greece leading the way. In other words, authors' research was done using samples with high awareness of the phenomenon.

Another issue is how openly the topic of Internet regulation is discussed in different countries, and to what extent this is related to how positive or negative Internet users are to the implementation of an IRS that will be controlled by the government or a state service. In almost every country, except Germany, the vast majority of the Internet users stated that they were not informed by official statements. Even in Germany, where the discussion of Internet regulation is an important aspect of the current political life (Wired, 1997; Efroni, 2008), only one out of five stated the opposite. So, we have a general rule that none of the surveyed countries' governments discussed publicly the need for Internet regulation or even the existence of related international laws that have to be implemented.

Another question, probably the most important one for this research, is "How positive or negative are the Internet users to the implementation of an IRS in their country?" Five out of six surveys (except German) recorded high rates of acceptance of such a development, in agreement with some of the past-related surveys (such as 2012 Internet Society survey, reviewed in section 2.1). In that sense, Internet users are ready to accept the implementation of an IRS, but under what conditions?

Greek, Russian, and Cypriot Internet users were positive for such an IRS to target hate-speech and pornographic content, but no copyright infringement and defamation content. This is partially due to a shared Orthodox Christian tradition, but at the same time shows that these societies share something common: they agree that there is a need for Internet regulation, but not against freedom of speech and free access to data.

On the other hand, Germans proved to be the most hesitant to accept the regulation of any kind of content, while the Kosovars are keen to accept regulation in many different topics.

The former is partially explained due to the fact that Germany was under the Nazi authoritarian regime only a few decades ago, and so it is expected to have (as a society) a very protective approach towards freedom of speech. This explanation is backed by another outcome of the German survey: as the participant's age increases, there is an almost smooth transition from answer "Yes" to the answer "No." More specifically, younger participants are keener to accept without conditions the implementation of an IRS while older ones are absolutely negative to such a development.

A quite interesting detail is that the Russian Internet users are the only ones to trust their government or a state-service to control such an IRS. No matter how incomprehensible it might seem from a Westerner's point of view, it is expected if we take into account that among the Russian society the liberal intelligentsia is still a quite small minority, and liberal ideas have not managed to win widespread support so far (Markwick & Gill, 2000; Rose, Munro & Mishler, 2004).

On the other hand, the Germans do not trust anyone to control and function an IRS in their country. In the middle stand the Greek, Indian, Kosovar, and Cypriot Internet users that show a preference for non-governmental organisations and/or university-based institutes.

Regarding trends and associations that emerged during the statistical analysis of the results, there are quite a few comments to make.

In the example of Germany, there is no association between education level or parenthood and the willingness to accept Internet regulation. On the other hand, religious beliefs are playing an important role as religious Internet users proved to be positive, while non-religious Internet users were negative to the implementation of an IRS. These findings verify the general opinion of media analysts that religion and free speech have a long history of conflict (Biddle, 2006; IoC, 2013).

In the example of Russia, an important association was spotted too: the participants who stated positive to the implementation of an IRS are the same as those stating that trust the Russian government. In India and Cyprus, the Internet users who are positive towards the implementation of an IRS are those who want hate-speech content to be targeted.

In Kosovo, the most interesting association is between agreement on the implementation of an IRS and religious belief. Even if it is expected that religious people are keener to accept content regulation (Biddle, 2006; IoC, 2013), it is important to state that even non-religious ones are keen to accept such a development "under conditions."

CONCLUSION

In conclusion, no matter the differences and similarities between the surveyed countries, the carrying out of these surveys proved how important it is to measure public opinion. Furthermore, the statistical analysis of these results proved that every society is different, and it is crucial to spot the "dos and don'ts" if we want to design a Fair IRS that will be accepted by the majority of a country's citizens.

As an example, Internet users in different countries are willing to accept different characteristics for their country's IRS. German, Greek, and Russian Internet users tend to agree on the kind of online content that should be regulated (pornographic and hate-speech websites), but they prefer different entities to control and run such an IRS. Greek Internet users tend to trust university-based research institutes and NGOs to control such an IRS, Russian Internet users tend to trust their government-controlled related Ministry, while German Internet users seem to trust no-one for such a role.

The aforementioned examples are only a small portion of the significant differences on Internet users' preferences between six countries. With that in mind, the authors present their FIRS blueprint (chapter 12), before theoretically implementing it in Greece, choosing the latter as a country-example (chapter 13).

REFERENCES

Ahmeti, B. (2014). *Internet Usage in Kosovo, Digital Spoiler, November 2014*. https://digitalspoiler.com/internet-usage-kosovo/

Anastasiou, A. (2017). UN wants Cyprus to prosecute more hate speech. *Cyprusail Online*. http://cyprus-mail.com/2017/05/13/un-wants-cyprus-prosecute-hate-speech/

Bhandari, M. K., & Bhatt, M. N. (2012). Hate Speech and Freedom of Expression: Balancing Social Good and Individual Liberty. *The Practical Lawyer*. http://www.supremecourtcases.com/index2.php?option=com_content&itemid=5&do_pdf=1&id=22819

Biddle, C. (2006). Religion vs. Free Speech. *The Objective Standard, 1*(2).

Binder, K. (2016). The Trans-Pacific Partnership (TPP) Potential regional and global impacts. *EPRS | European Parliamentary Research Service, European Parliament*. https://www.europarl.europa.eu/RegData/etudes/BRIE/2016/582028/EPRS_BRI(2016)582028_EN.pdf

Daniyal, S. (2017). Does India need stronger hate speech laws? The Law Commission seems to think so. *Scroll.in*. https://scroll.in/article/832978/does-india-need-stronger-hate-speech-laws-the-law-commission-seems-to-thinks-so

Efroni, Z. (2008). German Court Orders to Block Wikipedia.de Due to Offending Article. *Center for Internet and Society Blog, Stanford University Law School*. http://cyberlaw.stanford.edu/blog/2008/11/german-court-orders-block-wikipediade-due-offending-article

Evans, A. B. (2011, January). The failure of democratization in Russia: A comparative perspective. *Journal of Eurasian Studies*, *2*(1), 40–51. doi:10.1016/j.euras.2010.10.001

IoC. (2013). Religion and free speech: it's complicated. *Index on Censorship*. https://www.indexoncensorship.org/2013/03/free-expression-and-religion-overview/

Koumartzis, N. (2010). Greek Internet Regulation Survey. *WebObserver.net*.

Markwick, R. D., & Gill, G. (2000). *Russia's stillborn democracy? From Gorbachev to Yeltsin*. Oxford, UK: Oxford University Press.

Marusic, S. J. (2014). Kosovo Leads Balkans in Internet Addiction. *Balkan Insight*. http://www.balkaninsight.com/en/article/kosovars-lead-balkans-internet-usage-chart

Ottaway, M. (2003). *Democracy challenged: The rise of semi-authoritarianism*. Washington, DC: Carnegie Endowment for International Peace.

Psaltis, C., & Cakal, H. (2014). Social Identity in a Divided Cyprus. In S. McKeown, R. Haji, & N. Ferguson (Eds.), *Understanding peace and conflict through social identity theory: Contemporary and world-wide perspectives* (pp. 229–244). Springer.

RMVP. (1938). *Liste des schädlichen und unerwünschten Schrifttums*. Reichsministerium für Volksaufklärung und Propaganda.

Rose, R., Munro, N., & Mishler, W. (2004). Resigned acceptance of an incomplete democracy: Russia's political equilibrium. *Post-Soviet Affairs*, *20*(3), 195–218. doi:10.2747/1060-586X.20.3.195

Smith, H. (2017). Fear and loathing in Nicosia: will peace talks unify Europe's last divided capital? *The Guardian*. https://www.theguardian.com/cities/2017/jan/12/fear-loathing-nicosia-peace-talks-unify-divided-cypriot-capital

Solomou, A., Athinodorou, I., Patsalidou, A., & Tsekouras, C. (2013). Report of the Republic of Cyprus, International Legal Research Group on Online Hate Speech. *ELSA International.* https://www.academia.edu/7836525/Online_Hate_Speech_in_Cyprus

Stikk. (2013). Internet penetration and usage in Kosovo. *Kossovo Association of Information and Communication Technology (STIKK).* http://www.mfa-ks.net/repository/docs/STIKK_raport_eng_2013_short_web.pdf

Wired. (1997). Germany gets Radikal about extremists on web. *Wired Magazine.* https://www.wired.com/1997/01/germany-gets-radikal-about-extremists-on-web/

Section 4

Research, Design, and Blueprint of a Fair IRS

Chapter 12
Designing a Fair Internet Regulation System

ABSTRACT

Taking into consideration the IRSs, older surveys, and authors' surveys results discussed in previous chapters, this chapter presents a fair internet regulation system (FIRS) designed by the authors. Their aim is to be highly adaptable to each country's special political needs in order to be accepted by the general public. In that context, they propose that a blueprint should be used in the development of an effective, fast, and low cost system that will encourage internet users to participate in the whole procedure, giving them the opportunity to enrich and correct its "behaviour." At the same time, the proposed FIRS has to be able to handle specific kinds of online illegal content with "discretion."

INTRODUCTION

Taking into consideration the IRSs discussed in chapters 1 and 3, older surveys presented in chapter 2 and authors' surveys results in chapters 5 to 11, a Fair Internet Regulation System (FIRS) was designed by the authors. Their aim is to be highly adaptable to each country special political needs in order to be accepted by the general public.

In that context, the authors propose in this chapter that a blueprint should be used in the production of an cheap, quick but also efficient method that will support Internet users participation in the whole process, thus providing them

DOI: 10.4018/978-1-5225-9973-9.ch012

with the possibility to adjust and finetune its "behaviour." Simultaneously, the proposed FIRS has to be able to handle specific kinds of online illegal content with "discretion."

THE VALUE OF WELL-MADE SURVEYS

So, for public opinion to consent to the introduction of an Internet regulation system, from the initial steps of the design process, the needs of each society must be taken into consideration.

These needs may vary between countries (as it is clearly shown in chapters 5 to 11). In that sense, each society's needs must be identified via well-designed surveys, ideally conducted on a great proportion of the population. In case this is not possible for a researcher (i.e. due to no adequate funds), small samples that are familiarised with the use of the Internet can give some initial trends and act as proof that a bigger survey is feasible and worth funding (Teijlingen & Hundley, 2001).

Such surveys can produce valuable data regarding a. if the general public wants to embrace and engage in some sort of Internet regulation, b. who is thought to be best suited to running such a system, c. what kind of content should be aimed, and so on (Koumartzis & Veglis, 2012).

In Greece's example, a survey was conducted by the authors at Aristotle University of Thessaloniki (June 2010, see chapter 5) on a small but highly educated sample (Koumartzis, 2010) consisting mainly of MA and PhD students, and faculty members of the School of Journalism and Mass Communication. This provided useful results to be studied in detail, but in brief this revealed that 37.9 percent favored such a system to be run by university-based institutes (compared to just 11.5 percent who believed in a ministry-based government service). As far as the content that should be addressed the survey participants suggested: a) pornographic websites (35.1 percent), b) hate speech content (34 percent), c) defamation content (13.4 percent), and d) multimedia illegal sharing websites (7.2 percent).

FIRS FEATURES AND ORGANIZATION

Taking into consideration the outcome of the survey, a regulation body must be chosen in order to analyse Internet users' feedback and prepare the blocking lists of websites. Concerning Greece, survey's results shown that general public is more willing to accept a combination of university-based institutes and non-governmental organisations as the regulation body.

Authors' surveys (see chapters 5 to 11) and experts' opinion (Keny, 2016) show a clear preference to non-governmentally controlled bodies in many countries.

Targeted Content and Categorisation

Another important aspect of a FIRS design is to define what illegal content to target. Child pornography seems to be a widely accepted option worldwide for a regulation (Hamade, 2008). Further expansion of the online content to be targeted must be done following independent evaluation per country.

The authors suggest in this chapter the categorisation of the targeted online content to a. unquestionable must-be-filtered content and b. contradictable must-be-filtered content. In the case of Greece it is obvious that child pornography falls into category a., whereas the rest categories would fall into category b. Therefore, two different lists are formed: Blacklist A (including unquestionable must-be-filtered content) and Blacklist B (including contradictable must-be-filtered content).

System-User Interaction

As far as how the system will be interacted with the Internet users is concerned, this chapter proposes an IRS that will be hybrid in terms of technology it is using, content management and user feedback.

The IRS should, in principle, be able to determine whether the Internet user attempts to access a. websites which have not been blocked, b. contradictable must-be-filtered content and c. unquestionable must-be-filtered content.

In case (a), the IRS will grant free access. In case (b), it will block the access, inform the Internet user about the current Internet regulation policies, and gather complaints if the Internet user want to submit one. In case (c), the IRS will block the access with "discretion": it will serve a "404 error message" and, therefore, it will not inform the user that this particular website is blocked. The latter is quite important concerning the determined users: the system will not let them identify child pornography websites and, therefore, use circumvention methods to bypass the IRS and access the content (check chapter 3, section 4 for more details).

Technical Aspects

In technical terms, the FIRS is designed as a three-stage hybrid system. It uses IP blocking for its first two stages, a method that is quick but not accurate. During the third stage, URL blocking is being applied: a method that is quite precise, but time-consuming at the same time.

In order each stage to be effective, four lists are being produced based on the aforementioned Blacklist A, and Blacklist B. More specific, the four lists are IP1 List, IP2 List, URL1 List and URL2 List.

IP1 List: It is used during the Stage 1 Check, as described in Figure 1. It is derived from the URLs that are included in Blacklist A, and Blacklist B.

IP2 List: It is used during the Stage 2 Check, as described in Figure 2. It is derived from the URLs that are included in Blacklist A.

URL1 List: It is used during the Stage 3a Check, and it includes the URLs of Blacklist A.

URL2 List: It is used during Stage 3b Check, and it includes the URLs of Blacklist B.

Figure 1. How IP1 List derives from Blacklists A&B (blacklists A&B URLs of categories a&b; IP1 lists IPs of the URLs of category a&b)
(Koumartzis & Veglis, 2012)

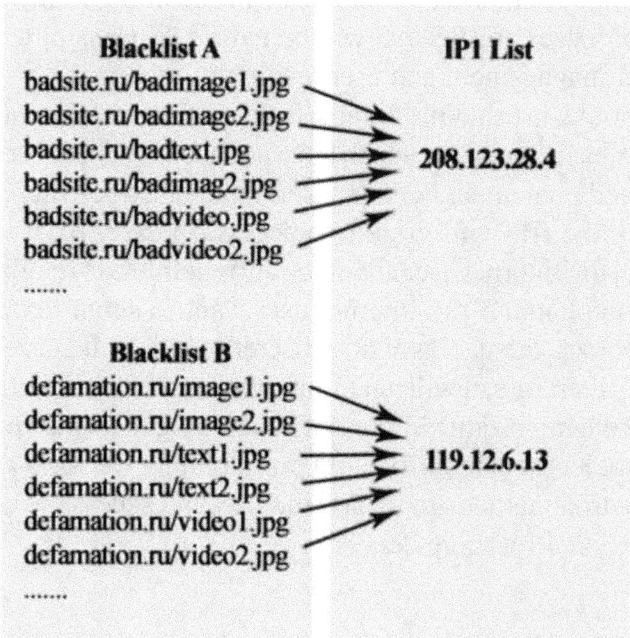

Figure 2. How IP2 List derives from Blacklist A (blacklist A URLs of category a unquestionable must-be-filtered content; IP1 list IPs of the URLs of category a) *(Koumartzis & Veglis, 2012)*

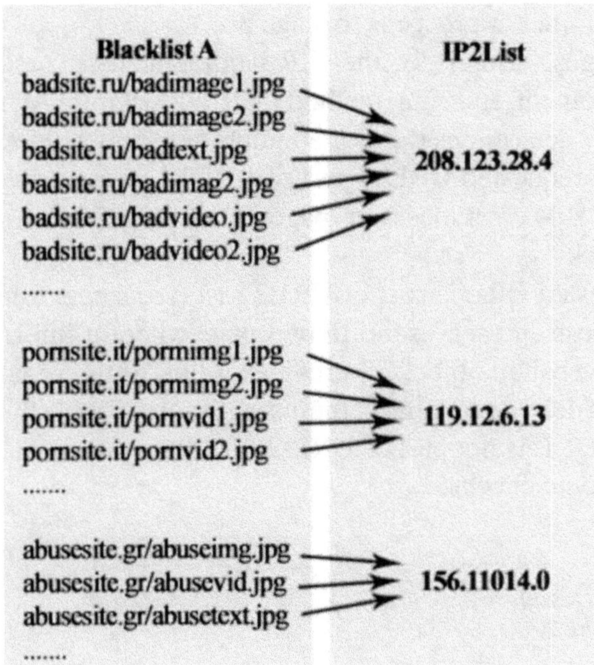

In order to understand the aforementioned four lists model, it is important to know how an IP and a URL are related. In brief, an IP address is the numerical name that computers use to locate each others through the Internet (ISI, 2017). On the other hand, a URL is the descriptive name that defines how a computer can fetch a resource on the Internet: a text, an image, etc. (Berners-Lee, T. et al, 1994). In that sense, a URL contains an IP address to define on which computer each resource is actually hosted. It is crucial here to comprehend that many URLs can share the same IP, while the opposite is not possible (Koumartzis, 2008).

As Figure 3 visually describes below, the FIRS's whole procedure is straightforward. During stage 1, the FIRS determines with packet dropping (i.e. IP blocking, a quick but not accurate method) when a user attempts to access a "suspicious" website. If the website is not hosted in an IP included in IP1 List, then the FIRS serves the content without additional checks. If the website is hosted on an IP of IP1 List, then the FIRS proceed to the next stage.

During stage 2, the FIRS decides if the "suspicious" website falls in category (a) or in category (b). This is done by using, once more, packet dropping. If the website's IP is part of IP2 List, then the FIRS proceeds in stage 3a. If not, then it proceeds to stage 3b.

During stages 3a and 3b, the FIRS implements a precise (but time-consuming) content filtering method: URL blocking. At that point, the system actually determines if a user attempts to access a blocked URL. More specific, if the requested URL is part of URL1 List (see stage 3a), then the FIRS serves a "404 error message" page. If not, it serves the website without additional checks.

If the requested URL is part of URL2 List (see stage 3b), then the FIRS blocks the access and serves a different page where it informs the Internet user that the website is blocked, provides a link to the regulation policies, and a way to file a complaint if the user disagrees with the regulation. If the requested URL is not part of URL 2 List, the system serves the website without additional checks.

Figure 3. FIRS Design
(Koumartzis & Veglis, 2012)

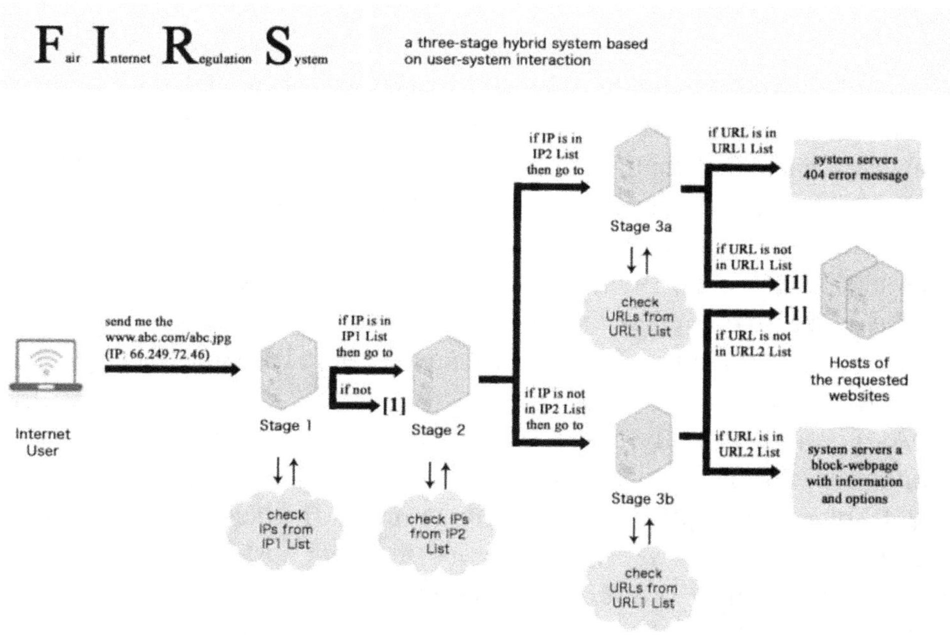

Situation:
[1] In this case, system stops further checking, get the requested webpage from the server and serves it to the user.

PROPOSED FIRS'S ADVANTAGES

The goal of this method is to be very efficient and to have low running costs, which is why the FIRS incorporates the efficiency of the IP blocking process with the accuracy of the URL filtering technique. The key advantages of the FIRS concept that is being introduced, is that it recommends the use of four separate lists to facilitate the involvement of Internet users, while at the same time it is able to manage particular forms of content with "discretion."

Nevertheless, the key advantage of FIRS, namely the three-stage design is also its biggest drawback, as it is technologically vulnerable and can be overtaken. In the next section, the authors briefly discuss this issue.

CIRCUMVENTING FIRS AND POSSIBLE SOLUTIONS

It is not possible for an IRS built for large scale usage in a democratic society to be entirely invulnerable. However widespread Internet user engagement will allow it to become gradually more effective.

Two of the circumvention methods that need to be discussed are the use of network proxy (which can fully bypass the system) and the use of URL variations (which can overcome the FIRS Phase 3) by Internet users, and website mirroring, multiple URLs, and the use of another port by the provider of the illegal content (Koumartzis & Veglis, 2012).

Several different methods can be used in order to address to a certain these problems. For example, the usage of web proxies may be handled by introducing web proxies URLs to the Blacklists A & B, or better yet by programming FIRS to reject all source routed packets (i.e. packets that attempt to reach the website through proxies (Clayton, 2008).

In comparison, the URL variations technique may be addressed due to the input of Internet users, or whether the system is designed to employ algorithms to generate various types of variants with the URLs already used in Blacklists A & B.

The authors believe that it is not meaningful to further elaborate on the issue as in Chapter 3 of this book they discuss in depth available circumvention techniques, such as Internet Archive services, web proxies, URL variations, content provider circumvention, mirroring, changing IP address, multiple URLs, use of another HTTP port, and others.

CONCLUSION

The authors suggest in this chapter an Internet regulation system (called FIRS) that can function at high speed and at low cost, while at the same time being "open" to Internet users ' involvement and assessment.

They also note the significance of performing well-devised surveys in each country prior to the FIRS design process, so that each system can be tailored to the national political setting and ultimately acknowledged by the general public. Subsequently a blueprint for this system is introduced (see figure 3) and outlined.

Since 2010, the authors have constantly been promoting the use of surveys as a tool to the design procedure of such systems through WebObserver.net website, welcoming international participation. Thanks to their efforts, many surveys were conducted around the world, while six of them managed to gather enough participants to present valuable results: Greece, Germany, Russia, Kosovo, India, and Cyprus (see chapters 5 to 11).

With all these data available, in the next chapter, the authors proceed to the final stage of their research by implementing the aforementioned FIRS blueprint, using Greece as a country example.

REFERENCES

Berners-Lee, T. (1990). Design Issue for the World Wide Web. *w3.org*. Retrieved from http://www.w3.org/DesignIssues/

Clayton, R. (2008). Failures of a Hybrid Content Blocking System. In G. Danezis & D. Martin (Eds.), *Privacy Enhancing Technologies, Fifth International Workshop, PET 2005*. Berlin: Springer Verlag.

Hamade, S. N. (2008). Internet Filtering and Censorship. In *Fifth International Conference on Information Technology: New Generations*. New York: IEEE Computer Society.

ISI. (2017). DOD Standard Internet Protocol. *Information Sciences Institute University of Southern California*. Retrieved from https://www.ietf.org/rfc/rfc0760.txt

Keny, A. (2016). UK Cleanfeed vs. Australian Cleanfeed. *Inside Internet Filtering*. Retrieved from http://www.insideinternetfiltering.com/2008/08/uk-cleanfeed-vs-australian-cleanfeed/

Koumartzis, N. (2008). *BT's CleanFeed and Online Censorship in UK: Improvements for a More Secure and Ethically Correct Systeym* (Doctoral dissertation). University of the Arts London, London College of Communication, London, UK.

Koumartzis, N. (2010). Greek Internet Regulation Survey. *WebObserver.net.*

Koumartzis, N., & Veglis, A. (2012). Internet Regulation, A New Approach: Outline of a system formed to be controlled by the Internet Users. *Computer Technology and Application, 3*(1), 16–23.

Teijlingen, E. R., & Hundley, V. (2001). The importance of pilot studies. *Social Research Update, 35*. Retrieved from http://sru.soc.surrey.ac.uk/SRU35.pdf

Chapter 13
Putting a FIRS to the Test:
The Case Study of Greece

ABSTRACT

In this chapter, the authors implement their fair internet regulation system (FIRS) blueprint using Greece as a country example. They discuss the results of Greece initial survey, and they present all the improvements that were implemented in the initial questionnaire. The improved questionnaire was then used for Greece's mass survey that was conducted in October 2013, gathering 446 responses, the results of which are being presented here. Taking the results of Greece's mass survey into account, the authors proceed with choosing the content and categorisation that FIRS will target and the technical aspects based on the aims and the budget. Furthermore, the blacklists of Greek FIRS are being presented, along with its interface and interaction with the internet users. Last, the authors present their conclusions and discuss possible improvements of the Greek FIRS in the future based on different financial and technical potentials.

INTRODUCTION

In this chapter, the authors implement their FIRS blueprint (discussed in chapter 12), using Greece as a country example.

They discuss the results of Greece's Survey presented in chapters 5 to 11, while later, they present all the improvements that were implemented in the questionnaire of the initial survey. The improved questionnaire was then used

DOI: 10.4018/978-1-5225-9973-9.ch013

for Greece's Mass Survey that was conducted in October 2013, gathering 446 responses, the results of which are then presented.

Taking the analysed results of Greece's Mass Survey into account, the authors proceed with choosing the content and categorisation that FIRS will target and the technical aspects based on the aims and the budget.

Furthermore, the blacklists of Greek FIRS (GFIRS) are being presented along with the GFIRS Interface and its interaction with the Internet users.

Last, the authors present their conclusions, and discuss possible improvements of the GFIRS in the future, based on different financial and technical potentials.

ANALYSING THE RESULTS OF THE GREEK SURVEY

Greek Survey's results are being presented in depth in chapter 5. In this section, the authors discuss only specific data that is highly relevant to the implementation of the FIRS blueprint in Greece's example.

Concerning the value of the collected data, it is important to state that 96.7 percent of the participants are Greek Internet users for more than 3 years (see figure 1), while 85 percent stated that they were informed of the global Internet regulation phenomenon to some extent (see figure 2). Last, the participants declared an important diversity regarding the means of information as 62.5 percent said that they were informed through mass media, while 52.1 percent through specialised researchers and related scientists (see figure 3).

Figure 1. For how many years are you a Greece based Internet user? (Greece Survey)

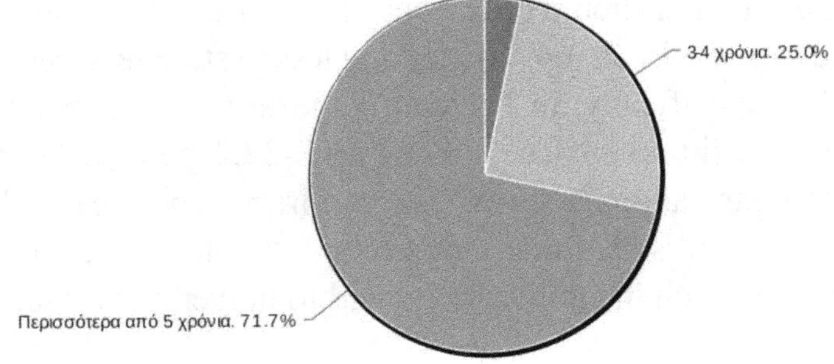

Figure 2. Are you aware of the global phenomenon of Internet regulation? (Greece Survey)

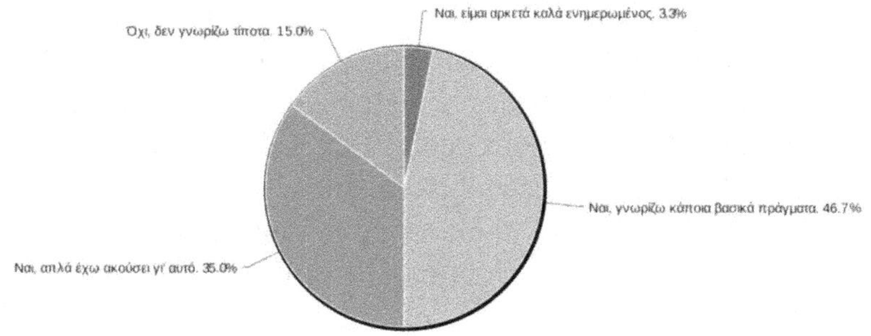

Figure 3. What were the means of your information? (Greece Survey)

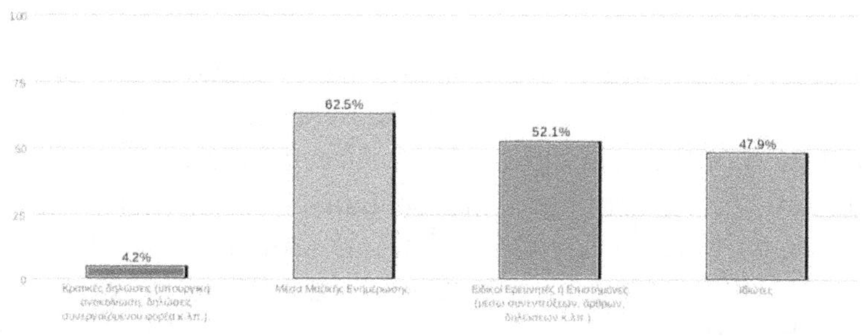

Regarding the possibility of implementing a Greek IRS at a national level, 79.7 percent of the participants were positive (see figure 4). Concerning the type of online content that a Greek IRS should target, 61 percent stated "hate-speech websites," 61 percent "pornographic websites," 25.4 percent "defamatory content," and only 13.6 percent stated "online piracy websites (movies, music, books, and so on)" (see figure 5).

As for the entity that should be in control of a Greek IRS, the participants showed more trust in Greek universities and less in state services and related ministries. More specifically, 59.3 percent of the respondents stated "Research or Educational Institutes inside universities," 32.2 percent "Related non-governmental organisations (such as *Reporters without borders,* and so forth)," and only 20.3 percent stated that they prefer a "State service in the related Ministry" or "Research institutes not related to universities" (see figure 6).

Figure 4. Do you agree with the implementation of an Internet regulation system by the state focusing on illegal content? (Greece Survey)

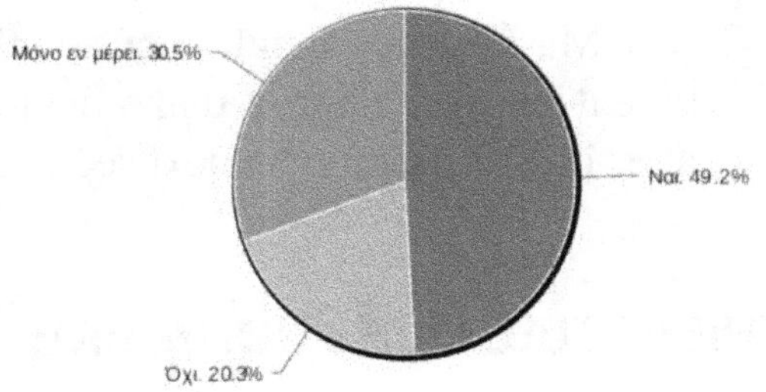

Figure 5. What kind of content should be regulated if your country's state decides to implement such a system? (Greece Survey)

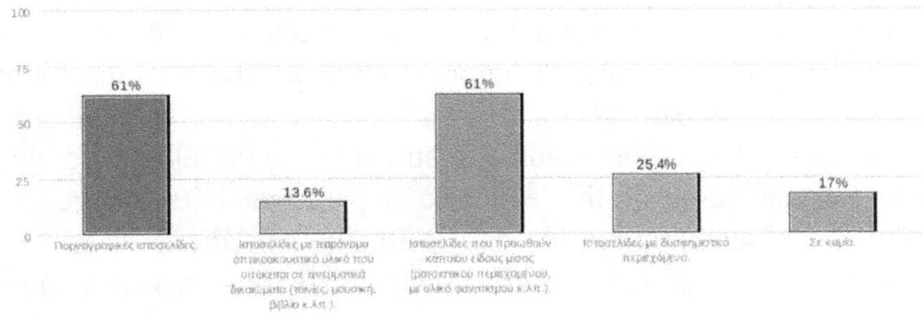

Figure 6. In case an Internet regulation system is implemented in Greece, from whom do you believe it must be operated in order to function with justice and to be accepted by the majority of [you country] citizens? (Greece Survey)

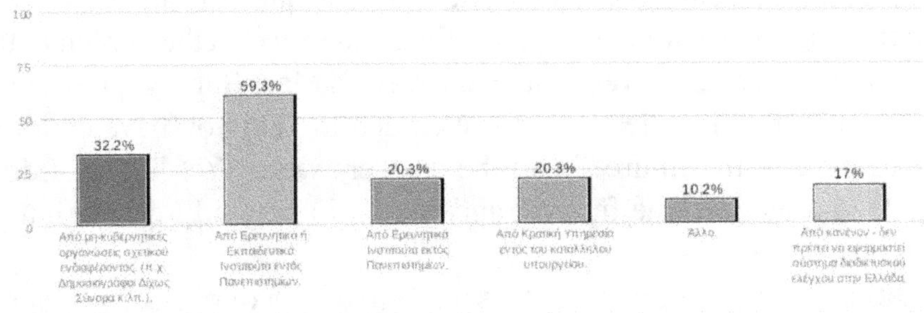

All the data presented above show possible characteristics of the ideal Greek FIRS (such as candidates for Blacklist A and Blacklist B, see section 12.3.1), but they have to be confirmed by conducting a mass survey with a greater sample. A Greece Mass Survey should focus on the aforementioned data, and at the same time it has to be improved in order to collect even more reliable results. The latter is discussed in the next section.

IMPROVING THE INITIAL QUESTIONNAIRE

It is important to state here that there always was a core questionnaire for all the surveys and the mass survey in Greece, which was partially adjusted to each country's needs and current conditions. Besides that, the initial surveys in each country are meant to play a key role for the whole process of implementing a FIRS at a national level, among others by testing the initial questionnaires and concluding to improvements for the final questionnaire of the country's mass survey.

In that sense, the authors made alterations to the initial questionnaire of Greece's Survey, based on the feedback by participants (see appendix 15) and experts. These alterations are discussed below in this section.

An important alteration was made to question 6 of the two questionnaires. In Greece's Survey, the question was "Do you have children?" with only two answers "Yes" and "No." As a result, the answer "No" was chosen by two completely different types of participants: a. people who do not have children, but are positive to that possibility, and b. people who do not have children, and negative to that possibility.

Taking into account the importance of that question in the search of correlations between parenthood and willingness to accept the implementation of an IRS, improvements were made to Greece's Mass Survey questionnaire. More specifically, the question was reworded to "Do you have children or intend to have in the future?" and the answers were "Yes," "No, I do not, but I intend to have in the future," and "No, I do not and I do not intend to have in the future."

Additionally, an improvement was made to the set of pre-defined answers of the question 11 of the two questionnaires: "What was the source of your information?" The reason was that the initial set (with only 5 options) proved confusing to some part of the participants. For that reason, in the final questionnaire of Greece's Mass Survey, the set of pre-defined answers for question 11 was expanded to include these options: "Statements by state employees–officials," "Statements by government's officials (ministers and others)," "Statements by politicians and political parties," "Statements by related non-governmental organisations (Human Rights, Free Speech, and so on.)," "Specialised researchers," "Journalists," and "Private conversations."

What's more, a major improvement was made to the last question of the two questionnaires: "In case an Internet regulation system is implemented in Greece, by whom do you believe it must be operated in order to function with justice and to be accepted by the majority of the Greek citizens?" The reason was to provide additional and more clearly pre-defined options for the participants. The initial set of answers consisted of 6 options, while the improved set has these 8 options: "Department inside Greek Police," "Department inside Greek Army," "Department inside the appropriate Greek Ministry," "Non-Governmental organisations (i.e. Reporters Without Borders and so on)," "Research or Educational Institute inside Universities," "Research or Educational Institute outside Universities," "Another department-agency that will not be controlled by the government," "Other."

Last, the difference in the number of questions between the two questionnaires is fictitious as it is credited to the fact that, due to technical reasons, some sub-questions of the old questionnaire became separate questions in the new questionnaire.

CONDUCTING A GREECE MASS SURVEY

Following the Greek Survey, another one was designed based on the initial results and feedback. The Greece Mass Survey (GMS) was conducted with the aid of many professional Greek journalists, leading to a massive participation. More specifically, the new survey was conduced between 27th of February and 2nd of October 2013, gathering 446 respondents.

The authors begin by presenting some of the survey's results that are related to their research topic, continue with statistical analysis to find trends and associations, and end with their conclusions. The rest of the survey's results can be found in Appendix 21. The statistical graphs that are shown are in the original language, with an explanation in English for each image.

Greek Internet Users and Internet Regulation Policies

Below, the authors include a series of related inquiries regarding their research topic.

Figure 7. Are you aware of the global phenomenon of Internet regulation? (Greece Mass Survey)

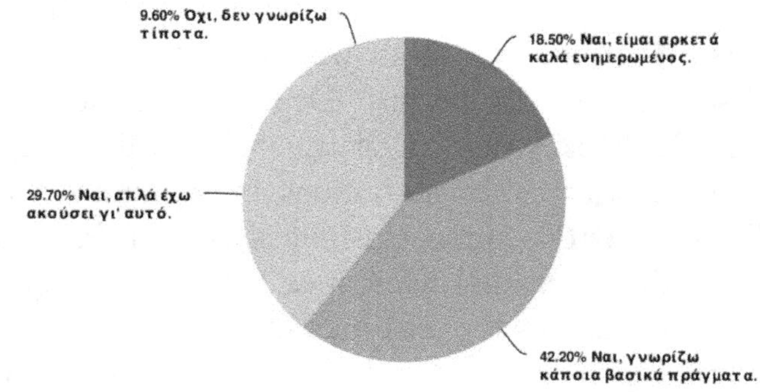

A question of major significance was "Are you aware of the global phenomenon of Internet regulation?," to which most of the respondents stated that they know the basics (42.2 percent), 18.5 percent that they are well-informed, and 29.7 percent that they just heard about it. Only 9.6 percent stated that they have not heard anything related before.

Figure 8. What were the means of your information? (Greece Mass Survey)

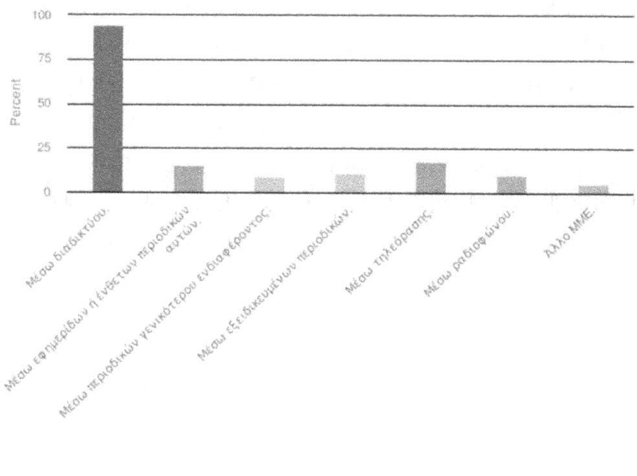

Regarding the means of their information, it is worth mentioning that the vast majority of the participants (94.2 percent) read about it online, 17.5 percent via television broadcasts, 15.4 percent through "Newspapers," and 10.7 percent via specialised magazines.

Figure 9. Who was the source of your information? (Greece Mass Survey)

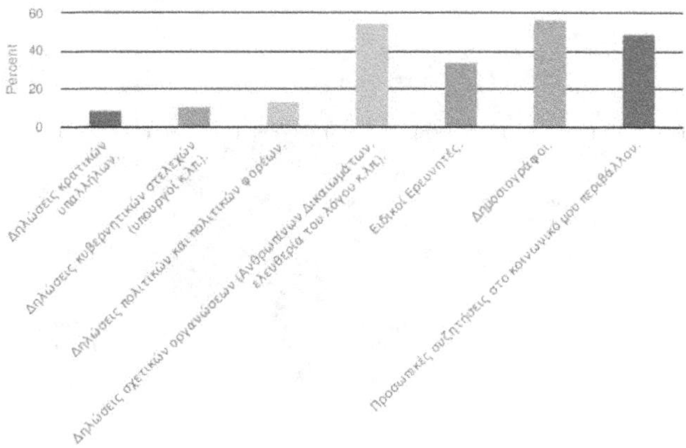

Concerning the source of information, 57 percent of the respondents stated that they get informed through journalists' work, 54.8 percent through statements by related organisations, 49.4 percent through discussion with individuals, and 33.8 percent through specialised researchers. Only 13.2 percent stated that they were informed via statements by politicians or related entities, and 10.6 through state representatives' statements.

Figure 10. Have you ever faced online censorship in the past? (Greece Mass Survey)

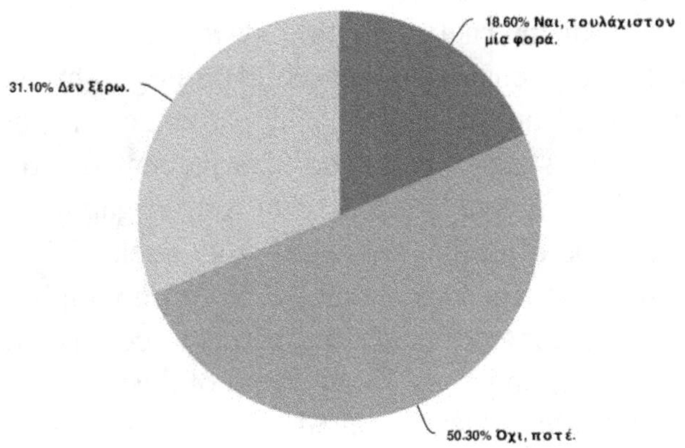

Another interesting question was “Have you ever faced online censorship in the past?” 18.6 percent stated “Yes, at least once,” 50.3 percent “No,” and 31.1 percent “I do not know.”

Figure 11. Were you using the Internet from Greece? (Greece Mass Survey)

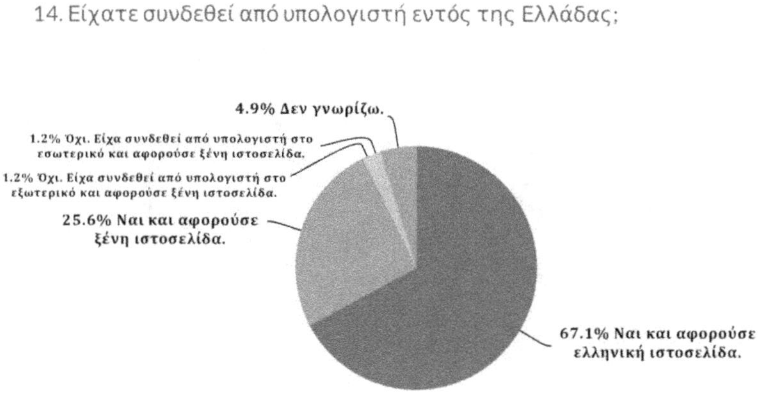

Of those who answered “Yes, at least once” to the previous question, 57.1 percent stated that they were using the Internet in Greece and they were trying to visit a Greek website, and 25.6 percent stated that they were using the Internet in Greece.

Are Internet users keen to accept the implementation of Internet regulation system in Greece?

The last part of this questionnaire focused on the possibility of an Internet Regulation System implementation in Greece, and under which conditions.

This question was the main one of this survey: “Do you agree with the implementation of an Internet regulation system by the state focusing on illegal content of highly sensitive issues (child pornography, hate-speech, and pro-terrorists websites, and so forth?.” 83.7 percent of the participants were positive (60.8 percent stated “Yes,” and 22.9 percent stated “Yes, but only under conditions”), while only 16.3 percent were negative (stating “No”).

Regarding the type of online content that a Greek IRS should regulate, 66.7 percent stated “hate speech content,” 62.6 “pornographic content,” 30.1 percent “defamatory content,” and 16.6 percent “copyrighted multimedia content.” On the other hand, only 13.4 percent of the respondents stated that “no type of content” should be regulated.

Figure 12. Do you agree with the implementation of an Internet regulation system by the state focusing on illegal content? (Greece Mass Survey)

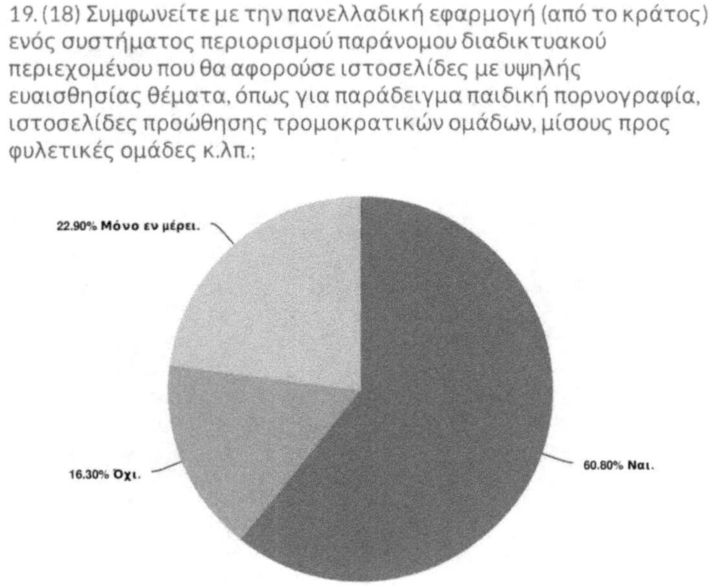

Figure 13. What kind of content should be regulated if your country's state decide to implement such a system? (Greece Mass Survey)

Figure 14. In case an Internet regulation system is implemented in Greece, from whom do you believe it must be operated in order to function with justice and to be accepted by the majority of [you country] citizens? (Greece Mass Survey)

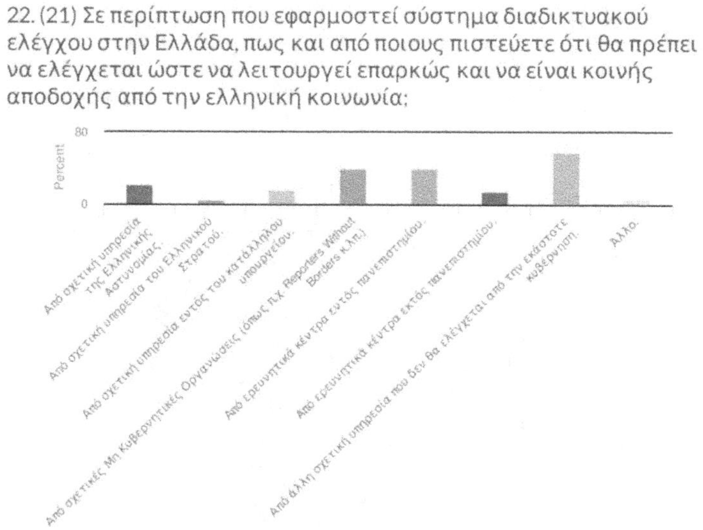

Last, concerning the entity that they prefer to be in control of such an IRS, 57.6 percent stated "public service not related with the government," 40.5 percent "related non-governmental organisation (Reporters without Borders, and so on), 40.5 percent "university-based research institutes," 21.7 percent "Hellenic Police related service," and 14.1 percent "non university-based research institutes." Only 16.1 percent of the participants stated "related Ministry's public agency."

Trends and Associations With the Aid of Statistical Analysis

In a questionnaire with so many questions, an exhausting statistical analysis can prove both time-consuming and lead to finding dozens of trends and associations more suitable for a research in the scientific field of statistics. This is why it is not in the scope of this book to present all the existing associations between groups and different answers, but only to focus on some of them, which the authors believe can play a key role in future research and development of a FIRS for Greece.

Table 1. Agreement on the implementation of an IRS & Gender (Pearson chi-square).

		Gender		Total
		Male	Female	
Do you agree an IRS to be implemented in a national level?	Yes	107	142	249
	No	41	25	66
	Yes, under conditions	55	39	94
Total		203	206	409

χ^2= 11.500, df= 2, α= 0.003

Pearson chi-square statistical analysis showed (χ^2=11.50) a significant association (a=0.003) between gender and agreement on the question set. Adjusted standardised residuals indicate that females are associated with positive answer (answer "Yes"), while males are associated with the answers "No" and "Yes, conditioned." The size of the coefficient V (V=0.335) confirms the aforementioned association.

Table 2. Agreement on the implementation of an IRS & religious belief (Pearson chi-square)

		Do You Consider Yourself Religious?		Total
		Yes	No	
Do you agree an IRS to be implemented in a national level?	Yes	130	119	249
	No	28	38	66
	Yes, under conditions	34	60	94
Total		192	217	409

χ^2= 7.693, df= 2, α= 0.021

Pearson chi-square statistical analysis showed (χ^2=7.693) a significant association (a=0.021) between religious belief and agreement on the question set. Adjusted standardised residuals indicate that religious people are associated with positive answer (answer "Yes"), while non-religious people are associated with the answer "Yes, conditioned."

Pearson chi-square statistical analysis showed (χ^2=14.637) a significant association (a=0.023) between awareness of the Internet regulation phenomenon and agreement on the question set. Adjusted standardised residuals indicate that well-informed people are associated with the positive

Table 3. Agreement on the implementation of an IRS & level of awareness of the global phenomenon of Internet regulation (Pearson chi-square)

		Level of Awareness of Global Phenomenon of Internet Regulation				Total
		Yes, I Am Well-Informed	Yes, I Know the Basics	Yes, I Just Heard About It	No, I Don't Know Anything	
Do you agree an IRS to be implemented in a national level?	Yes	38	101	84	26	249
	No	16	30	12	8	66
	Yes, under conditions	22	41	29	2	94
Total		76	172	125	36	409

χ^2= 14.637, df= 6, α= 0.023, G= 0.199

answers "Yes, conditioned" and "No," while people who know nothing about or have just heard about it are associated with the answer "Yes." The size of the Gudman-Kruskal Gamma (G= 0.199) confirms the aforementioned relationship.

Table 4. Agreement on the implementation of an IRS & Statements of non-governmental organizations related to human rights, freedom of speech etc. (Pearson chi-square)

		Statements of Non-Governmental Organizations (Human Rights, Freedom of Speech etc.)		Total
		Unchecked	Checked	
Do you agree an IRS to be implemented in a national level?	Yes	130	119	249
	No	27	39	66
	Yes, under conditions	34	60	94
Total		191	218	409

χ^2= 8.112, df= 2, α= 0.017

Pearson chi-square statistical analysis showed (χ^2=8.112) a significant association (a=0.017) between agreement on the question set and NGOs (human rights, freedom of speech, and so on) as a means of information. Adjusted standardised residuals indicate that participants who were informed by related NGOs are associated with the answer "Yes, under conditions," while participants who were not informed by related NGOs are associated with the answers "Yes."

Table 5. Agreement on the implementation of an IRS & pornographic online content (Pearson chi-square)

		Pornographic Content (What Kind of Content an IRS Should Target?)		**Total**
		Unchecked	**Checked**	
Do you agree an IRS to be implemented in a national level?	Yes	67	182	249
	No	47	19	66
	Yes, under conditions	40	54	94
Total		154	255	409

χ^2= 44.871, df= 2, α= 0.000

Pearson chi-square statistical analysis showed (χ^2=44.871) a significant association (a=0.000) between agreement on the question set and preference this IRS to target pornographic content. Adjusted standardised residuals indicate that participants who want an IRS to target pornographic content are associated with positive answer (answer "Yes") to the question set, while participants who do not are associated with the answer "No."

Table 6. Agreement on the implementation of an IRS & hate-speech online content (Pearson chi-square)

		Hate-Speech Content (What Kind of Content an IRS Should Target?)		**Total**
		Unchecked	**Checked**	
Do you agree an IRS to be implemented in a national level?	Yes	54	195	249
	No	50	16	66
	Yes, under conditions	33	61	94
Total		137	272	409

χ^2= 68.614, df= 2, α= 0.000

Pearson chi-square statistical analysis showed (χ^2=44.871) a significant association (a=0.000) between agreement on the question set and preference this IRS to target hate-speech content. Adjusted standardised residuals indicate that participants who want an IRS to target hate-speech content are associated with positive answer (answer "Yes") to the question set, while participants who do not are associated with the answer "No."

On the other hand, there is no association between agreement on the question set and neither age, education level, parenthood, level of awareness of the global phenomenon of Internet regulation, source of information, and so forth.

CONCLUSION

Summarising the survey's results in the 2013 Greek survey, the vast majority was aware of the global phenomenon of Internet regulation, with almost half of them stating a high level of awareness. This leads to the conclusion that Greek Internet users are among the most informed users compared to all the rest surveyed countries.

Furthermore, the vast majority of this sample (eight out of ten, if combining answers "Yes" and "Yes, under condition) was positive to the implementation of an IRS in Greece, targeting illegal content. In that scenario, the majority trusts services not controlled by the government to be responsible for the function of the IRS, followed by university-based research institutes and non-governmental organisations.

Concerning the content that should be targeted, the highest rates were recorded in hate-speech and child pornographic content. The exact preferences were recorded during the 2010 Greek survey and 2012 Cypriot survey too, verifying the general notion that the Cypriot and Greek societies share many similarities (Psaltis & Cakal, 2014). Copyright infringement and defamation content scored low rates, proving that Greek Internet users might be open to the implementation of an IRS, but at the same time are very concerned and protective concerning freedom of speech and free access to information.

There was no association between acceptance of an IRS implementation and education level or parenthood. On the other hand, statistical analysis showed that there are certain respondents' groups, which are associated with positive answer "Yes": people that are non-aware or less-aware of the global phenomenon of Internet regulation, females, and religious people. The latter verifies the general opinion of media analysts that religion and free speech have a long history of conflict (Biddle, 2006; IoC, 2013).

Finally, a quite important remark has to be made: the 2013 Greek Survey verified almost all the main conclusions of the specialised 2010 Greek survey that was conducted on a limited sample, i.e. acceptance of the implementation of an IRS, trusted body to function the system, and preference on the type of content to be targeted.

Choose Targeted Content and Categorization Based on the Results

As it is described in chapter 12, the FIRS blueprint categorises the targeted content to a. unquestionable must-be-filtered content and b. contradictable must-be-filtered content.

In Greece's example, results show (see figure 2.6) that the Greek Internet users are willing to accept Internet regulation to some extent in all the pre-defined categories. In that sense, Blacklist A should include child pornography content (as an unquestionable must-be-filtered content based on regional law and society's ethics), while category b. should include generic pornographic content, along with hate-speech content. Defamatory and piracy content gathered only 30.1 and 16.6 percent of the participant's responses, so it is not advisable to be included in any of the two blacklists.

As a result, two different URLs lists are formed: Blacklist A (including child pornography) and Blacklist B (including generic pornographic content and hate-speech content).

Figure 15. What kind of content should be regulated if your country's state decide to implement such a system? (Greece Mass Survey)

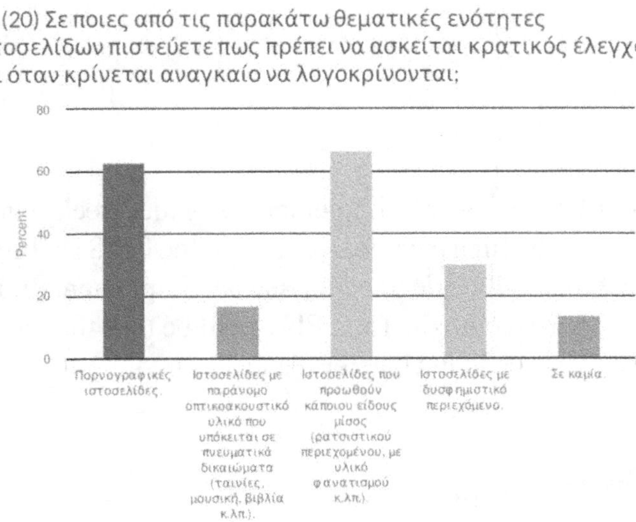

Regarding the entity that will control a Greek FIRS, the survey's results made it clear (see figure 16) that there is no trust by the citizens towards government or state controlled agencies. Research institutes inside universities and non-governmental related organisations are the two top choices for the Greek Internet users.

Figure 16. In case an Internet regulation system is implemented in Greece, from whom do you believe it must be operated in order to function with justice and to be accepted by the majority of [you country] citizens? (Greece Mass Survey)

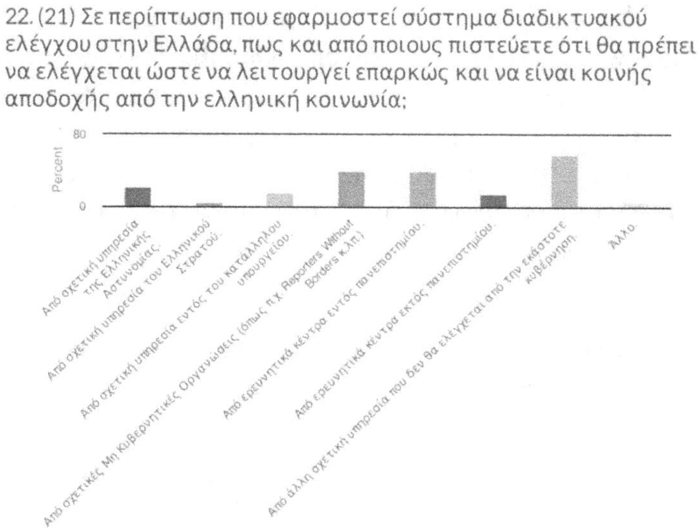

Last, such a FIRS can only be implemented by the Greek state at a national level. In that sense, the final technical aspects of the FIRS are highly related to the total budget that will be decided for such an implementation. The higher the budget, the more secure the final FIRS will be (see the disadvantages of two- and three-stage IRSs in Chapter 3 and 12).

CONCLUSION

There are many details to be decided for a real-life implementation of a Greek FIRS at a national level, details that are highly influenced by the total financial budget and current political and social conditions.

What it is provided, though, in chapter 13 is a step-by-step real-life example (using chapter 12's FIRS blueprint) for designing questionnaires, conducting surveys in the given country, and analysing gathered data in order to conclude to specific characteristics for the final FIRS (such as targeted content categorisation, and so on). What's more, diverse rich data is gathered during the surveys, able to lead to further conclusions and additional research. Last, Internet users are encouraged to state if they are willing to accept Internet regulation, and their responses can be indicative of how difficult or even possible the implementation of such a system is in their country.

REFERENCES

Biddle, C. (2006). Religion vs. Free Speech. *The Objective Standard, 1*(2).

IoC. (2013). *Religion and free speech: it's complicated, Index on Censorship*. https://www.indexoncensorship.org/2013/03/free-expression-and-religion-overview/

Psaltis, C., & Cakal, H. (2014). Social Identity in a Divided Cyprus. In S. McKeown, R. Haji, & N. Ferguson (Eds.), *Understanding peace and conflict through social identity theory: Contemporary and world-wide perspectives* (pp. 229–244). Springer.

Section 5
Outcome

Chapter 14
Concluding Remarks and Future Work

ABSTRACT

In this book, the authors examined the need for a fair internet regulation system (FIRS) to be developed and the possibility to implement it in different countries with the acceptance of the general public. The issue was examined with three different research methods: literature review, technical analysis of current IRSs, and surveys around the world. In this chapter, the authors present their concluding remarks along with their thoughts about future work regarding the need for a fair internet regulation system (FIRS) to be developed and implemented in different countries with the acceptance of the general public.

INTRODUCTION

In this book, the authors examined the need for a Fair Internet Regulation System (FIRS) to be developed, and the possibility to be implemented in different countries with the acceptance of the general public. The issue was examined with three different research methods: literature review, technical analysis of current IRSs, and surveys around the world.

In this last chapter, the authors present their concluding remarks along with their thoughts regarding future work.

DOI: 10.4018/978-1-5225-9973-9.ch014

FINAL REMARKS

Many widespread beliefs regarding Internet freedom are actually misconceptions as the Internet had been regulated from its very first steps, since 1990 (Ehrilch, 2014). Additionally, there are already in use two main categories of Internet regulation systems: the open and the silent IRSs (Ballard, 2006). Unexpectedly, the formers are quite popular among authoritarian regimes, while the latter are implemented mainly in Western democracies (CTV News, 2006; ABC, 2007; Pauli, 2008).

A great example is CleanFeed, a silent IRS that went live during 2004 in the United Kingdom by British Telecommunications. Many IT experts and media analysts criticised the UK government's choice to go with a silent IRS, expressing their fear that this could set a dangerous precedent for the rest of the democratic countries around the world (Thompson, 2004; Hunter, 2004). UK's Internet users seemed to agree too (Koumartzis, 2008): the majority of the participants of a 2010 UK Survey preferred the implementation of an open IRS, to no IRS or a silent IRS. Furthermore, all the improvements suggested by these respondents were focusing on making CleanFeed a more open IRS.

So, how do silent IRSs really function? Unfortunately, almost none of these systems are well documented, except the UK's CleanFeed (Clayton, 2005). Concerning the reasons behind the choice of a democratic country to develop a silent IRS, BT's few statements can give us the answer: due to the fact that it targets only child pornography, it was designed this way in order to minimise the chance of being circumvented (Bright, 2004; Koumartzis & Veglis, 2011). The latter proved wrong, though, as even non-determined and amateur users can quite easily circumvent UK's CleanFeed (Clayton, 2008). Furthermore, being silent means that it can be easily expanded to include additional online content categories (as past incidents indicate) apart from child pornography, without being noticed (Edwards, 2006 & 2010).

Is it possible, then, to develop and implement a Fair IRS that, on the one hand, would be accepted by the Internet users of each country, and on the other hand would be effective? In their effort to find an answer, the authors took in 2010 an international initiative to measure Internet users' opinion in many countries around the world. They managed to complete six surveys in Greece, Germany, Russia, India, Kosovo, and Cyprus, and present valuable data and statistically analyse it to find trends and associations (Koumartzis & Veglis, 2015).

Thanks to previous massive generic surveys (GlobalScan Incorporated, 2010; Whirlpool, 2010a & 2010b; Internet Society, 2012), and to authors' specialised surveys in 6 countries, it is clear that Internet users worldwide in their majority prefer an open IRS to no Internet regulation at all. They prefer the former, but only under conditions: in brief, they want to decide what kind of content would be targeted, and what entity will be responsible for functioning the implemented IRS.

What's more, there is a need for an open public discussion to take place in western democracies concerning Internet regulation. During this research, that was not the case in any of the surveyed countries as the vast majority of the participants stated that they have not heard about Internet regulation from official statements, even if they were aware of the global phenomenon (chapters 5 to 11 & section 13.4). The latter is probably one of the main reasons why most of the participants did not want a government-controlled entity to function such an IRS in their country.

Apart from the many similarities, there are significant differences too concerning the needs of the Internet users in each country, due to current and recent social and political developments. Statistical analysis of specialised surveys' results (chapter 11) showed that there is no association between agreement to the implementation of an IRS and educational level or parenthood. On the other hand, there is a significant association between the former and age or religious beliefs. For example, religious participants in specific countries were keener to accept the implementation of an IRS.

Further differences regarding public opinion between countries concern the kind of online content that should be targeted by an IRS. In general, an IRS that targets hate-speech or illegal pornographic content is much easier to be accepted by many countries' Internet users, while an IRS targeting copyright infringement or online defamation content is not. Another main difference is who they trust to control such an IRS: Indian and Cypriot users trust NGOs, Greek users trust research institutes and universities, Russian and Kosovar users trust government-controlled ministries and agencies, while German users trust no one.

Differences like the aforementioned showed that carrying out specialised surveys plays a crucial role during the design, development, and implementation process of a Fair IRS. After all, different needs mean different IRS's characteristics for each country, i.e. a differently designed Fair IRS.

Due to all the above, a Fair IRS is feasible, and a blueprint is already presented explaining how it has to function in order to maximise its effectiveness, keep a low implementation cost, and increase the probability of acceptance by each country's general public (chapter 12).

Furthermore, this book put the aforementioned FIRS blueprint to the test by theoretically implementing it in Greece as a country example (chapter 13). Additionally, the authors explain how a survey can be handled for defining initial research scope and for improving a country's questionnaire. What's more, the authors conducted a mass survey in Greece (section 13.4), and explained how the collected data and its statistical analysis should be used for defining crucial characteristics of a FIRS, such as types of targeted content and its further categorisation.

The 2013 massive Greek survey conducted for this purpose has verified many conclusions based on the limited specialised 2010 Greece survey:

1. The vast majority of the Greek Internet users were aware of the Internet regulation phenomenon.
2. The majority was positive to the implementation of a Fair IRS in Greece.
3. They want to be controlled by non-governmental services.
4. Illegal pornographic content and hate speech websites are to be targeted; no defamation or copyright infringement content.
5. Acceptance of the implementation of a Fair IRS is associated with the groups following: females, religious people, people that are not aware or less aware of the global phenomenon of Internet regulation.

Concerning the key area inquiries, all of them are answered in one or more chapters. More specifically:

How can the current IRSs implemented around the world be improved?

Several survey's results suggested quite a few improvements for the current silent IRSs:

1. In every content regulation incident, the IRS shall display a message stating that the website is blocked. Additionally, this message should state the reason of the blocking too.
2. The IRS can give access to a requesting form for unblocking the website.
3. The entities involved to IRS's function should provide better and more frequent information in order to raise the awareness of the public.
4. Academic researchers and research entities should have unlimited access to the silent IRS data and statistics, in order to ensure that the functioning

entities are continuously monitored and not able to silently expand the use of the IRS to additional types of content.

5. Broader and formal surveys should be completed, so that they could represent a larger number of each country's citizens.
6. Target specific types of content, taking into account the needs of each country's Internet users.
7. The IRS ought to be controlled by specific entities, which vary from country to country.

What do the Internet users actually believe regarding Internet Regulation? Can online citizens accept the implementation of an IRS?

Older generic and recent specialised surveys show that Internet users in many countries around the world prefer the implementation of an open IRS under conditions to no Internet regulation at all.

Can a Fair IRS really be developed and implemented? How can a Fair IRS be designed?

There are already in use open IRSs (in technical terms) that are implemented in authoritarian regimes, such as the IRS implemented in Saudi Arabia and China (Zittrain & Edelman, 2003· Hermida, 2002). Furthermore, already implemented silent IRSs, such as CleanFeed in the UK, can be improved in specific ways in order to become fair regulation systems of online content. The Fair IRS blueprint that the authors present is a strong candidate for open IRSs implementation in democratic societies, while its core layout can be used to design open and fair IRSs for different countries.

What kind of online content should a FIRS focus on?

On the one hand, each IRS is obligated to survey the legal framework of the country that is implemented (section 1.4). On the other hand, a Fair IRS has to be openly discussed and be accepted by the majority of the Internet users. In that sense, online citizens from different countries have different needs and are willing to accept different types of content to be targeted; as a general rule, hate-speech and illegal pornographic content are easily accepted as targeted content, while copyright infringement and defamation content are not. As a conclusion, carrying out specialised surveys on that matter can play a crucial role in the design and development of an IRS.

How will a Fair Internet Regulation System work?

An IRS that is intended to be used on a massive scale in a democratic society cannot be totally invulnerable, but extensive participation of the Internet users can help it become gradually more effective.

In order for the implementation of a Fair IRS to be feasible, its aim is to be very accurate and with low operational cost. Briefly, this can be done, according to the authors, by combining the speed of IP blocking mechanism and the precision of URL filtering technique (Cisco, 2017). What's more, in order to encourage Internet users' participation in the Internet regulation process and at the same time for the IRS to be able to handle with "discretion" specific kinds of content, the proposed Fair IRS uses four different lists (section 12.3.1): two IP lists for fast and low cost IP blocking (the first and second stage of check, where a website is classified as "suspicious" or not), and two URL lists for precise URL filtering (the third and last stage of check, where a website is blocked with discretion or by giving the Internet user the chance to interact with the IRS).

These four lists result from two blacklists that are prepared by the chosen controlling entities: blacklist A that includes unquestionable must-be-filtered content, and blacklist B that includes contradictable must-be-filtered content.

In conclusion, based on all the above and their ten-year research on the topic from 2007 to 2017, the authors strongly believe that a Fair Internet Regulation System can be designed, developed, and implemented in a way that Internet users will accept it and interact with it in order to gradually improve it. Such an IRS has to be designed, taking into account its main recipient: the end-user of the Internet.

LIMITATIONS AND FUTURE WORK

One of the most important limitations that the authors faced was the lack of funding for carrying out the surveys; a funding that would result in larger and better-formed samples for the specialised surveys, along with more countries to run the questionnaire. For future research, additional funding can be used to hire market research companies to conduct mass scale related surveys around the world.

As D. Altman (1991) once said, "Statistical analysis allows us to put limits on our uncertainty, but not to prove anything." In that sense, bigger samples can lead to less uncertainty and better chances to spot differences and similarities between different groups, so additional statistical analysis must be conducted in case new surveys' data is gathered.

Additionally, the possibility of biased questions in the survey's questionnaire is already thoroughly discussed. This issue was tackled by consulting different academics from various universities, with an expertise in different fields. The initial questionnaire used in 2007 UK survey was then improved in order to be used at specialised surveys in six different countries and the mass survey in Greece. In future research, further improvements can be made in collaboration with a statistical department in order to minimise the chance of biased questionnaires.

According to Choi & Pak (2008), among the three categories of main sources of bias is "the way a questionnaire is administered." In order to tackle that issue, related surveys in the future could be promoted or even run by a body capable of attracting the desired number of participants. A practical solution will be to include related questions to an annual broadband survey run by each country's ISPs, such as the 2007 Australian Broadband Survey (Whirpool, 2010a).

Regarding the design and development of a Fair IRS and the authors' suggested blueprint, there are quite a few limitations. The most important among them is definitely the conflict between IRS's circumvention immunity and its low cost effectiveness.

On the one hand, precise Internet regulation techniques, along with constant updates of the blacklists, can lead to a system that will prevent most types of the circumvention efforts, but at the same time it will need extensive resources to function at a national level and it will be vulnerable to DoS attacks (McDowell, 2013). On the other hand, a focus on the IRS's effectiveness can lead to low-cost systems in order to handle heavy traffic, but at the same time these systems are easily circumvented by, for example, a simple change in the URL by the content-provider (Clayton, 2008; Koumartzis & Veglis 2014).

In that sense, an IRS cannot be perfect taking into account the current technological developments. Its design is just an approach to finding the balance between effectiveness/feasibility, and precision/circumvention immunity. Authors' Fair IRS blueprint is such an approach, and its three-stage design is effective and can handle heavy traffic, but at the same time is vulnerable to expert and determined users.

So, by putting the proposed FIRS in practice in limited groups and in various countries, a future researcher can gather valuable feedback in order to further improve and adjust its design to each different society.

Last, during this research, there was limited access to key information of IRSs that are currently implemented around the world, with an exception being UK's CleanFeed, thanks to Dr. Clayton's work. Future research that will have access to more IRSs technical reports, data, and statistics can lead to better and more promising blueprints too.

Finaly, it is important to state that this book is based on research conducted from 2008 until 2017 in seven specific countries: United Kingdom, Greece, Germany, Russia, India, Kosovo and Cyprus. In that sense, the aim of this publication is to present the authors' original research and its outcome.

For readers/researchers interested in the current state (i.e. 2020) of the global phenomenon of Internet Regulation, below you can find an indicative list of recent selected publications and papers to start from:

Aceto, G., Montieri, A., & Pescapé, A. (2017, May). Internet censorship in italy: An analysis of 3g/4g networks. In 2017 IEEE International Conference on Communications (ICC) (pp. 1-6). IEEE.

Acharya, H. B., Ramesh, A., & Jalaly, A. (2019, April). The World from Kabul: Internet Censorship in Afghanistan. In IEEE INFOCOM 2019-IEEE Conference on Computer Communications Workshops (INFOCOM WKSHPS) (pp. 1061-1062). IEEE.

Agrawal, V., & Sharma, P. (2019). Internet Censorship in India. In Proceedings of 10th International Conference on Digital Strategies for Organizational Success.

Al-Saqaf, W. (2016). Internet censorship circumvention tools: Escaping the control of the Syrian regime. Media and Communication, 4(1), 39-50.

Banerjee, A. (2017). Internet censorship in India: the law and beyond. In Digital Democracy in a Globalized World. Edward Elgar Publishing.

Busch, A., Theiner, P., & Breindl, Y. (2018). Internet Censorship in Liberal Democracies: Learning from Autocracies?. In Managing democracy in the digital age (pp. 11-28). Springer, Cham.

Chen, I. C. (2020). Government Internet Censorship Measures and International Law (Vol. 26). LIT Verlag Münster.

Clark, J. D., Faris, R. M., Morrison-Westphal, R. J., Noman, H., Tilton, C. B., & Zittrain, J. L. (2017). The shifting landscape of global internet censorship.

Darer, A., Farnan, O., & Wright, J. (2018, May). Automated discovery of internet censorship by web crawling. In Proceedings of the 10th ACM Conference on Web Science (pp. 195-204).

Dixon, L., Ristenpart, T., & Shrimpton, T. (2016). Network traffic obfuscation and automated internet censorship. IEEE Security & Privacy, 14(6), 43-53.

Druzin, B., & Gordon, G. S. (2018). Authoritarianism and the Internet. Law & Social Inquiry, 43(4), 1427-1457.

Du, Y. R. (2016). Same events, different stories: Internet censorship in the Arab Spring seen from China. Journalism & Mass Communication Quarterly, 93(1), 99-117.

Faust, M. (2019). Does the democratic West 'learn'from the authoritarian East? Juxtaposing German and Chinese Internet censorship and filter bubbles. East Asian Journal of Popular Culture, 5(1), 55-78.

Gebhart, G., & Kohno, T. (2017, April). Internet censorship in Thailand: User practices and potential threats. In 2017 IEEE European symposium on security and privacy (EuroS&P) (pp. 417-432). IEEE.

Giuseppe Aceto and Antonio Pescapé. 2015. Internet Censorship detection: A survey. Computer Networks 83, C, 381--421.

Khattak, S. (2017). Characterization of Internet censorship from multiple perspectives (No. UCAM-CL-TR-897). University of Cambridge, Computer Laboratory.

Nisbet, E. C., Kamenchuk, O., & Dal, A. (2017). A psychological firewall? Risk perceptions and public support for online censorship in Russia. Social Science Quarterly, 98(3), 958-975.

Shen, F., & Tsui, L. (2016). Public opinion toward Internet freedom in Asia: A survey of Internet users from 11 jurisdictions. Berkman Center Research Publication, (2016-8).

Shi, G. (2019). MultiProxy: a collaborative approach to censorship circumvention.

Ververis, V., Isaakidis, M., Loizidou, C., & Fabian, B. (2017, December). Internet censorship capabilities in Cyprus: An investigation of online gambling blocklisting. In International Conference on e-Democracy (pp. 136-149). Springer, Cham.

Wang, Z., Cao, Y., Qian, Z., Song, C., & Krishnamurthy, S. V. (2017, November). Your state is not mine: a closer look at evading stateful internet censorship. In Proceedings of the 2017 Internet Measurement Conference (pp. 114-127).

Zhongjie Wang, Yue Cao, Zhiyun Qian, Chengyu Song, and Srikanth V. Krishnamurthy. 2017. Your state is not mine: a closer look at evading stateful internet censorship. In Proceedings of the 2017 Internet Measurement Conference (IMC '17). Association for Computing

Machinery, New York, NY, USA, 114–127. DOI:https://doi.org/10.1145/3131365.3131374

Zittrain, J. L. et al (2017). The Shifting Landscape of Global Internet Censorship, Berkman Klein Center Research Publication No. 2017-4

REFERENCES

ABC. (2007, Dec. 31). Conroy announces mandatory Internet filters to protect children. *ABC News*.

Altman, D. G. (1991). *Practical Statistics for Medical Research*. London: Chapman & Hall.

Ballard, M. (2006). *Govt sets target for blocking child porn sites*. https://www.theregister.co.uk/2006/05/18/uk_site_blocking/

Bright, M. (2004, June 6). BT puts block on child porn sites. *The Observer*.

Choi, B., & Pak, A. (2008). A Catalog of Biases in Questionnaires. *PubMed Central Journal List*. http://www.pubmedcentral.nih.gov/articlerender.fcgi?artid=1323316

Clayton, R. (2005). Anonymity and Traceability to Cyberspace (Technical Report UCAM-CL-TR-653). *University of Cambridge, Computer Laboratory*. https://www.cl.cam.ac.uk/techreports/UCAM-CL-TR-653.html

Clayton, R. (2008). Failures of a Hybrid Content Blocking System. In G. Danezis & D. Martin (Eds.), *Privacy Enhancing Technologies, Fifth International Workshop, PET 2005*. Berlin: Springer Verlag.

CTV News. (2006). *New initiative will see ISPs block child porn sites*. CTV News.

Edwards, L. (2006). From child porn to China, in one Cleanfeed. *SCRIPTed - A Journal of Law. Technology in Society*, *3*(3).

Edwards, L. (2010). Content Filtering and the New Censorship. In *2010 Fourth International Conference on Digital Society*. New York: IEEE Computer Society. 10.1109/ICDS.2010.72

Ehrlich, E. (2014). A Brief History of Internet Regulation. Progressive Policy Institute.

Cisco. (2017). *Access Control Rules: Filtering URL Firepower Management Center Configuration Guide, Version 6.0.* https://www.cisco.com/c/en/us/td/docs/security/firepower/60/configuration/guide/fpmc-config-guide-v60/Access_Control_Rules__URL_Filtering.pdf

GlobalScan Incordporated. (2010). *Four in Five Regard Internet Access as a Fundamental Right: Global Poll.* BBC World Service.

Hermida, A. (2002). *Saudis Block 2000 websites.* BBC News.

Hunter, P. (2004). Computer Fraud & Security 2004(8). Amsterdam: Elsevier.

Internet Society. (2012). Global Internet User Survey 2012. *InternetSociety.org*. https://www.internetsociety.org/internet/global-internet-user-survey-2012

Koumartzis, N. (2008). *BT's CleanFeed and Online Censorship in UK: Improvements for a More Secure and Ethically Correct Systeym* (Doctoral dissertation). University of the Arts London, London College of Communication, London, UK.

Koumartzis, N., & Veglis, A. (2011). Internet Regulation: The Need for More Transparent Internet Filtering Systems and improved measurement of public opinion on Internet Filtering. *First Monday, 16*(10). https://firstmonday.org/ojs/index.php/fm/article/view/3266/3071

Koumartzis, N., & Veglis, A. (2011). On the Pursue for a Fair Internet Regulation system. *Sixteenth IEEE Symposium on Computers and Communications (ISCC11).*

Koumartzis, N., & Veglis, A. (2011). The Future of Internet Regulation: Current Trends, a Dangerous Precedent and the Role of Internet Users. *Euro-NF International Workshop on Traffic and Congestion Control for the Future Internet.*

Koumartzis, N., & Veglis, A. (2014). Internet Regulation and Online Censorship. *International Journal of E-Politics*, *5*(4), 65–80. doi:10.4018/ijep.2014100104

Koumartzis, N., & Veglis, A. (2015). Internet Regulation and Online Censorship. *The First International Congress on the Internet, Trolling and Addiction (ITA15).*

McDowell, M. (2013). Understanding Denial-of-Service Attacks, Security Tip (ST04-015). *US-CERT.gov*. https://www.us-cert.gov/ncas/tips/ST04-015

Pauli, D. (2008). *No opt-out of filtered Internet*. ComputerWorld Australia.

Thompson, B. (2004, June 11). Doubts over web filtering plans. *BBC News*.

Whirlpool. (2010a). Australian Broadband Survey 2007. *Whirlpool*. https://whirlpool.net.au/survey/2007/

Whirlpool. (2010b). Australian Broadband Survey 2008. *Whirlpool*. https://whirlpool.net.au/survey/2008/

Zittrain, J., & Edelman, B. (2003). *Documentation of Internet Filtering Worldwide*. Cambridge, MA: Harvard Law School.

Appendix

APPENDIX 1: GREECE SURVEY'S QUESTIONNAIRE

Διαδικτυακός Έλεγχος και Λογοκρισία στην Ελλάδα (Internet Regulation in Greece)

Το φαινόμενο του ελέγχου του διαδικτύου και της διαδικτυακής λογοκρισίας είναι σε διαρκή άνοδο παγκοσμίως και εμφανίζεται σε πλήθος κρατών σε ολόκληρη την υφήλιο, από αυταρχικές χώρες της Ασίας (Κίνα, Σαουδική Αραβία κ.λπ.) έως κατά παράδοση δημοκρατικά κράτη της Ευρώπης (Γερμανία, Μεγάλη Βρετανία κ.λπ.).

Αν και ως φαινόμενο είναι γενικευμένο, εντούτοις το μεγαλύτερο μέρος της εκάστοτε κοινωνίας στην οποία εφαρμόζεται δεν γνωρίζει την ύπαρξη του (ούτε φυσικά την επιρροή που έχει στην καθημερινότητα του) λόγω της πολιτικής που ακολουθείται από τις εκάστοτε αρχές. Εξαιτίας αυτής ακριβώς την πολιτικής «σιωπηλού» ελέγχου του διαδικτύου που ακολουθείται, έχει αναπτυχθεί μία αρκετά δραστήρια ακαδημαϊκή κοινότητα που παρατηρεί και δημοσιεύει αξιολογήσεις για την κατάσταση που ισχύει σε κάθε κράτος.

Το παρόν ερωτηματολόγιο είναι κομμάτι μίας τέτοιας έρευνας που ξεκίνησε λίγο καιρό πριν στην Ελλάδα πάνω στο φαινόμενο του διαδικτυακού ελέγχου και της διαδικτυακής λογοκρισίας σε κρατικό, εταιρικό, πανεπιστημιακό ή/ και οικογενειακό επίπεδο. Εφόσον αποφασίσετε να αφιερώσετε λίγο χρόνο για τη συμπλήρωση του, παρακαλείσθε να απαντήσετε με υπευθυνότητα.

Σχετικά με το background σας

1. Ποιο είναι το φύλο σας;
   a. Γυναίκα
   b. Άνδρας

2. Σε ποια ηλικιακή ομάδα ανήκετε;
    a. 18-21
    b. 22-25
    c. 26-30
    d. 31-40
    e. 41-50
    f. 51-60
    g. 61 και πάνω
3. Ποιο είναι το μορφωτικό σας επίπεδο;
    a. Μικρότερο από Γυμνάσιο
    b. Γυμνάσιο/ Λύκειο
    c. ΙΕΚ ή παρεμφερές ινστιτούτο
    d. Προπτυχιακές πανεπιστημιακές σπουδές
    e. Μεταπτυχιακές σπουδές
    f. Διδακτορικές σπουδές
4. Πόσο καιρό χρησιμοποιείτε το διαδίκτυο εντός Ελλάδας;
    a. Λιγότερο από 1 χρόνο
    b. 1-2 χρόνια
    c. 3-4 χρόνια
    d. Περισσότερα από 5 χρόνια
5. Θεωρείτε τον εαυτό σας θρήσκο άτομο (ανεξαρτήτως θρησκείας);
    a. Ναι
    b. Όχι
6. Έχετε παιδιά;
    a. Ναι
    b. Όχι

Σχετικά με τη χρήση του internet

7. Πόσες περίπου ώρες αφιερώνεται καθημερινά στο internet;
    a. Λιγότερο από 30 λεπτά
    b. 1 ώρα
    c. 2-3 ώρες
    d. 4-5 ώρες
    e. Περισσότερες από 6 ώρες
8. Για ποιους λόγους χρησιμοποιείτε κυρίως το internet;
    a. Διασκέδαση (gaming, video, μουσική κ.λπ.)
    b. Download (software, μουσική, video κ.λπ.)
    c. Επαγγελματικούς λόγους (ως κομμάτι της δουλειάς μου)

d. Εκπαιδευτικούς λόγους (ως κομμάτι των σπουδών μου)
e. Μέσο πληροφόρησης (ειδήσεις, ανταποκρίσεις, αναλύσεις κ.λπ.)
f. Άλλο: ________________________________

Διαδικτυακός Έλεγχος και Λογοκρισία Παγκοσμίως

9. Γνωρίζετε για το παγκόσμιο φαινόμενο της διαδικτυακής λογοκρισίας;
   a. Ναι, είμαι αρκετά καλά ενημερωμένος.
   b. Ναι, γνωρίζω κάποια βασικά πράγματα.
   c. Ναι, απλά έχω ακούσει γι' αυτό.
   d. Όχι, δεν γνωρίζω τίποτα.
10. Αν απαντήσατε *ναι* στην προηγούμενη ερώτηση, από ποια μέσα ενημέρωσης αντλήσατε τις πληροφορίες σας;
   a. Μέσω διαδικτύου.
   b. Μέσω εφημερίδων ή ένθετων περιοδικών αυτών.
   c. Μέσω περιοδικών γενικότερου ενδιαφέροντος.
   d. Μέσω εξειδικευμένων περιοδικών.
   e. Μέσω τηλεόρασης.
   f. Μέσω ραδιοφώνου.
   g. Μέσω συζήτησης με γνωστό.
   h. Άλλο: ______________________
11. Αν απαντήσατε *ναι* στην ερώτηση 9, ποια ήταν η πηγή των πληροφοριών;
   a. Κρατικές δηλώσεις (υπουργική ανακοίνωση, δηλώσεις συνεργαζόμενου φορέα κ.λπ.).
   b. Μέσα Μαζικής Ενημέρωσης.
   c. Ειδικοί Ερευνητές ή Επιστήμονες (μέσω συνεντεύξεις, άρθρων, δηλώσεων κ.λπ.).
   d. Ιδιώτες.

Διαδικτυακός Έλεγχος και Λογοκρισία στην Ελλάδα

12. Έχετε πέσει ποτέ θύμα διαδικτυακής λογοκρισίας κατά το παρελθόν;
   a. Ναι, τουλάχιστον μία φορά.
   b. Όχι, ποτέ.
   c. Δεν ξέρω.
13. Αν ναι, είχατε συνδεθεί από υπολογιστή εντός Ελλάδας;
   a. Ναι και αφορούσε ελληνική ιστοσελίδα.
   b. Ναι και αφορούσε ξένη ιστοσελίδα.

c. Όχι. Είχα συνδεθεί από υπολογιστή στο εξωτερικό, αλλά αφορούσε ελληνική ιστοσελίδα.
d. Όχι. Είχα συνδεθεί από υπολογιστή στο εξωτερικό και δεν αφορούσε ελληνική ιστοσελίδα.
e. Δεν γνωρίζω.

14. Σε τι δίκτυο ανήκε ο υπολογιστής που χρησιμοποιούσατε;
a. Συνδέθηκα μέσω πανεπιστημιακού δικτύου (εντός σχολής, πανεπιστημιούπολης κ.λπ.).
b. Συνδέθηκα μέσω δικτύου κάποιας βιβλιοθήκης.
c. Συνδέθηκα μέσω internet cafe.
d. Συνδέθηκα μέσω προσωπικής σύνδεσης (εταιρία: ________).
e. Συνδέθηκα μέσω προσωπικής σύνδεσης των γονιών μου, οι οποίοι είχαν εγκαταστήσει φίλτρο δικτύου για παιδιά.
f. Άλλο: ____________________

15. Αν απαντήσατε *ναι* στην ερώτηση 12, περιγράψτε με λίγα λόγια την εν λόγω κατάσταση/ εμπειρία (γράψτε στοιχεία όπως τι ιστοσελίδα αφορούσε, από τι δίκτυο είχατε συνδεθεί, αν ήταν ολική απαγόρευση πρόσβασης ή μερική κ.λπ.):

____
____
____
____
____
____
____

16. Έχετε ακούσει ποτέ για περιπτώσεις διαδικτυακής λογοκρισίας σε χώρες του εξωτερικού; Αν ναι, δώστε μερικά παραδείγματα:

____
____
____
____
____
____
____

Σχετικά με την Εφαρμογή Διαδικτυακού Ελέγχου στην Ελλάδα

17. Συμφωνείτε με την πανελλαδική εφαρμογή (από το κράτος) ενός συστήματος περιορισμού παράνομου διαδικτυακού περιεχομένου που θα αφορούσε ιστοσελίδες με υψηλής ευαισθησίας θέματα όπως π.χ. παιδική πορνογραφία;

    a. Ναι.
    b. Όχι.
    c. Εν μέρει.

Γιατί; ____

____

____

18. Σε ποιες από τις παρακάτω θεματικές ενότητες ιστοσελίδων πιστεύετε ότι πρέπει να ασκείτε κρατικός έλεγχος και όταν κρίνεται αναγκαίο (είναι παράνομες, προωθούν τον φανατισμό, τον φυλετικό ρατσισμό, την τρομοκρατία κ.λπ.) να λογοκρίνονται;
    a. Πορνογραφικές ιστοσελίδες
    b. Ιστοσελίδες με παράνομο οπτικοακουστικό υλικό που υπόκειται σε πνευματικά δικαιώματα (ταινίες, μουσική, βιβλία κ.λπ.)
    c. Ιστοσελίδες που προωθούν κάποιου είδους μίσος (ρατσιστικού περιεχομένου, με υλικό φανατισμού κ.λπ.)
    d. ????????
19. Σε περίπτωση που εφαρμοστεί σύστημα διαδικτυακού ελέγχου στην Ελλάδα, πως και από ποιους πιστεύετε ότι θα πρέπει να ελέγχεται ώστε να λειτουργεί επαρκώς και να είναι της κοινής αποδοχής της ελληνικής κοινωνίας;
    a. Από μη-κυβερνητικές οργανώσεις σχετικού ενδιαφέροντος. (π.χ. Δημοσιογράφοι Δίχως Σύνορα κ.λπ.)
    b. Από Ερευνητικά ή Εκπαιδευτικά Ινστιτούτα εντός Πανεπιστημίων
    c. Από Ερευνητικά Ινστιτούτα εκτός Πανεπιστημίων
    d. Από Κρατική Υπηρεσία εντός του κατάλληλου υπουργείου
    e. Άλλο: ______________________

Το παρόν ερωτηματολόγιο είναι ανώνυμο και τα αποτελέσματα του δεν θα συνδεθούν με οποιονδήποτε τρόπο με συγκεκριμένα πρόσωπα και ονόματα. Η έρευνα όμως πάνω στο φαινόμενο της διαδικτυακής λογοκρισίας στην Ελλάδα έχει πολλά στάδια και ως εκ τούτου θα χρειαστεί να συγκεντρωθούν στοιχεία για όσο το δυνατόν περισσότερες περιπτώσεις λογοκρισίας.

Για το λόγο αυτό, εφόσον έχετε βιώσει κάποιου είδους διαδικτυακού ελέγχου ή λογοκρισίας σε πανελλαδικό, εταιρικό, πανεπιστημιακό, οικογενειακό κ.λπ. περιβάλλον και επιθυμείτε να βοηθήσετε στην παρούσα έρευνα, παρακαλώ αναγράψτε στο κατάλληλο πεδίο παρακάτω ένα email επικοινωνίας.

Η όποια πιθανή μελλοντική επικοινωνία με το ερευνητικό μας team θα είναι για συμπληρωματικές ερωτήσεις σχετικά με την εμπειρία σας, ενώ και σε αυτή την περίπτωση θα διατηρήσετε την ανωνυμία σας.

Email Επικοινωνιασ:

APPENDIX 2: GERMANY SURVEY'S QUESTIONNAIRE

Internetregulierung in Deutschland

Internetregulierung ist ein Phänomen, das weltweit immer mehr an Bedeutung gewinnt. Regulierungssysteme sind in vielen Ländern schon umgesetzt, sowohl von autoritären Regimen (z.B. in China und Saudi Arabien) als auch von demokratischen Regierungen (z.B. in Großbritannien und Deutschland).

Ungeachtet der Tatsache, dass diese Systeme heute intensiv genutzt werden, zeigen aktuelle Studien, dass nur wenigen Bürgern bewusst ist, dass sie existieren und wie sie ihren Alltag beeinflussen. Der Hauptgrund dafür ist, dass die "stille" Umsetzung von vielen Regierungen bevorzugt wird. Um diese beunruhigende Tatsache anzugehen, hat sich bereits eine sehr aktive wissenschaftliche Gemeinschaft gebildet, die das Phänomen beobachtet und regelmäßige Länderstudien veröffentlicht, um die öffentliche Aufmerksamkeit für das Thema zu erhöhen.

Diese Umfrage ist ein Teil dieser weltweiten Anstrengung und misst die öffentliche Meinung hinsichtlich der politischen Maßnahmen zur Internetregulierung und ihrer Umsetzung in technischen Systemen (Hardware und Software) im nationalen, unternehmerischen, universitären und familiären Umfeld. Falls Sie an der Umfrage teilnehmen möchten, so tun Sie dies bitte verantwortungsvoll.

Demographische Fragen

1. Sind Sie männlich oder weiblich?
    a. Männlich
    b. Weiblich
2. Wie alt sind Sie?
    a. 18-21
    b. 22-25
    c. 26-30
    d. 31-40
    e. 41-50
    f. 51-60
    g. 61 und älter
3. Was ist ihr höchster Bildungsabschluss?
    a. Kein Schulabschluss
    b. Hauptschulabschluss/Mittlere Reife/Abitur
    c. Abgeschlossene Berufsausbildung
    d. Begonnene Universitätsausbildung
    e. Bachelor-Abschluss oder M.A.-Zwischenprüfung/Vordiplom
    f. Master-Abschluss oder M.A./Diplom
    g. Promotion
    h. Habilitation
4. Wie lange nutzen Sie das Internet in Deutschland?
    a. Seit weniger als einem Jahr
    b. 1-2 Jahre
    c. 3-4 Jahre
    d. Über 5 Jahre
5. Sind Sie religiös?
    a. Ja
    b. Nein
6. Haben Sie Kinder oder möchten Sie Kinder haben?
    a. Ja, ich habe bereits Kinder.
    b. Nein, ich habe keine Kinder, möchte aber in Zukunft Kinder haben.
    c. Nein, ich habe keine Kinder und möchte auch in Zukunft keine haben.

Internetbezogene demographische Fragen

7. Wie viele Stunden verbringen sie täglich im Internet?
    a. Unter 30 Minuten.
    b. 1 Stunde
    c. 2-3 Stunden
    d. 4-5 Stunden
    e. Über 6 Stunden
8. Wofür nutzen Sie das Internet?
    a. Zur Unterhaltung (Spiele, Videos, Musik etc.)
    b. Zum Herunterladen (Software, Musik, Videos etc.)
    c. Für die Arbeit (Teil des Berufs)
    d. Für Bildung (Teil meiner Schul-/Universitätsausbildung)
    e. Zur Informationssammlung (Online-Zeitungen lesen etc.)
    f. Für anderes: _______

Internetregulierung allgemein

9. Ist Ihnen das globale Phänomen der Internetregulierung bekannt?
    a. Ja, ich bin gut informiert.
    b. Ja, ich kenne die Grundlagen.
    c. Ja, ich habe gerade davon gehört.
    d. Nein, darüber weiß ich nichts.
10. Falls Sie Frage 9 mit Ja beantwortet haben, wie haben Sie diese Information erhalten?
    a. Über das Internet
    b. In Zeitungen
    c. Aus allgemeinen Nachrichtenmagazinen
    d. Aus spezialisierten Zeitschriften
    e. Aus dem Fernsehen
    f. Im Radio
    g. Aus Gesprächen
    h. Auf anderem Wege: ______________________
11. Falls Sie Frage 9 mit Ja beantwortet haben, was war die Quelle ihrer Information?
    a. Die Regierung.
    b. Die Medien
    c. Wissenschaftler und Forscher (über Interviews, Zitate, Artikel etc.)
    d. Andere Individuen

Internetregulierung in Deutschland

12. Haben Sie in der Vergangenheit Internetzensur erfahren?
    a. Ja, in mindestens einem Fall.
    b. Nein.
    c. Ich weiß nicht.
13. Falls Sie Frage 12 mit Ja beantwortet haben, ging die Zensur von Deutschland aus?
    a. Ja, und es handelte sich um eine deutsche Internetseite.
    b. Ja, und es handelte sich um eine ausländische Internetseite.
    c. Nein, ich nutzte eine Verbindung außerhalb Deutschlands, aber es handelte sich um eine deutsche Internetseite.
    d. Nein, ich nutzte eine Verbindung außerhalb Deutschlands, und es handelte sich um eine ausländische Internetseite.
    e. Ich weiß nicht.
14. Falls Sie Frage 12 mit Ja beantwortet haben, von wo griffen Sie auf das Internet zu?
    a. Aus einer Universität.
    b. Aus einer Bibliothek.
    c. Aus einem Internetcafe.
    d. Von zu Hause (Internetprovider: ___?).
    e. Von zu Hause mit einer auf meinem Computer installierten Filtersoftware.
    f. Von einem anderen Ort aus: ______________________________
15. Falls Sie Frage 12 mit Ja beantwortet haben, beschreiben Sie kurz: a. die URL der zensierten Internetseite, b. die Information über Ihren Zugang, c. ob es sich um eine vollständige oder teilweise Zensur der Inhalte der Internetseite handelte etc.:

____

____

____

____

____

____

____

16. Haben Sie jemals von Beispielen für Internetregulierung außerhalb Deutschlands gehört? Falls ja, bitte nennen Sie einige Beispiele:

____

____

____

____

____

____

____

Die Umsetzung des Internetregulierungssystems in Deutschland betreffend

17. Stimmen Sie der Umsetzung eines Systems zur Internetregulierung gegen illegale Inhalte durch den Staat zu?
    a. Ja.
    b. Ja, aber nur unter bestimmten Voraussetzungen.
    c. Nein.

Begründung: ________________________________

18. Welche Arten von Inhalten sollten reguliert werden, wenn der deutsche Staat sich entscheidet, solch ein System umzusetzen?
    a. Pornographische Inhalte
    b. Hassbotschaften (Rassismus, Extremismus etc.)
    c. Defamierende Inhalte
    d. Keine Inhalte
    e. Urheberrechtsgeschützte Medien-Inhalte (Filme, Musik, Bücher etc.)
19. Falls ein System zur Internetregulierung in Deutschland umgesetzt wird, wer sollte es Ihrer Meinung nach betreiben, damit es rechtsstaatlichen Prinzipien folgt und von der Mehrheit der deutschen Bevölkerung akzeptiert wird?
    a. Nicht-Regierungsorganisationen (z.B. Reporter Ohne Grenzen)
    b. Forschungs- oder Bildungseinrichtungen innerhalb von Universitäten
    c. Forschungs- oder Bildungseinrichtungen außerhalb von Universitäten

d. Von der Regierung kontrolliert innerhalb eines Ministeriums
e. Eine andere Stelle: ______________________________

Epilog

Die vorliegende Umfrage ist anonym und die Ergebnisse werden nicht mit den Teilnehmern in Verbindung gebracht. Allerdings benötigen wir, um diese Umfrage weiter durchführen zu können, genaue Daten zu Beispielen der Internetregulierung in Deutschland.

Falls Sie also Maßnahmen der Internetregulierung erfahren haben und diese zum Wohle unserer Forschung teilen möchten, tragen Sie bitte Ihre E-Mail-Adresse in das dazugehörige Feld ein.

Die Kommunikation mit unserem Forscherteam wird zusätzliche Fragen zu Ihren Erfahrungen betreffen und Ihre Antworten werden vertraulich behandelt.

E-Mail-Adresse:

____

APPENDIX 3: RUSSIA SURVEY'S QUESTIONNAIRE

Интернет-Регулирование в [Вашей стране]

Интернет-регулирование - явление, растущее во всем мире. Такие системы уже созданы во многих странах и с авторитарными режимами (то есть в Китае и Саудовской Аравии) и демократических правительствах (то есть в Великобритании и Германии).

Несмотря на то, что такие системы сегодня широко применяются, текущие исследования показывают, что совсем немного граждан знают об их существовании и о том, как это влиет на их повседневную жизнь. Главная причина этого состоит в том, что во всем мире многие правительства предпочитают проводить эту политику “тихо”. Для исследования этой актуальной проблемы уже сформировалось очень активное академическое сообщество которое, наблюдая за этим явлением и регулярно издавая региональные отчеты пытается повысить уровень осведомленность общественности.

Это исследование - часть этого глобального усилия измерить общественное мнение относительно политики регулирования интернета как на национальном уровне, так и на уровне организаций, университетов и семьи. Если Вы готовы участвовать, пожалуйста, сделайте это ответственно.

Демографические вопросы

1. Вы - Мужчина или Женщина?
   a. Мужчина
   b. Женщина
2. Каков Ваш возраст?
   a. 18-21
   b. 22-25
   c. 26-30
   d. 31-40
   e. 41-50
   f. 51-60
   g. 61 и выше
3. Каков высший уровень образования, которое Вы закончили?
   a. Незаконченное среднее (школа)
   b. Законченное среднее (школа)
   c. Колледж
   d. Учусь на бакалавриате.
   e. Степень бакалавра (4 года)
   f. Степень магистра
   g. Докторская степень
   h. Профессиональная степень (MD, JD)
4. Сколько лет Вы являетесь пользователем Интернета (в пределах вашей страны) ?
   a. Меньше года
   b. 1-2 года
   c. 3-4 года
   d. Больше 5 лет
5. Вы считаете себя религиозным человеком?
   a. Да
   b. Нет
6. У Вас есть / намерение иметь детей?
   a. Да, у меня уже есть дети.
   b. Нет, у меня нет детей, но я намереваюсь иметь их в будущем.
   c. Нет, у меня нет детей, и я не намереваюсь иметь их в будущем.

Демографические вопросы, связанные с интернетом

7. Приблизительно, сколько часов Вы тратите в Интернете каждый день?
   a. Меньше чем 30 минут.
   b. 1 час
   c. 2-3 часа
   d. 4-5 часов
   e. Больше чем 6 часов
8. Что Вы делаете в Интернете?
   a. Развлечение (Игры / видео / музыка / и т.д.)
   b. Скачивание (программное обеспечение, музыка, видео, и т.д.)
   c. Профессиональные цели (как часть моей работы)
   d. Образовательные цели (как часть моего обучения в колледже / университете / средней школе / на курсах)
   e. Информационные цели (читаю газеты онлайн, и т.д.)
   f. Другое: ____________

Интернет-Регулирование в целом.

9. Вы знаете о глобальном явлении интернет-регулирования?
   a. Да, я хорошо информирован об этом.
   b. Да, я знаю основную информацию.
   c. Да, я слышал об этом.
   d. Нет, я ничего не знаю об этом.
10. Если Вы ответили "да" в вопросе 9, каковы были средства получения Вами информации об интернет-регулировании?
   a. Интернет
   b. Газеты
   c. Журнал массового содержания.
   d. Специализированные журналы.
   e. Телевидение.
   f. Радио.
   g. "Сарафанное радио".
   h. Другой источник информации: ______________________
11. Если Вы ответили "да" в вопросе 9, кто был источником Вашей информации?
   a. Правительственные заявления.
   b. СМИ.

c. Исследователи и ученые (через интервью, цитаты, статьи и т.д.)
d. Люди.

Интернет-Регулирование в России.

12. Вы когда-либо сталкивались с он-лайн цензурой ранее?
    a. Да, по крайней мере однажды.
    b. Нет.
    c. Я не знаю.
13. Если Вы ответили "да" в вопросе 12, то отметьте, существует ли он-лайн цензура в России ?
    a. Да и это имеет отношение российским веб-сайтам.
    b. Да и это имеет отношение к иностранным веб-сайтам.
    c. Нет. Я был в сети за пределами России, а она имеет отношение к российским веб-сайтам.
    d. Нет. Я был в сети за пределами России, а цензура касалась иностранных веб-сайтов.
    e. Я не знаю.
14. Если Вы ответили "да" на вопрос 12, какую сеть Вы использовали?
    a. Университетская сеть.
    b. Сеть в библиотеке (не университетской).
    c. Сеть в интернет-кафе.
    d. Личная связь (ISP: ___?).
    e. Личная связь с интернет-фильтрующим программным обеспечением, установленным в моем компьютер.
    f. Друге: ____________________________
15. Если Вы ответили "да" на вопрос 12, опишите вкратце свой опыт:
    a. укажите url (адрес) подвергнутого цензуре веб-сайта,
    b. информация о Вашей сети,
    c. ситуацию, если Вы столкнулись с полной или частичной цензурой содержания веб-сайта и т.д.:

____

____

____

____

____

____

____

16. Вы когда-либо слышали об случаях регулирования интернета вне пределов России ? Если да, пожалуйста, укажите некоторые примеры:

____
____
____
____
____
____
____

Вопросы касающиеся интернет-регулирования в вашей стране.

17. Вы согласны с выполнением системы регулирования интернета в государстве, если она касается незаконного содержания?
    a. Да.
    b. Да, но только при определенных условиях.
    c. Нет.

Объясните свой ответ: ___________________________________

18. Какое содержание должно быть контролироваться, если государство Вашей страны решит осуществить такую систему?
    a. Порнографическое содержание.
    b. Выражение ненависти (расизм, экстремизм и т.д.)
    c. Содержащее клевету.
    d. Никакой вид содержания не должен контролироваться.
    e. Защищенное авторским правом мультимедийное содержание (фильмы, музыка, книги и т.д.)
19. В случае, если система интернет регулирования будет существовать в России, кто, по Вашему мнению, должен этим управлять, чтобы осуществлять правосудие и быть принятым большинством российских граждан ?
    a. Неправительственные организации (например, Репортеры Без Границ и т.д.).

b. Исследовательские или Образовательные структуры в университетах.
c. Исследовательские или Образовательные структуры вне университетов.
d. Правительство в соответствующем министерстве
e. Другое: ______________________________

Заключение

Текущий обзор является анонимным, и результаты не будут связаны ни с одним из участников никаким образом. С другой стороны, для продолжения этого обзора мы нуждаемся в определенных данных относительно примеров интернет-регулирования внутри России. Поэтому в случае, если у Вас есть опыт относительно некоторых форм интернет-политики регулирования, и Вы хотите поделиться этим, чтобы помочь этому исследованию, пожалуйста, укажите адрес своей электронной почты в соответствующей области.

Дальнейшая коммуникация с нашей исследовательской группой будет иметь отношение к дополнительным вопросам относительно Вашего опыта, и Ваши ответы будут анонимными.

электронная почта:

APPENDIX 4: INDIA SURVEY'S QUESTIONNAIRE

Internet Regulation in India

Internet regulation is a phenomenon on the rise worldwide. Such systems are already implemented in many countries with both authoritarian regimes (i.e. China and Saudi Arabia) and democratic governments (i.e. UK and Germany).

Despite the fact that such systems are in an extensive use today, current surveys shows that quite few citizens are aware of their existence and how they influence their everyday life. The main reason behind this is that «silent» implementation is being preferred by many governments around the globe. In order to tackle this disturbing issue, a very active academic community has already been formed observing the phenomenon and publishing country reviews regularly to raise public awareness.

This survey is part of this global effort to measure the public opinion regarding the implementation of Internet regulation policies and systems in national, company, university and family level. If you are willing to participate, please do so with the appropriate responsibility.

Demographical Questions

1. Are you Male or Female?
    a. Male
    b. Female
2. What is your age?
    a. 18-21
    b. 22-25
    c. 26-30
    d. 31-40
    e. 41-50
    f. 51-60
    g. 61 and above
3. What is the highest level of education you have completed?
    a. Less than High School
    b. High School/ GED
    c. Some College
    d. 2 year College Degree (Associates)
    e. 4 year College Degree (BA/ BS)
    f. Master's Degree
    g. Doctoral Degree
    h. Professional Degree (MD, JD)
4. For how many years are you a India based Internet user?
    a. Less than a year
    b. 1-2 years
    c. 3-4 years
    d. More than 5 years
5. Do you consider yourself a religious man?
    a. Yes
    b. No

6. Do you have/ intent to have children?
   a. Yes, I have children already.
   b. No, I don't have children but I am intending to have in the future.
   c. No, I don't have children and I am not intending to have in the future neither.

Internet Related Demographic Questions

7. Approximately how many hours do you spend on Internet every day?
   a. Less than 30 minutes.
   b. 1 hour
   c. 2-3 hours
   d. 4-5 hours
   e. More than 6 hours
8. What are you doing on Internet?
   a. Entertainment (Gaming/ videos/ music/ etc.)
   b. Download (software, music, videos, etc.)
   c. Professional purposes (part of my job)
   d. Educational purposes (part of my college/ university/ high school courses)
   e. Informational purposes (reading online newspapers, etc.)
   f. Other: _______

Internet Regulation in General

9. Are you aware of the global phenomenon of Internet regulation?
   a. Yes, I am well informed.
   b. Yes, I know the basics.
   c. Yes, just heard about it.
   d. No, I know nothing about this.
10. If you answered yes at question 9, what were the means of your information?
    a. Internet
    b. Newspapers
    c. Magazine of general interest.
    d. Specialized (niche) magazines.
    e. TV.
    f. Radio.
    g. Word of mouth.
    h. Other: ________________________

11. If you answered yes at question 9, who was the source of your information?
    a. Government statements.
    b. Media.
    c. Researchers and scientists (via interviews, quotes, articles etc.)
    d. Individuals.

Internet Regulation in India

12. Have you ever faced online censorship in the past?
    a. Yes, at least once.
    b. No.
    c. I don't know.
13. If you answered yes in question 12, was the censorship based in India?
    a. Yes and it has to do with an India website.
    b. Yes and it has to do with a foreign website.
    c. No. I was connected outside India but it has to do with an India country] website.
    d. No. I was connected outside India but it has to do with a foreign website.
    e. I don't know.
14. If you answered yes in question 12, what kind of network did you use?
    a. University network.
    b. Library network.
    c. Internet cafe network.
    d. Personal connection (ISP: ___?).
    e. Personal connection with an Internet filtering software installed in my computer.
    f. Other: ____________________________
15. If you answered yes in question 12, describe in brief your experience: a. provide the url of the website censored, b. information about your network, c. state if you faced full or partial censorship of the website's content etc.:

____

____

____

____

____

____

16. Have you ever heard about Internet regulation examples outside India? If yes, please provide some examples:

____
____
____
____
____
____
____

Concerning the Implementation of Internet

Regulation System in India

17. Do you agree with the implementation of an Internet regulation system by the state focusing on illegal content?
    a. Yes.
    b. Yes, but only under conditions.
    c. No.

Explain your answer: ______________________________

18. What kind of content should be regulated if your country's state decides to implement such a system?
    a. Pornographic content.
    b. Hate speech content (racism, extremism etc.)
    c. Defamation content.
    d. No kind of content.
    e. Copyrighted multimedia content (movies, music, books etc.)
19. In case an Internet regulation system is implemented in Greece, from whom do you believe it must be operated in order to function with justice and to be accepted by the majority of India citizens?
    a. Non-government organizations (i.e. Reporters Without Borders etc.).
    b. Research or Educational Institute inside Universities.
    c. Research or Educational Institute outside Universities.
    d. Government controlled service inside the appropriate ministry
    e. Other: ________________________

Epilogue

The current survey is anonymous and the results will not be connected with any of the participants in any kind of form. From the other hand, for this survey to continue we need specific data regarding examples of Internet regulation inside India.

For this reason, in case you have experience some form of Internet regulation policies and wants to share it in order to help this research, please fill your email in the appropriate field.

Further communication with our research team will have to do with supplementary questions concerning your experience and your answers will be anonymous.

e-mail:

____

APPENDIX 5: KOSOVO SURVEY'S QUESTIONNAIRE

Politikat mbi rregullimin e Internetit në Kosovë

Politika e Rregullimit të Internetit po paraqitet si fenomen në rritje në mbarë botën. Këto politika janë duke u implementuar në shumicën e vendeve të botës me regjime autoritare (p.sh. Kinë dhe Arabin Saudite) si dhe në qeveritë demokratike (p.sh. Mbretërinë e Bashkuar dhe Amerikë).

Pavarësisht faktit se këto sisteme (politika) sot kanë gjetur zbatim të gjerë, studimet tregojnë që shumë pak qytetarë janë të informuar për ekzistencën e tyre dhe për mënyrën sesi e influencojnë jetën e tyrë të përditshme. Arsyeja kryesore prapa këtij fakti është se shumica e qeverive në botë sot preferojnë implementim ''të pazhurshëm'' të këtyre politikave.

Prandaj, për ta luftuar këtë dukuri shqetësuese, një komunitet shumë aktiv akademik është formuar me qëllim të vëzhgimit të këtij fenomeni, gjithashtu edhe për të publikuar pasqyra të gjendjes rreth këtij fenonomeni nga vende të ndryshme të botës me qëllim të rritjes së vetëdijës së publikut.

Ky studim (anket) është pjesë e përpjekjeve globale për të matur opinionin publik në lidhje me implementinin e politikave të rregullimit të internetit dhe sistemeve në nivelin kombëtar, të kompanisë, universitetit, dhe familjes. Nësë jeni të gatshëm të merrni pjësë, të lutem të plotësoni anketën me përgjegjësi të duhur.

Pyetjet demografike

1. A jeni Mashkull apo Femër?
    a. Mashkull
    b. Femër
2. Grupmosha juaj?
    a. më pak se 18
    b. 18-24
    c. 25-34
    d. 35-54
    e. 55 e sipër
3. Cili është niveli më i lartë i arsimimit që keni përfunduar?
    a. Më pak se shkolla e mesme
    b. Shkolla e mesme
    c. Shkolla e lartë 2 vjet
    d. Studimet bazike 3 vjet (bachelor)
    e. Studimet bazike 4 vjet (diplomë)
    f. Studimet master
    g. Studimet e doktoraturës
    h. Kualifikime profesionale (Doktor i mjekësisë, Avokaturë)
    i. Tjetër: ___________________
4. Sa vjet deri më tani e keni shfrytëzur internetin gjatë qëndrimit si rezident në Kosovë?
    a. Më pak se një vit
    b. 1-2 vite
    c. 3-4 vite
    d. Më shumë se 5 vite
5. A e konsideroni vetën si person fetar?
    a. Po
    b. Jo
6. A synoni të keni/ keni fëmijë?
    a. Po, unë tashmë veq kam fëmijë.
    b. Jo, nuk kam fëmijë por synojë të kem në të ardhmen.
    c. Jo, nuk kam fëmijë dhe nuk synojë të kem në të ardhmen.

Pytjet demografike në lidhje me internetin

7. Përafërsisht sa orë në ditë e shfrytëzoni internetin?
   a. Më pak se 30 minuta
   b. 1 orë
   c. 2-3 orë
   d. 4-5 orë
   e. Më shumë së 6 orë
8. Çfarë bëni zakonisht në internet?
   a. Argëtoheni (lojra/ video/ muzik/ etj.)
   b. Shkarkoni (programe kompjuterike, muzik, video, etj.)
   c. Qëllime profesionale (pjesë e punës)
   d. Qëllime edukimi (pjesë e lëndëve të universitetit/kolegjit/ shkollës se mesme)
   e. Qëllime informimi (leximi i shtypit online, etj.)
   f. Tjera: _______

Rregullimi i internetit (në përgjithësi)

9. A jeni të vetëdijshëm për fenonomenin global të rregullimit të internetit?
   a. Po, jam i mirë-informuar.
   b. Po, di pak a shumë në përgjithësi.
   c. Po, sapo kam dëgjuar për të.
   d. Jo, nuk di asgjë për këtë.
10. Nëse jeni përgjigjur me PO në pyetjen e 9, cila kanë qenë mjetet e informimit?
    a. Interneti
    b. Gazetat
    c. Revistat e përgjithshme.
    d. Revistat e specializuara (IT, kulturë, sport)
    e. TV.
    f. Radio.
    g. Fjala e gojës.
    h. Tjera: ________________________
11. Nëse jeni përgjigjur me PO në pyetjen e 9, kush ka qenë burim i informacionit tuaj?
    a. Deklaratat qeveritare.
    b. Mediat.

c. Hulumtuesit dhe shkencëtarët (përmes intervistave, thënievedeklaratave, artikujve etj.)
d. Individët.

Cenzurimi i internetit në Kosovë

12. A keni hasur ndonjëherë në cenzur gjatë përdorimit të internetit në të kaluarën?
    a. Po, së paku njëher.
    b. Jo.
    c. Nuk e di.
13. Nëse jeni përgjigjur me PO në pyetjen e 12, a ishte bërë cenzurimi në Kosovë?
    a. Po dhe kishte të bëjë me uebfaqe në Kosovë.
    b. Po dhe kishte të bëjë me uebfaqe nga jashtë Kosovës.
    c. Jo. E shfrytëzoja internetit jashtë Kosovës por kishtë të bëjë me uebfaqe në Kosovë.
    d. Jo. E shfrytëzoja internetit jashtë Kosovës por kishtë të bëjë me uebfaqe jashtë Kosovës.
    e. Nuk e di.
14. Nëse jeni përgjigjur me PO në pyetjen e 12, çfarë rrjeti të internetit shfrytëzoje?
    a. Rrjetin e universitetit.
    b. Rjetin e librarisë.
    c. Rrjetin e internet kafesë.
    d. Rrjetin personal (ISP: ___?).
    e. Rrjetin personal me një softuer për filtrimin e internetit të instaluar në kompjuterin tim.
    f. Tjetër: ______________________________
15. Nëse jeni përgjigjur me PO në pyetjen e 12, përshkruani shkurtimisht eksperiencën tuaj: a. tregoni linkun e ueb faqës së cenzoruar, b. Informat rreth rrjetit tuaj të Internetit, c. tregoni nësë jeni ballafaquar me cenzurë të plotë ose të pjesshme të përmbajtjes së ueb-faqes etj.:

____

____

____

____

____

16. A keni ndëgjuar ndonjëherë për praktikat (shembujt) e politikave të rregullimit të internetit jashtë Kosovës? Nëse po, paraqitni ndonjë rast:

____
____
____
____
____
____
____

Lidhur me zbatimin (rregullimit) e politikave të internetit në Kosovë

17. A jeni dakort me zbatimin e një sistemi për rregullim (cenzurim) të internetit nga ana e shtetit duke u fokusuar në përmbajtjen e paligjshme të ueb-faqeve?
    a. Po.
    b. Po, por me disa kushte.
    c. Jo.

Shpjegoni përgjigjen tuaj: ___________________________________

18. Çfarë lloji i përmbajtjes duhet të cenzurohet në Kosovë, nëse vendoset për implementim të një sistemi të tilllë?
    a. Përmbajtja pornografike.
    b. Përmbajtja me karakter të urrejtjes (racizimit, ekstremizmit etj.)
    c. Përmbajtje shpifëse.
    d. Pa asnjë përmbajtje.
    e. Përmbatjet multimediale me të drejtë të autorit (filmat, muzika, librat elektronik etj.)
19. Nëse sistemi për cenzurimin e internetit implementohet në Kosovë, nga kush duhet të operohet për të funksionuar me drejtësi dhe të pranohet nga shumica e qytetarëve në Kosovë?
    a. Organizatat joqeveritare (p.sh. Raporterët pa Kufinj etj.).
    b. Institutet Hulumtuese dhe Edukative brenda universiteteve.
    c. Institutet Hulumtuese dhe Edukative jashtë universiteteve.
    d. Shërbimit të kontrolluar nga qeveria brenda ministrisë së duhur.
    e. Tjera: ___________________________

Epilogu

Kjo anketë është krejtësisht anonime dhe rezultatet nuk do të jenë të lidhura me ndonjërin nga pjesmarrësit e kësaj ankete në asnjë lloj forme. Në anën tjetër, për vazhdimin/realizimin e kësaj ankete duhen të dhëna specifike në lidhje me praktikat dhe shembujtë e politikave të rregullimit të internetit brenda Kosovës.

Për këtë arsye në rast se keni ndonjë përjetuar ndonjë formë të politikave të rregullimit (kufizimit) të internetit dhe dëshironi ta ndani për ti kontribuar këtij hulumtimi, të lutem shënoni emailin tuaj në pjësën ku kërkohet. Pjesa tjetër e komunikimit me ekipin tonë hulumtues do të mërret me pyetje plotësuese në lidhje me eksperiencat, ndërsa përgjigjet do të jenë krejtësisht anonime.

e-maili:

____

APPENDIX 6: CYPRUS SURVEY'S QUESTIONNAIRE

Διαδικτυακός Έλεγχος και Λογοκρισία στην Ελλάδα

Internet Regulation in Greece

Το φαινόμενο του ελέγχου του διαδικτύου και της διαδικτυακής λογοκρισίας είναι σε διαρκή άνοδο παγκοσμίως και εμφανίζεται σε πλήθος κρατών σε ολόκληρη την υφήλιο, από αυταρχικές χώρες της Ασίας (Κίνα, Σαουδική Αραβία κ.λπ.) έως κατά παράδοση δημοκρατικά κράτη της Ευρώπης (Γερμανία, Μεγάλη Βρετανία κ.λπ.).

Αν και ως φαινόμενο είναι γενικευμένο, εντούτοις το μεγαλύτερο μέρος της εκάστοτε κοινωνίας στην οποία εφαρμόζεται δεν γνωρίζει την ύπαρξη του (ούτε φυσικά την επιρροή που έχει στην καθημερινότητα του) λόγω της πολιτικής που ακολουθείται από τις εκάστοτε αρχές. Εξαιτίας αυτής ακριβώς την πολιτικής «σιωπηλού» ελέγχου του διαδικτύου που ακολουθείται, έχει αναπτυχθεί μία αρκετά δραστήρια ακαδημαϊκή κοινότητα που παρατηρεί και δημοσιεύει αξιολογήσεις για την κατάσταση που ισχύει σε κάθε κράτος.

Το παρόν ερωτηματολόγιο είναι κομμάτι μίας τέτοιας έρευνας που ξεκίνησε λίγο καιρό πριν στην Ελλάδα πάνω στο φαινόμενο του διαδικτυακού ελέγχου και της διαδικτυακής λογοκρισίας σε κρατικό, εταιρικό, πανεπιστημιακό ή/ και οικογενειακό επίπεδο. Εφόσον αποφασίσετε να αφιερώσετε λίγο χρόνο για τη συμπλήρωση του, παρακαλείσθε να απαντήσετε με υπευθυνότητα.

Σχετικά με το background σας

1. Ποιο είναι το φύλο σας;
    a. Γυναίκα
    b. Άνδρας
2. Σε ποια ηλικιακή ομάδα ανήκετε;
    a. 18-21
    b. 22-25
    c. 26-30
    d. 31-40
    e. 41-50
    f. 51-60
    g. 61 και πάνω
3. Ποιο είναι το μορφωτικό σας επίπεδο;
    a. Μικρότερο από Γυμνάσιο
    b. Γυμνάσιο/ Λύκειο
    c. ΙΕΚ ή παρεμφερές ινστιτούτο
    d. Προπτυχιακές πανεπιστημιακές σπουδές
    e. Μεταπτυχιακές σπουδές
    f. Διδακτορικές σπουδές
4. Πόσο καιρό χρησιμοποιείτε το διαδίκτυο εντός Κύπρου;
    a. Λιγότερο από 1 χρόνο
    b. 1-2 χρόνια
    c. 3-4 χρόνια
    d. Περισσότερα από 5 χρόνια
5. Θεωρείτε τον εαυτό σας θρήσκο άτομο (ανεξαρτήτως θρησκείας);
    a. Ναι
    b. Όχι
6. Έχετε παιδιά;
    a. Ναι
    b. Όχι

Σχετικά με τη χρήση του internet

7. Πόσες περίπου ώρες αφιερώνεται καθημερινά στο internet;
   a. Λιγότερο από 30 λεπτά
   b. 1 ώρα
   c. 2-3 ώρες
   d. 4-5 ώρες
   e. Περισσότερες από 6 ώρες
8. Για ποιους λόγους χρησιμοποιείτε κυρίως το internet;
   a. Διασκέδαση (gaming, video, μουσική κ.λπ.)
   b. Download (software, μουσική, video κ.λπ.)
   c. Επαγγελματικούς λόγους (ως κομμάτι της δουλειάς μου)
   d. Εκπαιδευτικούς λόγους (ως κομμάτι των σπουδών μου)
   e. Μέσο πληροφόρησης (ειδήσεις, ανταποκρίσεις, αναλύσεις κ.λπ.)
   f. Άλλο: ______________________________

Διαδικτυακός Έλεγχος και Λογοκρισία Παγκοσμίως

9. Γνωρίζετε για το παγκόσμιο φαινόμενο της διαδικτυακής λογοκρισίας;
   a. Ναι, είμαι αρκετά καλά ενημερωμένος.
   b. Ναι, γνωρίζω κάποια βασικά πράγματα.
   c. Ναι, απλά έχω ακούσει γι’ αυτό.
   d. Όχι, δεν γνωρίζω τίποτα.
10. Αν απαντήσατε *ναι* στην προηγούμενη ερώτηση, από ποια μέσα ενημέρωσης αντλήσατε τις πληροφορίες σας;
    a. Μέσω διαδικτύου.
    b. Μέσω εφημερίδων ή ένθετων περιοδικών αυτών.
    c. Μέσω περιοδικών γενικότερου ενδιαφέροντος.
    d. Μέσω εξειδικευμένων περιοδικών.
    e. Μέσω τηλεόρασης.
    f. Μέσω ραδιοφώνου.
    g. Μέσω συζήτησης με γνωστό.
    h. Άλλο: ____________________
11. Αν απαντήσατε *ναι* στην ερώτηση 9, ποια ήταν η πηγή των πληροφοριών;
    a. Κρατικές δηλώσεις (υπουργική ανακοίνωση, δηλώσεις συνεργαζόμενου φορέα κ.λπ.).
    b. Μέσα Μαζικής Ενημέρωσης.

c. Ειδικοί Ερευνητές ή Επιστήμονες (μέσω συνεντεύξεις, άρθρων, δηλώσεων κ.λπ.).
d. Ιδιώτες.

Διαδικτυακός Έλεγχος και Λογοκρισία στην Κύπρο

12. Έχετε πέσει ποτέ θύμα διαδικτυακής λογοκρισίας κατά το παρελθόν;
    a. Ναι, τουλάχιστον μία φορά.
    b. Όχι, ποτέ.
    c. Δεν ξέρω.
13. Αν ναι, είχατε συνδεθεί από υπολογιστή εντός Κύπρου;
    a. Ναι και αφορούσε ελληνική ιστοσελίδα.
    b. Ναι και αφορούσε ξένη ιστοσελίδα.
    c. Όχι. Είχα συνδεθεί από υπολογιστή στο εξωτερικό, αλλά αφορούσε ελληνική ιστοσελίδα.
    d. Όχι. Είχα συνδεθεί από υπολογιστή στο εξωτερικό και δεν αφορούσε ελληνική ιστοσελίδα.
    e. Δεν γνωρίζω.
14. Σε τι δίκτυο ανήκε ο υπολογιστής που χρησιμοποιούσατε;
    a. Συνδέθηκα μέσω πανεπιστημιακού δικτύου (εντός σχολής, πανεπιστημιούπολης κ.λπ.).
    b. Συνδέθηκα μέσω δικτύου κάποιας βιβλιοθήκης.
    c. Συνδέθηκα μέσω internet cafe.
    d. Συνδέθηκα μέσω προσωπικής σύνδεσης (εταιρία: _________).
    e. Συνδέθηκα μέσω προσωπικής σύνδεσης των γονιών μου, οι οποίοι είχαν εγκαταστήσει φίλτρο δικτύου για παιδιά.
    f. Άλλο: ________________________
15. Αν απαντήσατε *ναι* στην ερώτηση 12, περιγράψτε με λίγα λόγια την εν λόγω κατάσταση/ εμπειρία (γράψτε στοιχεία όπως τι ιστοσελίδα αφορούσε, από τι δίκτυο είχατε συνδεθεί, αν ήταν ολική απαγόρευση πρόσβασης ή μερική κ.λπ.):

____
____
____
____
____
____
____

16. Έχετε ακούσει ποτέ για περιπτώσεις διαδικτυακής λογοκρισίας σε χώρες του εξωτερικού; Αν ναι, δώστε μερικά παραδείγματα:

____
____
____
____
____
____
____

Σχετικά με την Εφαρμογή Διαδικτυακού Ελέγχου στην Κύπρο

17. Συμφωνείτε με την πανελλαδική εφαρμογή (από το κράτος) ενός συστήματος περιορισμού παράνομου διαδικτυακού περιεχομένου που θα αφορούσε ιστοσελίδες με υψηλής ευαισθησίας θέματα όπως π.χ. παιδική πορνογραφία;
    a. Ναι.
    b. Όχι.
    c. Εν μέρει.

Γιατί; ____
____
____

18. Σε ποιες από τις παρακάτω θεματικές ενότητες ιστοσελίδων πιστεύετε ότι πρέπει να ασκείτε κρατικός έλεγχος και όταν κρίνεται αναγκαίο (είναι παράνομες, προωθούν τον φανατισμό, τον φυλετικό ρατσισμό, την τρομοκρατία κ.λπ.) να λογοκρίνονται;
    a. Πορνογραφικές ιστοσελίδες
    b. Ιστοσελίδες με παράνομο οπτικοακουστικό υλικό που υπόκειται σε πνευματικά δικαιώματα (ταινίες, μουσική, βιβλία κ.λπ.)
    c. Ιστοσελίδες που προωθούν κάποιου είδος μίσους (ρατσιστικού περιεχομένου, με υλικό φανατισμού κ.λπ.)
    d. Ιστοσελίδες με δυσφημιστικό υλικό

19. Σε περίπτωση που εφαρμοστεί σύστημα διαδικτυακού ελέγχου στην Κύπρο, πως και από ποιους πιστεύετε ότι θα πρέπει να ελέγχεται ώστε να λειτουργεί επαρκώς και να είναι της κοινής αποδοχής της ελληνικής κοινωνίας;
    a. Από μη-κυβερνητικές οργανώσεις σχετικού ενδιαφέροντος. (π.χ. Δημοσιογράφοι Δίχως Σύνορα κ.λπ.)
    b. Από Ερευνητικά ή Εκπαιδευτικά Ινστιτούτα εντός Πανεπιστημίων
    c. Από Ερευνητικά Ινστιτούτα εκτός Πανεπιστημίων
    d. Από Κρατική Υπηρεσία εντός του κατάλληλου υπουργείου
    e. Άλλο: ___________________________

Το παρόν ερωτηματολόγιο είναι ανώνυμο και τα αποτελέσματα του δεν θα συνδεθούν με οποιονδήποτε τρόπο με συγκεκριμένα πρόσωπα και ονόματα. Η έρευνα όμως πάνω στο φαινόμενο της διαδικτυακής λογοκρισίας στην Κύπρο έχει πολλά στάδια και ως εκ τούτου θα χρειαστεί να συγκεντρωθούν στοιχεία για όσο το δυνατόν περισσότερες περιπτώσεις λογοκρισίας.

Για το λόγο αυτό, εφόσον έχετε βιώσει κάποιου είδους διαδικτυακού ελέγχου ή λογοκρισίας σε πανελλαδικό, εταιρικό, πανεπιστημιακό, οικογενειακό κ.λπ. περιβάλλον και επιθυμείτε να βοηθήσετε στην παρούσα έρευνα, παρακαλώ αναγράψτε στο κατάλληλο πεδίο παρακάτω ένα email επικοινωνίας.

Η όποια πιθανή μελλοντική επικοινωνία με το ερευνητικό μας team θα είναι για συμπληρωματικές ερωτήσεις σχετικά με την εμπειρία σας, ενώ και σε αυτή την περίπτωση θα διατηρήσετε την ανωνυμία σας.

Email Επικοινωνιασ:

APPENDIX 7: GREECE MASS SURVEY'S QUESTIONNAIRE

Διαδικτυακός Έλεγχος και Λογοκρισία στην Ελλάδα

Internet Regulation in Greece

Το φαινόμενο του ελέγχου του διαδικτύου και της διαδικτυακής λογοκρισίας είναι σε διαρκή άνοδο παγκοσμίως και εμφανίζεται σε πλήθος κρατών σε ολόκληρη την υφήλιο, από αυταρχικές χώρες της Ασίας (Κίνα, Σαουδική Αραβία κ.λπ.) έως κατά παράδοση δημοκρατικά κράτη της Ευρώπης (Γερμανία, Μεγάλη Βρετανία κ.λπ.).

Αν και ως φαινόμενο είναι γενικευμένο, εντούτοις το μεγαλύτερο μέρος της εκάστοτε κοινωνίας στην οποία εφαρμόζεται δεν γνωρίζει την ύπαρξη του (ούτε φυσικά την επιρροή που έχει στην καθημερινότητα του) λόγω της πολιτικής που ακολουθείται από τις εκάστοτε αρχές. Εξαιτίας αυτής ακριβώς την πολιτικής «σιωπηλού» ελέγχου του διαδικτύου που ακολουθείται, έχει αναπτυχθεί μία αρκετά δραστήρια ακαδημαϊκή κοινότητα που παρατηρεί και δημοσιεύει αξιολογήσεις για την κατάσταση που ισχύει σε κάθε κράτος.

Το παρόν ερωτηματολόγιο είναι κομμάτι μίας τέτοιας έρευνας που ξεκίνησε λίγο καιρό πριν στην Ελλάδα πάνω στο φαινόμενο του διαδικτυακού ελέγχου και της διαδικτυακής λογοκρισίας σε κρατικό, εταιρικό, πανεπιστημιακό ή/ και οικογενειακό επίπεδο. Εφόσον αποφασίσετε να αφιερώσετε λίγο χρόνο για τη συμπλήρωση του, παρακαλείσθε να απαντήσετε με υπευθυνότητα.

Σχετικά με το background σας

1. Ποιο είναι το φύλο σας;
   a. Γυναίκα
   b. Άνδρας
2. Σε ποια ηλικιακή ομάδα ανήκετε;
   a. 18-21
   b. 22-25
   c. 26-30
   d. 31-40
   e. 41-50
   f. 51-60
   g. 61 και πάνω
3. Ποιο είναι το μορφωτικό σας επίπεδο;
   a. Βασική εκπαίδευση (δημοτικό/ γυμνάσιο/ λύκειο)
   b. ΙΕΚ ή παρεμφερές ινστιτούτο
   c. Πανεπιστήμιο (προπτυχιακές σπουδές)
   d. Μεταπτυχιακές σπουδές
   e. Διδακτορικές σπουδές
4. Πόσο καιρό χρησιμοποιείτε το διαδίκτυο εντός Ελλάδας;
   a. Λιγότερο από 1 χρόνο
   b. 1-2 χρόνια
   c. 3-4 χρόνια
   d. Περισσότερα από 5 χρόνια

5. Θεωρείτε τον εαυτό σας θρήσκο άτομο (ανεξαρτήτως θρησκείας);
    a. Ναι
    b. Όχι
6. Έχετε παιδιά;
    a. Ναι, έχω παιδιά.
    b. Όχι, δεν έχω παιδιά αλλά σκοπεύω να αποκτήσω.
    c. Όχι, δεν έχω παιδιά και δεν σκοπεύω να αποκτήσω.

Σχετικά με τη χρήση του internet

7. Πόσες περίπου ώρες αφιερώνεται καθημερινά στο internet;
    a. Λιγότερο από 30 λεπτά
    b. 1 ώρα
    c. 2-3 ώρες
    d. 4-5 ώρες
    e. Περισσότερες από 6 ώρες
8. Για ποιους λόγους χρησιμοποιείτε κυρίως το internet;
    a. Διασκέδαση (gaming, video, μουσική κ.λπ.)
    b. Download (software, μουσική, video κ.λπ.)
    c. Επαγγελματικούς λόγους (ως κομμάτι της δουλειάς μου)
    d. Εκπαιδευτικούς λόγους (ως κομμάτι των σπουδών μου)
    e. Μέσο πληροφόρησης (ειδήσεις, ανταποκρίσεις, αναλύσεις κ.λπ.)
    f. Άλλο: ________________________________

Διαδικτυακός Έλεγχος και Λογοκρισία Παγκοσμίως

9. Είστε ενήμερος για το παγκόσμιο φαινόμενο της διαδικτυακής λογοκρισίας;
    a. Ναι, είμαι αρκετά καλά ενημερωμένος.
    b. Ναι, γνωρίζω κάποια βασικά πράγματα.
    c. Ναι, απλά έχω ακούσει γι' αυτό.
    d. Όχι, δεν γνωρίζω τίποτα.
10. Από ποια ΜΜΕ αντλήσατε τις πληροφορίες σας;
    a. Μέσω διαδικτύου.
    b. Μέσω εφημερίδων ή ένθετων περιοδικών αυτών.
    c. Μέσω περιοδικών γενικότερου ενδιαφέροντος.
    d. Μέσω εξειδικευμένων περιοδικών.
    e. Μέσω τηλεόρασης.

f. Μέσω ραδιοφώνου.
g. Άλλο ΜΜΕ.

11. Ποια ήταν η πηγή των πληροφοριών σας;
    a. Δηλώσεις κρατικών υπαλλήλων.
    b. Δηλώσεις κυβερνητικών στελεχών (υπουγοί κ.λπ.).
    c. Δηλώσεις πολιτικών και πολιτικών φορέων.
    d. Δηλώσεις σχετικών οργανώσεων (Ανθρωπίνων Δικαιωμάτων, ελευθερία του λόγου κ.λπ.).
    e. Ειδικοί ερευνητές.
    f. Δημοσιογράφοι.
    g. Προσωπικές συζητήσεις στο κοινωνικό μου περιβάλλον.

Διαδικτυακός Έλεγχος και Λογοκρισία στην Ελλάδα

12. Έχετε πέσει ποτέ θύμα διαδικτυακής λογοκρισίας κατά το παρελθόν;
    a. Ναι, τουλάχιστον μία φορά.
    b. Όχι, ποτέ.
    c. Δεν ξέρω.
13. Είχατε συνδεθεί από υπολογιστή εντός Ελλάδας;
    a. Ναι και αφορούσε ελληνική ιστοσελίδα.
    b. Ναι και αφορούσε ξένη ιστοσελίδα.
    c. Όχι. Είχα συνδεθεί από υπολογιστή στο εξωτερικό, αλλά αφορούσε ελληνική ιστοσελίδα.
    d. Όχι. Είχα συνδεθεί από υπολογιστή στο εξωτερικό και αφορούσε ξένη ιστοσελίδα.
    e. Δεν γνωρίζω.
14. Σε τι δίκτυο ανήκε ο υπολογιστής που χρησιμοποιούσατε;
    a. Συνδέθηκα μέσω πανεπιστημιακού δικτύου (εντός σχολής, πανεπιστημιούπολης κ.λπ.).
    b. Συνδέθηκα μέσω δικτύου κάποιας βιβλιοθήκης.
    c. Συνδέθηκα μέσω internet cafe.
    d. Συνδέθηκα μέσω προσωπικής σύνδεσης (εταιρία: _________).
    e. Συνδέθηκα μέσω προσωπικής σύνδεσης των γονιών μου, οι οποίοι είχαν εγκαταστήσει φίλτρο δικτύου για παιδιά.
    f. Άλλο: ____________________

15. Περιγράψτε με λίγα λόγια την εν λόγω κατάσταση/ εμπειρία (γράψτε στοιχεία όπως τι ιστοσελίδα αφορούσε, από τι δίκτυο είχατε συνδεθεί, αν ήταν ολική απαγόρευση πρόσβασης ή μερική κ.λπ.):

____

____

____

____

____

____

____

16. Έχετε ακούσει ποτέ για περιπτώσεις διαδικτυακής λογοκρισίας σε χώρες του εξωτερικού;
    a. Ναι.
    b. Όχι.
17. Αναφέρετε μερικά παραδείγματα τέτοιων περιπτώσεων στο εξωτερικό:

____

____

____

____

____

____

____

Σχετικά με την Εφαρμογή Διαδικτυακού Ελέγχου στην Ελλάδα

18. Συμφωνείτε με την πανελλαδική εφαρμογή (από το κράτος) ενός συστήματος περιορισμού παράνομου διαδικτυακού περιεχομένου που θα αφορούσε ιστοσελίδες με υψηλής ευαισθησίας θέματα, όπως για παράδειγμα παιδική πορνογραφία, ιστοσελίδες προώθησης τρομοκρατικών ομάδων, μίσους προς φυλετικές ομάδες κ.λπ.;
    a. Ναι.
    b. Όχι.
    c. Εν μέρει.

Γιατί; ____

____

____

19. Σε ποιες από τις παρακάτω θεματικές ενότητες ιστοσελίδων πιστεύετε ότι πρέπει να ασκείτε κρατικός έλεγχος και όταν κρίνεται αναγκαίο (είναι παράνομες, προωθούν τον φανατισμό, τον φυλετικό ρατσισμό, την τρομοκρατία κ.λπ.) να λογοκρίνονται;
    a. Πορνογραφικές ιστοσελίδες
    b. Ιστοσελίδες με παράνομο οπτικοακουστικό υλικό που υπόκειται σε πνευματικά δικαιώματα (ταινίες, μουσική, βιβλία κ.λπ.)
    c. Ιστοσελίδες που προωθούν κάποιου είδους μίσος (ρατσιστικού περιεχομένου, με υλικό φανατισμού κ.λπ.)
    d. Ιστοσελίδες με δυσφημιστικό περιεχόμενο.
    e. Σε καμία.
20. Σε περίπτωση που εφαρμοστεί σύστημα διαδικτυακού ελέγχου στην Ελλάδα, πως και από ποιους πιστεύετε ότι θα πρέπει να ελέγχεται ώστε να λειτουργεί επαρκώς και να είναι της κοινής αποδοχής της ελληνικής κοινωνίας;
    a. Από σχετική υπηρεσία της Ελληνικής Αστυνομίας.
    b. Από σχετική υπηρεσία του Ελληνικού Στρατού.
    c. Από σχετική υπηρεσία εντός του κατάλληλου υπουργείου.
    d. Από σχετικές Μη Κυβερνητικές Οργανώσεις (όπως π.χ. Reporters Without Borders κ.λπ.).
    e. Από ερευνητικά κέντρα εντός πανεπιστημίου.
    f. Από ερευνητικά κέντρα εκτός πανεπιστημίου.
    g. Από άλλη σχετική υπηρεσία που δεν θα ελέγχεται από την εκάστοτε κυβέρνηση.
    h. Άλλο.

Το παρόν ερωτηματολόγιο είναι ανώνυμο και τα αποτελέσματα του δεν θα συνδεθούν με οποιονδήποτε τρόπο με συγκεκριμένα πρόσωπα και ονόματα. Η έρευνα όμως πάνω στο φαινόμενο της διαδικτυακής λογοκρισίας στην Ελλάδα έχει πολλά στάδια και ως εκ τούτου θα χρειαστεί να συγκεντρωθούν στοιχεία για όσο το δυνατόν περισσότερες περιπτώσεις λογοκρισίας.

Για το λόγο αυτό, εφόσον έχετε βιώσει κάποιου είδους διαδικτυακού ελέγχου ή λογοκρισίας σε πανελλαδικό, εταιρικό, πανεπιστημιακό, οικογενειακό κ.λπ. περιβάλλον και επιθυμείτε να βοηθήσετε στην παρούσα έρευνα, παρακαλώ αναγράψτε στο κατάλληλο πεδίο παρακάτω ένα email επικοινωνίας.

Η όποια πιθανή μελλοντική επικοινωνία με το ερευνητικό μας team θα είναι για συμπληρωματικές ερωτήσεις σχετικά με την εμπειρία σας, ενώ και σε αυτή την περίπτωση θα διατηρήσετε την ανωνυμία σας.

Email Επικοινωνιασ:

APPENDIX 8: INTERVIEW WITH DR. RICHARD CLAYTON

As it was mentioned in the Acknowledgements, Dr. Richard Clayton of Cambridge University Computer Laboratory accepted my invitation for an interview from the very beginning of my research. But, as he was able to answer my inquiries almost immediately, soon the interview transformed to a discussion via emails. As it is a common thing for academics to computer related fields, his answers were with few words and to the point. Below is a part of our discussion.

Email Exchange 1

From: nkoumartzis@hotmail.com
Sent: Sunday, July 06, 2008 5:05:58 PM
To: richard.clayton@cl.cam.ac.uk;

Dear Dr. R. Clayton,

my name is Nikolaos Koumartzis and I am currently a MA student in London College of Communication (University of the Arts London). At the present, I am conducting a research on various levels regarding Cleanfeed software and online censorship in UK as part of my dissertation.

Due to the fact that my first degree is on Computer Science (4year undergraduate course in Aristotle University of Thessaloniki, Greece), I strongly believe that I have to focus equally on technical terms of Cleanfeed, apart from design and ethical issues.

So, I have made an initial online research and I found a technical report of yours (Anonymity and traceability on cyberspace), partly focused on Cleanfeed too. I would like to ask you if you can exchange a couple of emails with me, answering some questions focusing on the technical aspects of Cleanfeed and technical improvements of the current software.

The interview method that I am proposing to use is that: an initial email with all my questions (you can propose a maximum number of questions concerning your time) and then, after your initial answers, I will send you a second email with a couple of additional questions or request for more clarification on some parts.

I hope to get an answer from you, even if you don't have the time to help me out (just saying that). Moreover, please inform me if you know any other experts/ academics/ etc. who have conducted research on Cleanfeed in the past.

If you accept my proposal for an interview via emails, it will take place during the second half of August. If you don't have free time then or if you are on vacation, we can conduct the interview during the first half of September (or you can suggest a different time, more suitable to you).

Best Regards,
Nikolaos Koumartzis,
MA Publishing course, LCC.

P.S. I have attached my research proposal, in case you want to know more about my research.

From: richard@highwayman.com
Sent: Sunday, July 06, 2008 5:29:06 PM
To: nkoumartzis@hotmail.com

In message <BAY111-W390F91A3458A8BC4441FCFBA950@phx.gbl>, =?iso-8859-7?B?zenq/Oth7/Igyu/1P2Hx9Obe8g==?= <nkoumartzis@hotmail.com> writes
> So, I have made an initial online research and I found a
> technical report of yours (Anonymity and traceability on
> cyberspace), partly focused on Cleanfeed too. I would like to ask
> you if you can exchange a couple of emails with me, answering some
> questions focusing on the technical aspects of Cleanfeed
up to a point, BT say that my description is mainly accurate, but not entirely so
> and
> technical improvements of the current software.
I recommend reading
http://www.cl.cam.ac.uk/~rnc1/takedown.pdf

Email Exchange 2

From: richard@highwayman.com
Sent: Thursday, August 21, 2008 3:12:17 AM
To: nkoumartzis@hotmail.com

In message <BAY111-W2685B5D11D7A24B70A8A1BA680@phx.gbl>, =?iso-
8859-7?B?zenq/Oth7/Igyu/1P2Hx9Obe8g==?= <nkoumartzis@hotmail.com> writes
> P.S. Regarding my research, right now I am trying to get in touch
> with someone inside IWF (Internet Watch Foundation)
Peter Robbins <peter@iwf.org.uk>
> or Cleanfeed
> software team,
sorry, no
>in case you have some related contacts.
>
> Connect to the next generation of MSN Messenger Get it now!
>
>[A MIME application / msword part was included here.]
Dr. R. Clayton
Cambridge University
Initial Questions:

1. First of all, I read in one of your papers that you have

managed to use Cleanfeed software as an “oracle” in order to extract the list of banned websites. This is a crucial drawback for such a program and so I am interested in replicating this procedure as an “experiment” for my dissertation.

feel free

Of course there will be a full and detailed reference of your job. Can you please explain to me how I can replicate the procedure or point me to a paper or article of yours?

there’s sufficient information in the paper (in fact there’s two techniques described because I attack Brightview). Essentially you just create packets with the right property send them and see what comes back

2. I read in a couple of online articles that Cleanfeed censored

some forums (http://dis.4chan.org/read.php/newpol/1150560346/1-40) that are not hosting intentionally "child abuse" content, but some individual users uploaded such images before moderators could take them down (average time of action: 30 sec). Have you found out such examples; that Cleanfeed censored non "child abuse" website?
no, but I haven't been looking

3. What changes in design terms do you believe that have to be

made to Cleanfeed software in order for it to be more ethically correct? (i.e. message stating that the website is blocked, form for user to fill in in order to unblock the website, etc.)
I don't think blocking is a solution to this problem

4. Is it true that you can overpass Cleanfeed with the use of

really simple tools such as a proxy?
yes (provided the proxy is not itself blocked)

5. What changes in technical terms do you believe that must be

made to Cleanfeed software in order for it to be more stable and secure? (not being easy to overpass it or use it as an oracle, etc.)
the oracle comes from it being a two-stage system. One stage systems are expensive and impractical

6. Is it true that many of the technical and design weaknesses of

Cleanfeed are due to financial issues?
I doubt it -- they hadn't considered the oracle attack, as for the other evasion issues; they knew about these but did not care.

7. Is it true that many ISP providers with limited financial

sources can't afford using Cleanfeed, because of the installation's high cost?
Yes, they've tended to go for DNS poisoning as a result.

What is the solution to this problem?
<URL:http://www.cartoonstock.com/blowup_stock.asp?imageref=sea0568&artist=Eales,+Stan&topic=money+tree+>

Email Exchange 3

From: richard@highwayman.com
Sent: Thursday, August 28, 2008 6:47:37 AM
To: nkoumartzis@hotmail.com

> 1. In your previous answers, you stated that many ISPs goes for DNS
> poisoning because of the high cost of CleanFeed implementation. Can
> you give me some specific examples of ISPs or some sources for that
> conclusion?
I suggest you read the Pennsylvania case from the US

> 2. In the 3rd questions of my first questions you said that you
> don't think blocking is a solution to online child abuse content.
> What would be a solution from your point of view?
remove the websites -- almost no ISPs are interested in hosting them
those that are can be prosecuted as well

> 3. At the page 139 of your technical report, you mention the case
> of Ashcroft v Free Speech Coalition in USA.
> Are you aware of any other cases regarding online blocking,
> existing blocking systems and/ or child abuse content?
cases no, but I am not a lawyer

Email Exchange 4

From: richard@highwayman.com
Sent: Wednesday, September 17, 2008 5:06:06 PM
To: nkoumartzis@hotmail.com

>1. After the publication of your technical paper, IWF and BT spokesmen stated
>that CleanFeed doesn't focus on determined paidophiles and advanced internet
>users. What your opinion about that?

I think they meant that they accepted it was easy to evade if you were determined to do so.

>If a content provider circumvent CleanFeed,

>then a user doesn't need to be neither determined nor to have advanced computer

>knownledge.

correct

>2. Is there a countermeasure if a content provider uses mirroring to circumvent

>CleanFeed system?

block the mirror ... this of course doesn't work for fast-flux hosting on botnets

>I hope you find the time to answer to those last questions. Thanks again for

>your time and your will.

APPENDIX 9: INTERVIEW WITH DR. PHIL ARCHER

1. First of all, are you aware of Cleanfeed software and its use by UK government and BT?

Yes, very aware of it. The person who instigated it at BT is someone I know. It's something that BT did by choice, not because the government asked them to. It is bad for business and brand image if your users are accessing illegal material, hence, it makes sense for BT to have brought this in. It takes just 5 servers to run the system for the whole of BT.

The majority of UK ISPs now operate CleanFeed or some other system that blocks access to sites on the IWF list. AS I'd like to emphasise, it's entirely voluntary – for now. However… if the few remaining ISPs (5% I think it is) do not start blocking access to the IWF list voluntarily, it's likely to become law that they have to. Illegal material is illegal however you get it, so blocking access is not a major change in the law.

2. Has FOSI ever been asked for Cleanfeed before its implementation?

I one had a brief e-mail exchange with (IWF CEO) Peter Robinson asking whether we had a method of blocking sites on their list,. We didn't so we didn't take it any further.

3. Does FOSI have any kind of relationship with Cleanfeed or Internet Watch Foundation (IWF)?

Formally, no – although we used to. IWF, under its founding CEO, David Kerr, was instrumental in setting up ICRA (which was renamed FOSI in 2006). I see Peter at many functions and a lot of our members are also IWF members but there's no formal relationship.

4. Do you agree with the use of such a piece of "silent censorship" software in UK?

In this specific area, yes. Anything that hinders the production and spread of images of child abuse has my full support. I guess the only argument is whether it should be more transparent – should you know that you've been blocked from a site because it contains illegal material. Possibly, but doing so would, of course, advertise its presence and thereby potentially serve to encourage circumventing CleanFeed (which is pretty easy to get round anyway to be honest).

The are of most concern is 'mission creep.' Might BT and others choose to use CleanFeed to legal but – in someone's eyes – undesirable content. I'm satisfied that this is very unlikely. CleanFeed, as intimated already, and like most online safety measures, is all about brand and business protection. Blocking access to anything beyond the clearly illegal and indefensible (child abuse images being the prime example) would be bad for business.

I'm not sure of the progress made but there's a new law concerning illegal violent (adult) pornography. Websites known to offer that might end up on the IWF list as well – but it's them – the IWF – that create the list, not BT or any other ISP. That's the only way that works commercially. You have an independent organisation that creates one list that everyone uses. You can bet that if there were a site on the IWF list that an ISP thought shouldn't be,. they'd soon get it removed.

5. What kind of actions, methods or tools does FOSI use in order to protect children and families through the internet?

We are still completing a period of transition. We used to offer labelling as a means of enabling filtering. i.e. you have a label on your website that a filter can then use to block or allow access according to user settings. We tried (hard) to make that work but it's never had the support it would need to be effective. it's an idea that gets reinvented every so often with things like the RTA and NSFW tags and politicians like it because it is least like censorship. It's the end user that gets to set the filter.

These days I'm working hard to bring a new metadata platform to the Web that will replace the old PICS system. Called POWDER, it's about recognising resources that meet given criteria or standards. Machine-readable trustmarks like this can help to highlight and promote quality resources. Couple that with user preferences and you get a more personalised, safer online experience. We also work to facilitate the online safety conversation between various organisations, we organise events, offer consultancy and more.

6. Are you using any kind of censorship method for protection reasons? If yes, is it implemented only on personal computers or is it internet based?

No, we don't, and never, been involved with censorship of any kind.

7. In FOSI's website you are stating that you try to protect children and families "without restricting wider online freedom". How do you manage to do this?

See Q5. We exist primarily to serve the interests of our members who you'll see are mostly from the industry. They want to offer their customers the widest possible range of content and services so restrictions on online activity is against their interest. By fostering and promoting good practice within the industry, and by developing systems and standards like POWDER, we believe we can make a contribution to efforts to allow users to enjoy what's available online without themselves or their children getting into danger.

Websites

http://www.rtalabel.org/
http://www.getnetwise.org/blog/2008/07/22/nsfw-tag-the-new-content-rating-for-the-net/
http://www.w3.org/PICS/
http://www.w3.org/2007/powder/
http://www.fosi.org/members

APPENDIX 10: EMAIL EXCHANGE WITH PAUL FORREST HICKMAN

From: nkoumartzis@hotmail.com
Sent: Sunday, September 07, 2008 3:32:43 PM
To: info@archive.org

Dear Sir,

my name is Nikolaos Koumartzis and I am conducting a research concerning CleanFeed content blocking system in UK as a postgraduate researcher at London College of Communication (University of the Arts London). Among the other, I am researching for circumvention techniques based on technical weaknesses of CleanFeed and what countermeasures can be taken in order CleanFeed to be more safe and stable in technical terms.

So, among the easiest circumvention techniques for a user is to use an internet archiving service in order to access older versions of blocked webpages. Currently, CleanFeed blocks only webpages with child abuse content. I would like to ask you 1) if you archiving webpages with this kind of content or you have an examination procedure in order to avoid them, 2) if you are in touch with IWF and CleanFeed software team in any way in order to be informed about IWF's list of blocked websites, 3) if there are any other internet archiving services like yours and 4) what can be done in your opinion in order your service not to be used by users who wants to access this kind of blocked content?

I hope for a reply soon. Thanks in advance for your time and your will to help me.

Best,
Nikolaos Koumartzis,
London College of Communication,
University of the Arts London.

From: paul@archive.org
Sent: Wednesday, September 10, 2008 12:15:57 AM
To: nkoumartzis@hotmail.com

Hello Nikolaos,

Thank you for contacting the Internet Archive. As we have an opt-out system, sometimes we capture pages that are pornographic in nature. As soon as people notify us about this information, we remove it from our Wayback Machine immediately. I have not been in touch with either one of the organizations that you mention, though it's possible other people in the Archive are (though I usually handle these issues, so I doubt

it). As far as I know, we are the only organization who does what we do. I'd be very interested in knowing if there is another. As far as accessing excluded materials, that's not a possibility. The sites are excluded from the Wayback Machine and depending on how it was excluded, that exclusion is not under our control (robots.txt files and such). Even for manual exclusions, that material is completely inaccessible to everyone (including us).

If you have any more questions or concerns, please let me know.

Paul Forrest Hickman
Office Manager
Internet Archive
www.archive.org

APPENDIX 11: EMAIL EXCHANGE WITH PETER ROBBINS

From: nkoumartzis@hotmail.com
Sent: Thursday, August 21, 2008 1:55:36 PM
To: peter@iwf.org.uk

Dear Peter Robbins,

my name is Nikolaos Koumartzis and I am a postgraduate researcher in London College of Communication (University of the Arts). I am conducting a research regarding Cleanfeed, its usage by UK government and BT, its relationship with IWF, its technical and design weaknesses (if any), etc. as part of my dissertation (Online Censorship in UK).

I have already organized interviews with many IT experts, such as Dr. R. Clayton of Cambridge University (many technical papers on Cleanfeed) and P. Archer (Technical Manager of FOSI - Family Online Safety Institute). So, I would like to speak with an expert (IT or something else) inside IWF or close to Cleanfeed software, in order my research to be more objective. Dr R. Clayton proposed me to get in touch with you.

In case you accept my invitation for an interview, it will take via emails sometime between 25th of August and 15th of September (whenever it suits you best). I will send you some initial questions, and I you have a little more time I will send some additional/ complementary based on your initial answers.

I hope for a reply soon.

Best,
Nikolaos Koumartzis,
Ma Publishing,
London College of Communication, University of the Arts London.

From: peter@iwf.org.uk
Sent: Thursday, August 28, 2008 11:43:23 AM
To: nkoumartzis@hotmail.com

Hello Nikolaos,

We receive many requests like this. Regrettably we don't have the resources to respond to interviews and surveys for dissertation purposes. I'm sure you'll be able to find all the information you require about us and the child sexual abuse URL list that we supply to our members on our website.

Good luck with your research.

Peter Robbins OBE, QPM
Chief Executive
Internet Watch Foundation
www.iwf.org.uk
mailto:peter@iwf.org.uk
t:+44 (0) 1223 237700

APPENDIX 12: EMAIL EXCHANGE WITH GEORGE SIARDOS

Dr. George Siardos, Emeritus Professor of Dept. Statistics in Aristotle University of Thessaloniki, helped me a lot to understand what kind of statistical analysis should I conduct to survey's results.

In this Appendix is part of the theory he shared with me for the needs of my research.

[Email 1]

Ακριβείς έλεγχοι

Χρησιμοποιούνται όταν το μέγεθος του δείγματος είναι μικρό, όταν οι διασταυρούμενοι πίνακες εμφανίζονται με διάσπαρτα δεδομένα ή με πολλά κενά στα φατνία τους, ή τα φατνία φέρουν πολλές τιμές που ταυτίζονται (ύπαρξη δεσμών) ή είναι μη ισορροπημένα ως προς την κατανομή των τιμών τους. Η ασυμπτωτική μέθοδος υπολογισμού του χ^2 ή των λοιπών μη παραμετρικών μεθόδων είναι σχεδόν αδύναμη να δώσει αξιόπιστα αποτελέσματα, γι' αυτό και στις περιπτώσεις αυτές υπολογίζεται το επίπεδο στατιστικής σημαντικότητας με βάση την ακριβή κατανομή του διερευνούμενου στατιστικού, χωρίς την ανάγκη να βασίζεται κανείς στις αναγκαίες υποθέσεις (Siegel, 1956: 96-104, Mehta and Patel/SPSS, 1996).

Η μέθοδος του ακριβούς ελέγχου (exact test) και η προσεγγιστική με αυτήν μέθοδος Monte Carlo (Mehta and Patel/SPSS, 1996) χρησιμοποιούνται για την απόκτηση αποτελεσμάτων ως προς την ακρίβεια, ή όταν τα δεδομένα αδυνατούν να ικανοποιήσουν οποιαδήποτε από τις υποθέσεις που είναι αναγκαίες για την απόκτηση αξιόπιστων αποτελεσμάτων τα οποία θα μπορούσαν να ληφθούν με την εφαρμογή των ασυμπτωτικών ελέγχων (π.χ. του κλασικού ελέγχου με το χ^2) - Cochran, 1954, Fisher, 1925, 1935, Kendall and Stuart, 1979, Mehta and Patel, 1996 και Mehta and Paton/SPSS Inc., 1996.

Μολονότι τα αποτελέσματα με ακριβή έλεγχο είναι πάντοτε αξιόπιστα, μερικές ομάδες δεδομένων είναι τόσο μεγάλες για την εφαρμογή του ακριβούς ελέγχου στον υπολογισμό της τιμής του p, ούτε όμως, από την άλλη, πληρούν τις αναγκαίες προϋποθέσεις για την εφαρμογή ασυμπτωτικής μεθόδου. Στην περίπτωση αυτή η μέθοδος Monte Carlo παρέχει μια ανεπηρέαστη εκτίμηση της ακριβούς τιμής p χωρίς, ωστόσο, τις απαιτήσεις της ασυμπτωτικής μεθόδου.

Η μέθοδος Monte Carlo είναι μια επαναληπτική μέθοδος δειγματοληψίας. Για οποιονδήποτε πίνακα υπάρχουν πολλοί παρόμοιοι πίνακες, ο καθένας με τις ίδιες διαστάσεις και με τα ίδια αθροίσματα σειρών και στηλών με εκείνα του εξεταζόμενου. Με τη μέθοδο Monte Carlo λαμβάνεται, ύστερα από μεγάλο αριθμό επαναλήψεων, δείγμα ορισμένου αριθμού από τους παραπάνω πίνακες, ώστε να αποκτηθεί μια ανεπηρέαστη εκτίμηση της ακριβούς τιμής p. Ο υπολογισμός ξεκινά με κάποιο πολύ μεγάλο τυχαίο ακέραιο αριθμό επαναλήψεων, μεγέθους διαφορετικού κάθε φορά που ξεκινά κάποια ανάλυση.

Βιβλιογραφία

Fisher, R.A. 1925. Statistical methods for research workers. Edinburgh: Oliver and Boyd.

Fisher, R.A. 1935. The design of experiments. Edinburgh: Oliver and Boyd.

Hinkle, D.E., W. Wiersna, and S. Jurs. 1979. Applied Statistics for Behavioral Sciences. Rand Mc Nally College Publishing Co., Chicago.

Mehta, C.R. and N.R. Patel/SPSS. 1996. SPSS Exact Tests 7.0 for Windows. SPSS Inc. Chicago

Siegel, Sidney. 1956. Nonparametric Statistics for the Behavioral Sciences. Mc Graw-Hill Kogakusha Ltd., Tokyo.

Snedecor, G. and W.G. Cochran. 1974. Statistical Methods, 6th ed., The Iowa State University Press, Ames, Iowa.

SPSS, 2003. SPSS Users Guide 12.0. SPSS Inc., Chicago Press.

[Email 2]

Έλεγχος ανεξαρτησίας των κριτηρίων κατάταξης - έλεγχος χ^2

Χρησιμοποιείται για τη σύγκριση μεταξύ δύο μεταβλητών οι οποίες διακρίνονται σε κατηγορίες ποιοτικών μεταβλητών. Ο έλεγχος αυτός αφορά σε δεδομένα που έχουν καταχωρηθεί σε πίνακες διαστάσεων RXC και αποσκοπεί στη διερεύνηση ύπαρξης στατιστικά σημαντικής σχέσης μεταξύ των κριτηρίων κατατάξεως (Siegel, 1956: 104-110 και SPSS, 2003:ch.34).

Ύστερα από την καταχώρηση των δεδομένων σε πίνακες, οι σχετικοί υπολογισμοί γίνονται με τη χρησιμοποίηση της σχέσης:

$$\chi^2 = \frac{\left(O_i - E_i\right)^2}{E_i}$$

όπου: O_i = οι συχνότητες που παρατηρήθηκαν στα φατνία
E_i = οι θεωρητικές (αναμενόμενες) συχνότητες.

Οι τιμές του χ^2 που προκύπτουν από την παραπάνω σχέση σε κάθε περίπτωση, αξιολογούνται από ειδικούς πίνακες ως προς το επίπεδο της στατιστικής τους σημαντικότητας P και για τους αντίστοιχους βαθμούς ελευθερίας Β.Ε.= (R-1)(C-1), όπου R=αριθμός σειρών και C= αριθμός στηλών.

Βιβλιογραφία

Siegel, Sidney. 1956. Nonparametric Statistics for the Behavioral Sciences. Mc Graw-Hill Kogakusha Ltd., Tokyo.

SPSS, 2003. SPSS Users Guide 12.0. SPSS Inc., Chicago Press.

[Email 3]

Έλεγχος Kruskal-Wallis

Είναι μη παραμετρικός έλεγχος που χρησιμοποιείται για τη διακρίβωση κατά πόσο διάφορα (περισσότερα των δύο) ανεξάρτητα δείγματα που έχουν μετρηθεί σε τακτική κλίμακα προέρχονται από τον ίδιο πληθυσμό (SPSS, 2003:ch 34).

Ο έλεγχος αυτός είναι προέκταση του ελέγχου Mann-Whitney, αντίστοιχος του ελέγχου της μονόδρομης ανάλυσης της διακύμανσης και ελέγχει διαφορές μεταξύ των ομάδων των παρατηρήσεων. Ο έλεγχος βασίζεται στο επίπεδο στατιστικής σημαντικότητας της τιμής χ^2, κατανομή την οποία ακολουθούν οι παρατηρήσεις και το οποίο επίπεδο σημαντικότητας συγκρίνεται με το θεωρητικό α=0,05. Σε περίπτωση όπου ο έλεγχος αυτός δείξει σημαντικότητα, η διαδικασία συνεχίζεται με τον έλεγχο Mann-Whitney κατά τον οποίο ελέγχονται οι μέσες τακτικές τιμές των παρατηρήσεων των ομάδων ανά δύο.

Έλεγχος των Mann-Whitney

Χρησιμοποιείται για τη διακρίβωση του βαθμού κατά τον οποίο δύο ανεξάρτητα δείγματα (ομάδες) προέρχονται από τον ίδιο πληθυσμό. (SPSS, 2003:ch 34).

Είναι μη παραμετρικός έλεγχος για τη διακρίβωση κατά πόσο δύο ανεξάρτητες ομάδες παρατηρήσεων που έχουν μετρηθεί σε τακτική κλίμακα προέρχονται από τον ίδιο πληθυσμό. Κατ' αυτόν οι παρατηρήσεις και των δύο ομάδων συνδυάζονται και λαμβάνουν τακτικές τιμές και ο έλεγχος βασίζεται στο επίπεδο στατιστικής σημαντικότητας της τιμής U (των διαφορών των μέσων τακτικών τιμών) το οποίο συγκρίνεται με το θεωρητικό α=0,05.

APPENDIX 13: 2007 UK SURVEY, QUESTION 24'S RESPONSES

Table 1. 24. What changes (in every aspect) would like to see regarding Cleanfeed and its usage?

1	As well as a message stating that the website is blocked, some indication of the reason why it is blocked would be helpful.
2	more info about it
3	Should precise the reason for the website being not available instead of mentioning website not available.
4	I think before commenting I would want to know what is the logic behind the decision that Cleanfeed should not show that the site has been censored. Perhaps there is a good reason why in this case they do not want to state that a website is blocked? WIthout knowing this, it is impossible to comment reasonably.
5	I would like to know that a website is censored, and preferably also why.
6	Cleanfeed should cease. If people choose to seek out and view illegal material such as child abusive pornography or terrorist training, there are other ways of combating and tracing them as recently reported in several high profile cases by the media. Cleanfeed is open to abuse by the powers that be (governments and other organizations). What exactly do they NOT want us to see and why? Cleanfeed software and its use should be made known to the general public and on line users. Most people are unaware that the state is censoring their activity and what they can access. My concern is that Cleanfeed software is not just used to filter out child porn, but may be being used for other more sinister purposes by parties unknown.
7	Reasons should be given as to why a particular Website has been blocked.
8	I want it stopped
9	a message saying something like - 'this page you are trying to access has been censored or blocked by UK government, IT program called Cleanfeed'
10	If a site is blocked, there should be a clear reason why this is the case. This would then provide a much better basis for any request to unblock the site. It would also, incidentally, provide information if one is taken to the site by sleath or deceit. It is also not clear whether any record is kept of those who try to access these sites. If there is, this should be made very clear.
11	it is not needed!!! we should try to educate people to be against child abuse!!! not manipulate them a politics that UK should try in a lot of domains!!!!
12	Awareness amongst the public of the use of Cleanfeed should be increaded, perhaps through advertising. Independent researchers and bodeis should be allowed unlimited access to Cleanfeed data and statistics, so that Cleanfeed and it's users (BT) are continuously monitored to make sure Cleanfeed is used ONLY to block child abuse material.
13	the ones ticked above!
14	Blocking of child porn sites is a must. But this software will be used by the government to gain total control of the internet.
15	I personally do not second censorship on the Internet in any way. Even though Cleanfeed is made with honest purposes, I would like it best if none had the ability to block sites. People have their own opinions.
16	If only research is concerned, what BT should do, they should provide special success features on the clean feed software. In this case, this thing won't be spreading among society and researchers will also be able to research into it.
17	I would like to see Cleanfeed being closely monitored and moderated so that censorship does not exceed the set boundaries such that freedom of speech on the internet is null and void.
18	same as question 23

continues on following page

Table 1. Continued

19	More information about it on the UK web. DA.
20	General awareness of the software being used.
21	Do be more open with their monitoring practices and how they block sites. Also to have a strong ethical portfolio that lays out exactly how they go about blocking sites and for what reasons.
22	The use of such software is innapropriate and subject to abuse by government. Existing legal sanctions already exist to target illegal websites through international agreements. Where necessary, hosting companies that host illegal websites can be targeted through the courts (in the UK), or by threatening to block the hosting company at national level where the host is abroad (by modification of the top-level UK DNS servers, if necessary), hence putting it under pressure to remove offending websites. The use of Cleanfeed-type software at ISP level is a potentialy sinister move that could have ramifications far beyond child pornography. ISP's should resist being compelled to implement it. This is the WRONG solution to the problem.
23	Some of the questions are hard to give an accurate answer to, as an approriate choice is not there. For instance, comparing the Cleanfeed system in the UK to Saudi Arabian internet censorship is comparing apples with pears.
24	A more transparent method of informing citizens of UK concerning any unblocking website. Request forms could probably work in UK however I am not sure to what extent they could be taken seriously in order to have an effect on Cleanfeeds policy. If broader and formal surveys could be completed so that they could represent a larger number of UK citizens who are using the internet on a daily basis and have knowledge on the subject then I would like to see Cleanfeed changing its policy towards a more fair and transparent method of blocking internet content.
25	Be completely shut-down. Every compromise in free-speech should be fought. Child abuse web-sites should be shut down if are based in the UK or diplomatic action should be taken if there are outside the UK.
26	It is comparable to denying that the holocaust ever took place, which is punishable in some countries. Stopping people because they take pleasure in which something the greater public considers unethical is a good approach but from the ashes of this project comes state control. The greater public also considers fundamentalists being a menace but they are free to express their hatred online - better to block those sites. By this premise alone they should drop the whole endeavour because it compromises freedom of speech and information. I trust that law enforcement can do their job with or without Cleanfeed stopping a few pedophiles from accessing their past time leisure. They are helping a few to the detriment of many.
27	From an ISP point of view I would like to see it being easier to use Cleanfeed rather than having to spend large amounts of money to use it which means all people wanting to view child abuse/etc needs to do is find an ISP with limited finances/small subscriber numbers to bypass Cleanfeed in the future.
28	give access based on a " request form " that will be reivised by a third party authourity [a trasted organisation]
29	I think your questions are leading. This survey is not impartial. People that do not know about Cleanfeed cannot be expected to give answers to some of these questions.
30	Apart from a message stating that the specific website attempted to be acessed is blocked, I firmly believe that this message should also include a reasonable explanation of the reasons for such blocking.
31	Be better tracked and monitored by legal system, the public should know more about it.

APPENDIX 14: GREECE MASS SURVEY – FULL RESULTS

In this appendix, Greece Mass Survey's full results are being presented through charts and pies.

Following the Greek Survey, this one was designed based on the initial results and feedback (see appendix 15). The Greece Mass Survey was conducted with the aid of many professional Greek journalists, leading to a massive participation. More specific, the new survey was conduced between 27th of February and 2nd of October 2013, gathering 446 respondents.

Demographic Data

As in the surveys mentioned before, the first part includes a series of demographic questions for the participants regarding gender, age, level of education, parenthood, religiosity etc. Below is a brief presentation of this data. The graphs in the original language are shown, with an explanation in English below each image.

Figure 1. Are you male or female? (Greece Mass Survey)

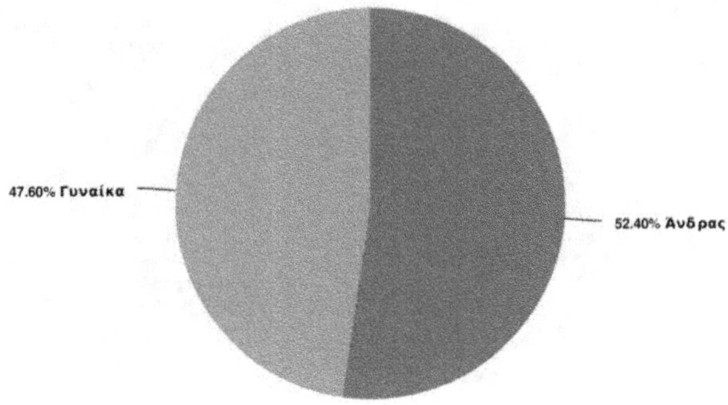

Regarding their gender, 52.4 percent of the respondents were males and 47.6 percent females.

Figure 2. What is your age? (Greece Mass Survey)

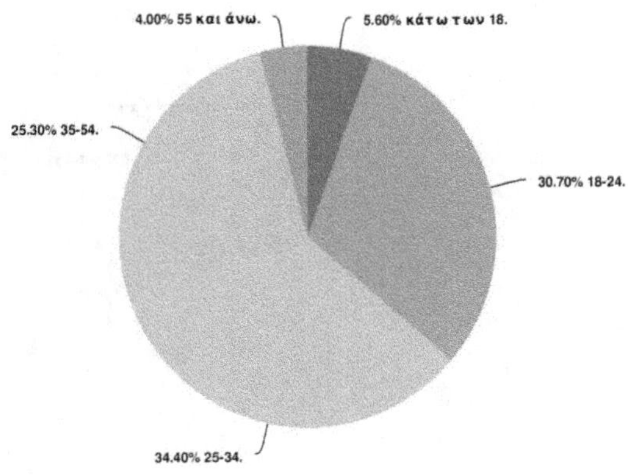

Concerning the age group, 5.6 percent of the participants stated that they were under 18 years old, 30.7 percent between 18 and 24, 34.4 percent were between 25 and 34 years old, 25.3 percent between 35 and 54, and only 4 percent stated that they were less than 18 years old.

Figure 3. What is the highest level of education you have completed? (Greece Mass Survey)

As for the education level, the great majority of the respondents were highly educated with 4.9 percent indicating that they are PhD candidates or graduates, 22.9 percent Master students or graduates, and 49.8 Bachelor students or graduates. Only 15.8 percent stated that they have no kind of higher education.

Figure 4. For how many years are you a Greece based Internet user? (Greece Mass Survey)

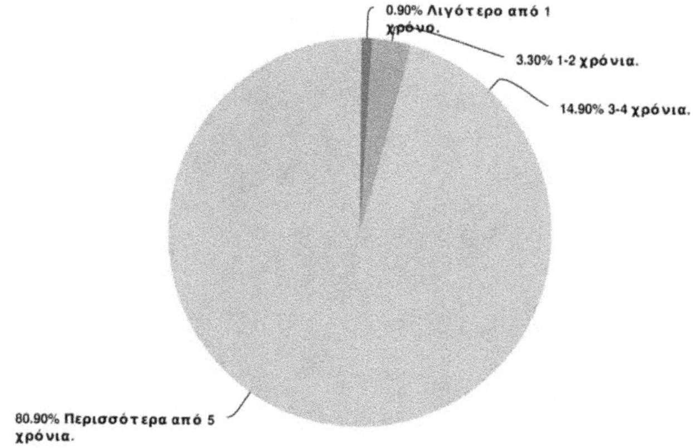

What's more, the vast majority of the respondents (80.9 percent) were Internet users based in Greece for more than 5 years, 14.9 percent 3-4 years, and only 4.2 percent less than 2 years.

Figure 5. Do you consider yourself a religious man? (Greece Mass Survey)

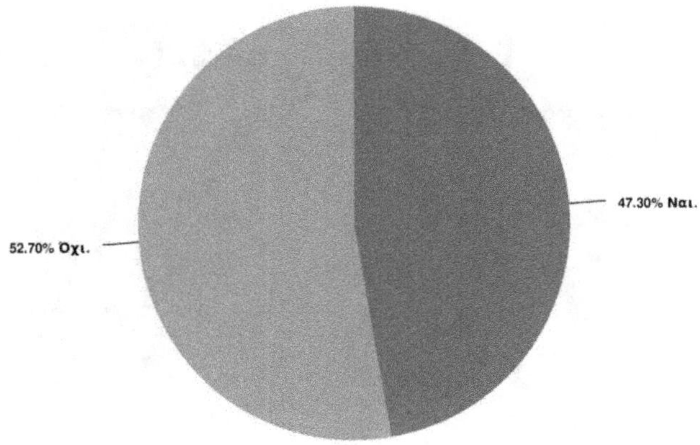

Regarding religiosity, the slight majority of the participants stated non-religious (52.7 percent), and 47.3 percent stated religious.

Figure 6. Do you have/ intent to have children? (Greece Mass Survey)

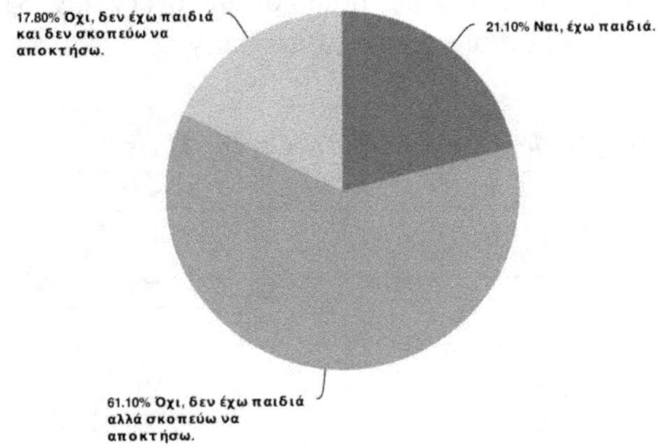

Concerning parenthood, the majority of the respondents stated they intent to have children in the future (61.1 percent), 21.1 percent were already parents, and only 17.8 percent stated that they don't want to have children in the future.

Figure 7. Approximately how many hours do you spend on Internet every day? (Greece Mass Survey)

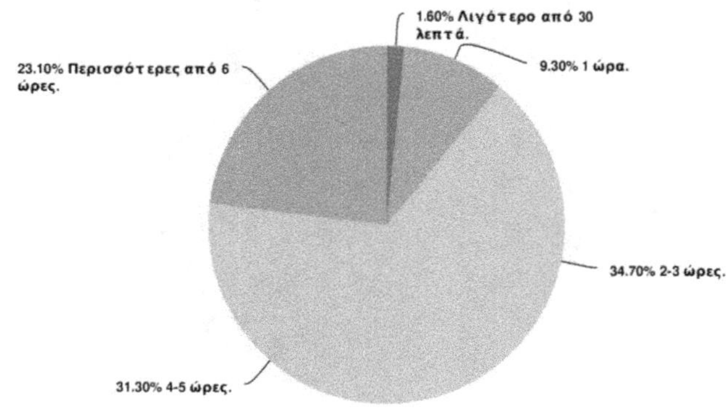

Another question was about how many hours the participants spend online daily. Only 1.6 percent stated that they stay online for less than 30 minutes daily, and 9.3 percent from 30 minutes to 1 hour. The vast majority of the participants (89.1 percent) stated that they spend from 2 up to 6+ hours online in a daily basis. More specific, 34.7 percent of the respondents stated that they spend approximately 2-3 hours online every day, 31.3 percent 4-5 hours, and 23.1 percent more than 6 hours daily.

Figure 8. What are you doing on Internet? (Greece Mass Survey)

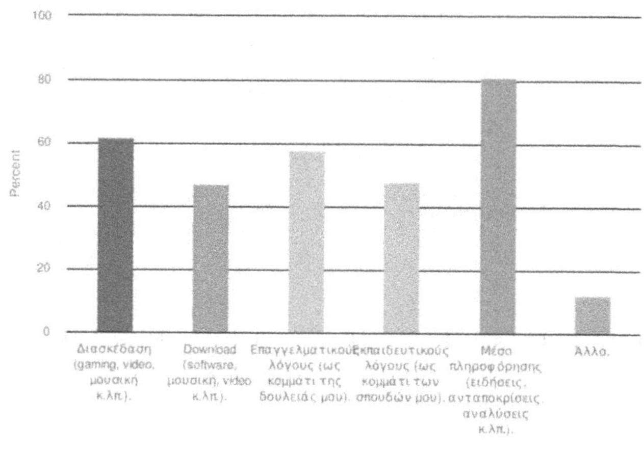

A question was included regarding their activities online, where 81.1 percent stated they use the Internet as a means of information (reading news etc.), 61.8 percent for fun (gaming, video, music etc.), 57.8 percent for professional reasons, 48 percent for educational reasons, and 47.3 for downloading data (software, music, videos etc.).

Greek Internet Users and Internet Regulation Policies

Except the aforementioned demographic-related questions, the authors included a series of related inquiries regarding their research topic.

Figure 9. Are you aware of the global phenomenon of Internet regulation? (Greece Mass Survey)

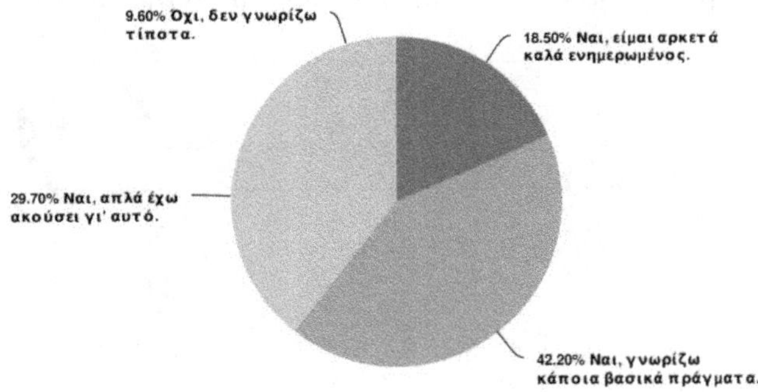

A question of major significance was "Are you aware of the global phenomenon of Internet regulation?", in which most of the respondents stated that they know the basics (42.2 percent), 18.5 percent that they are well-informed, and 29.7 percent thatthey just heard about it. Only 9.6 percent stated that they haven't heard anything related before.

Regarding the means of their information, it is worth-mentioning that the vast majority of the participants (94.2 percent) read about it online, 17.5 percent via television broadcasts, 15.4 percent through "Newspapers" and 10.7 percent via specialized magazines.

Concerning the source of information, 57 percent of the respondents stated that they get informed through journalists' work, 54.8 percent through statements by related organizations, 49.4 percent through discussion with individuals, and 33.8 percent through specialized researchers. Only 13.2

Figure 10. What were the means of your information? (Greece Mass Survey)

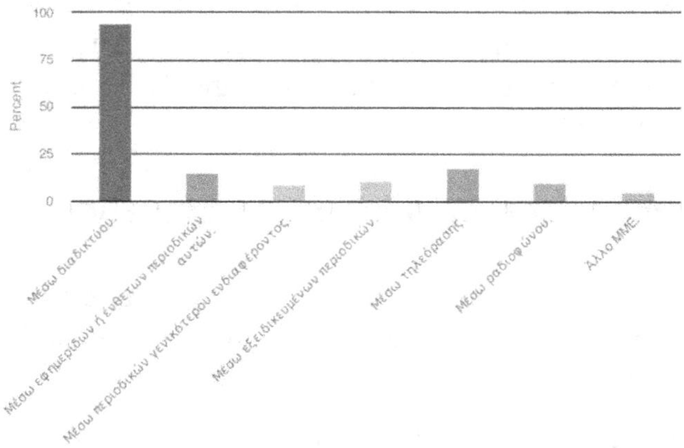

Figure 11. Who was the source of your information? (Greece Mass Survey)

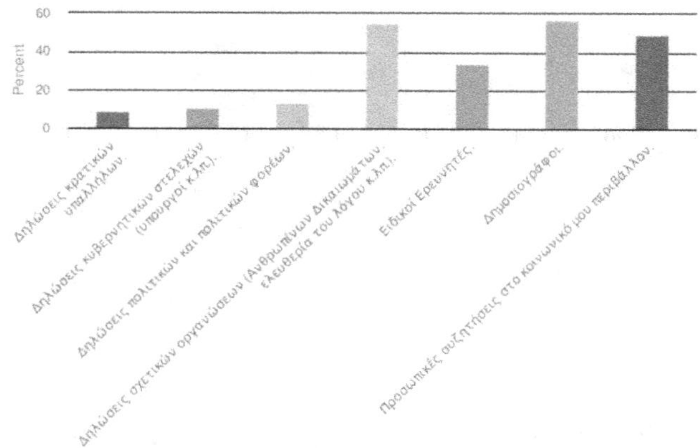

percent stated that they were informed via statements by politicians or related entities, and 10.6 through state representatives' statements.

Another interesting question was "Have you ever faced online censorship in the past?". 18.6 percent stated "Yes, at least once", 50.3 percent "No" and 31.1 percent "I don't know".

From those who answered "Yes, at least once" in the previous question, 57.1 percent stated that they were using the Internet in Greece and they were trying to visit a Greek website, and 25.6 percent stated that they were using the Internet in Greece.

Figure 12. Have you ever faced online censorship in the past? (Greece Mass Survey)

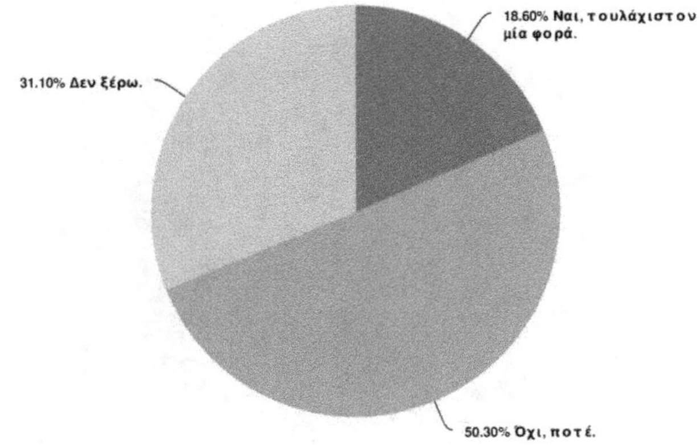

Figure 13. Were you using the Internet from Greece? (Greece Mass Survey)

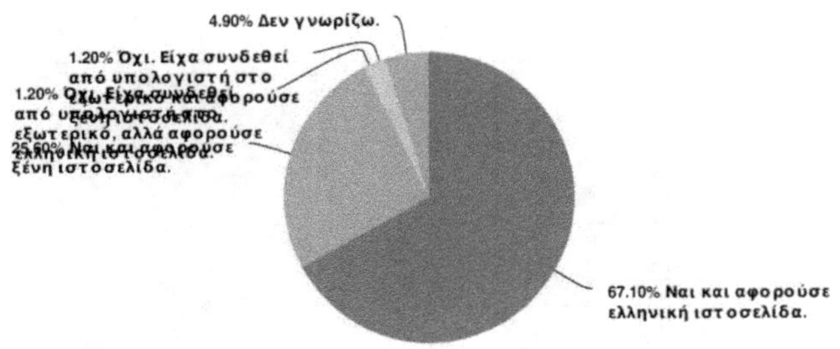

Are Internet Users Keen to Accept the Implementation of Internet Regulation System in Greece?

The last part of this questionnaire focused on the possibility of an Internet Regulation System implementation in Kosovo, and under which conditions.

This question was the main one of this survey: "Do you agree with the implementation of an Internet regulation system by the state focusing on illegal content of highly sensitive issues (child pornography, hate-speech and pro-terrorists websites etc.?". 83.7 percent of the participants were positive (60.8 percent stated "Yes", and 22.9 percent stated "Yes, but only under conditions"), while only 16.3 percent were negative (stating "No").

Figure 14. Do you agree with the implementation of an Internet regulation system by the state focusing on illegal content? (Greece Mass Survey)

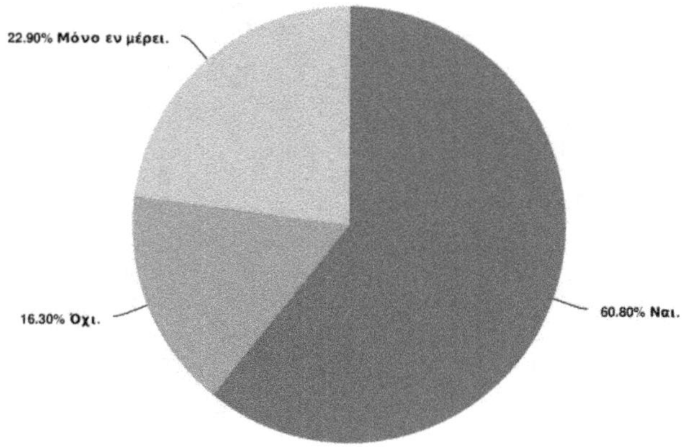

Figure 15. What kind of content should be regulated if your country's state decide to implement such a system? (Greece Mass Survey)

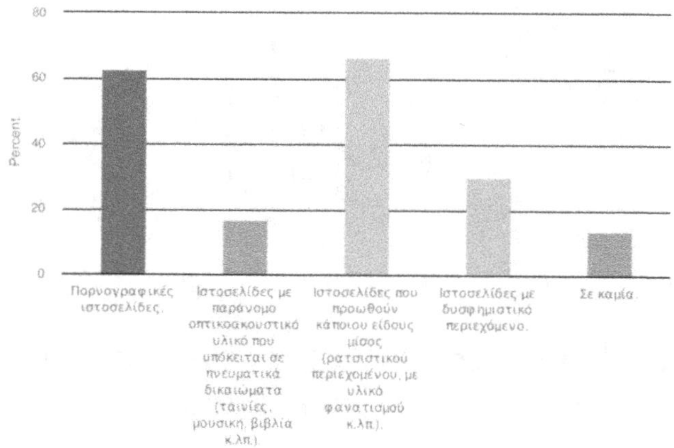

Regarding the type of online content that a Greek IRS should regulate, 66.7 percent stated "hate speech content", 62.6 "pornographic content", 30.1 percent "defamatory content", and 16.6 percent "copyrighted multimedia content". On the other hand, only 13.4 percent of the respondents stated that "no type of content" should be regulated.

Figure 16. In case an Internet regulation system is implemented in Greece, from whom do you believe it must be operated in order to function with justice and to be accepted by the majority of [you country] citizens? (Greece Mass Survey)

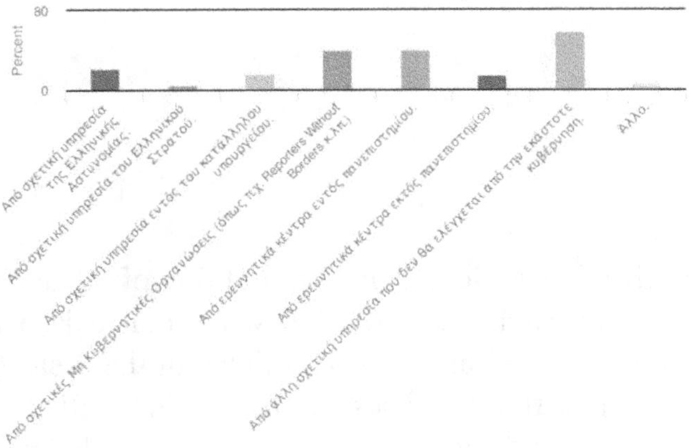

Last, concerning the entity that they prefer to be in-control of such an IRS, 57.6 percent stated "public service not related with the government", 40.5 percent "related non-governmental organization (Reporters without Borders etc.), 40.5 percent "university-based research institutes", 21.7 percent "Hellenic Police related service", and 14.1 percent "non university-based research institutes". Only 16.1 percent of the participants stated "related Ministry's public agency".

Related Readings

To continue IGI Global's long-standing tradition of advancing innovation through emerging research, please find below a compiled list of recommended IGI Global book chapters and journal articles in the areas of censorship, democracy, and online filtering. These related readings will provide additional information and guidance to further enrich your knowledge and assist you with your own research.

Abaya, A. S. (2016). A Critical Political Discourse Analysis of President Goodluck Jonathan's Declaration of State of Emergency on Adamawa, Borno, and Yobe States of Nigeria. In D. Orwenjo, O. Oketch, & A. Tunde (Eds.), *Political Discourse in Emergent, Fragile, and Failed Democracies* (pp. 165–177). Hershey, PA: IGI Global. doi:10.4018/978-1-5225-0081-0.ch009

Adeyanju, A. (2016). Symbols and Not Manifestoes Are the Selling Point Here: A Multimodal Critical Discourse Analysis of Two Contemporary Nigerian Political Parties' Images and Slogans. In D. Orwenjo, O. Oketch, & A. Tunde (Eds.), *Political Discourse in Emergent, Fragile, and Failed Democracies* (pp. 265–285). Hershey, PA: IGI Global. doi:10.4018/978-1-5225-0081-0.ch015

Adikpo, J. A. (2019). Fake Online News: Rethinking News Credibility for the Changing Media Environment. In I. Chiluwa & S. Samoilenko (Eds.), *Handbook of Research on Deception, Fake News, and Misinformation Online* (pp. 152–166). Hershey, PA: IGI Global. doi:10.4018/978-1-5225-8535-0.ch010

Adria, M., Messinger, P. R., Andrews, E. A., & Ehresman, C. (2020). Participedia as a Ground for Dialogue. In M. Adria (Ed.), *Using New Media for Citizen Engagement and Participation* (pp. 219–239). Hershey, PA: IGI Global. doi:10.4018/978-1-7998-1828-1.ch012

Ahrari, S., Zaremohzzabieh, Z., & Abu Samah, B. (2017). Influence of Social Networking Sites on Civic Participation in Higher Education Context. In R. Luppicini & R. Baarda (Eds.), *Digital Media Integration for Participatory Democracy* (pp. 66–86). Hershey, PA: IGI Global. doi:10.4018/978-1-5225-2463-2.ch004

Anggraeni, A. (2019). Factors Influencing Gossiping Behavior in Social Chatting Platforms. In I. Chiluwa & S. Samoilenko (Eds.), *Handbook of Research on Deception, Fake News, and Misinformation Online* (pp. 33–44). Hershey, PA: IGI Global. doi:10.4018/978-1-5225-8535-0.ch003

Aririguzoh, S. A. (2019). The Art of Deception in Political Advertising: A Study of Nigeria's 2015 Presidential Election Campaigns. In I. Chiluwa & S. Samoilenko (Eds.), *Handbook of Research on Deception, Fake News, and Misinformation Online* (pp. 349–374). Hershey, PA: IGI Global. doi:10.4018/978-1-5225-8535-0.ch019

Assay, B. E. (2019). Social Media and the Challenges of Curtailing the Spread of Fake News in Nigeria. In I. Chiluwa & S. Samoilenko (Eds.), *Handbook of Research on Deception, Fake News, and Misinformation Online* (pp. 226–263). Hershey, PA: IGI Global. doi:10.4018/978-1-5225-8535-0.ch014

Ayad, S. M., Dunn, R. A., & Marshall, S. W. (2020). Political Advertising Effects on Perceived Bias, Value, and Credibility in Online News. In K. Dalkir & R. Katz (Eds.), *Navigating Fake News, Alternative Facts, and Misinformation in a Post-Truth World* (pp. 184–202). Hershey, PA: IGI Global. doi:10.4018/978-1-7998-2543-2.ch008

Baarda, R. (2017). Digital Democracy in Authoritarian Russia: Opportunity for Participation, or Site of Kremlin Control? In R. Luppicini & R. Baarda (Eds.), *Digital Media Integration for Participatory Democracy* (pp. 87–100). Hershey, PA: IGI Global. doi:10.4018/978-1-5225-2463-2.ch005

Banerjee, S., & Chua, A. Y. (2019). Toward a Theoretical Model of Authentic and Fake User-Generated Online Reviews. In I. Chiluwa & S. Samoilenko (Eds.), *Handbook of Research on Deception, Fake News, and Misinformation Online* (pp. 104–120). Hershey, PA: IGI Global. doi:10.4018/978-1-5225-8535-0.ch007

Bartlett, J. C. (2020). Information Literacy and Science Misinformation. In K. Dalkir & R. Katz (Eds.), *Navigating Fake News, Alternative Facts, and Misinformation in a Post-Truth World* (pp. 1–17). Hershey, PA: IGI Global. doi:10.4018/978-1-7998-2543-2.ch001

Beneventi, P. (2018). *Technology and the New Generation of Active Citizens: Emerging Research and Opportunities* (pp. 1–173). Hershey, PA: IGI Global. doi:10.4018/978-1-5225-3770-0

Bessant, J. (2017). Digital Humour, Gag Laws, and the Liberal Security State. In R. Luppicini & R. Baarda (Eds.), *Digital Media Integration for Participatory Democracy* (pp. 204–221). Hershey, PA: IGI Global. doi:10.4018/978-1-5225-2463-2.ch010

Bhardwaj, A., & Cyphert, D. (2020). Direct Benefit Transfer Using Aadhaar: Improving Transparency and Reducing Corruption. In V. Kumar & G. Malhotra (Eds.), *Examining the Roles of IT and Social Media in Democratic Development and Social Change* (pp. 185–210). Hershey, PA: IGI Global. doi:10.4018/978-1-7998-1791-8.ch008

Blanton, R., & Carbajal, D. (2019). Not a Girl, Not Yet a Woman: A Critical Case Study on Social Media, Deception, and Lil Miquela. In I. Chiluwa & S. Samoilenko (Eds.), *Handbook of Research on Deception, Fake News, and Misinformation Online* (pp. 87–103). Hershey, PA: IGI Global. doi:10.4018/978-1-5225-8535-0.ch006

Camilleri, V., Dingli, A., & Montebello, M. (2017). Empowering Citizens Through Virtual and Alternate Reality. In R. Luppicini & R. Baarda (Eds.), *Digital Media Integration for Participatory Democracy* (pp. 188–203). Hershey, PA: IGI Global. doi:10.4018/978-1-5225-2463-2.ch009

Chajdas, T. (2019). Misleading Media Portrayals in a Globalized World: Justification of State Control Through an Orientalist Lens. In I. Chiluwa & S. Samoilenko (Eds.), *Handbook of Research on Deception, Fake News, and Misinformation Online* (pp. 45–64). Hershey, PA: IGI Global. doi:10.4018/978-1-5225-8535-0.ch004

Chiluwa, I. E. (2019). Deception in Online Terrorist Propaganda: A Study of ISIS and Boko Haram. In I. Chiluwa & S. Samoilenko (Eds.), *Handbook of Research on Deception, Fake News, and Misinformation Online* (pp. 520–537). Hershey, PA: IGI Global. doi:10.4018/978-1-5225-8535-0.ch028

Chiluwa, I. E., Ovia, E., & Uba, E. (2019). "Attention Beneficiary…!": Assessing Types and Features of Scam Emails. In I. Chiluwa & S. Samoilenko (Eds.), *Handbook of Research on Deception, Fake News, and Misinformation Online* (pp. 421–438). Hershey, PA: IGI Global. doi:10.4018/978-1-5225-8535-0.ch022

Chiluwa, I. M. (2019). "Truth," Lies, and Deception in Ponzi and Pyramid Schemes. In I. Chiluwa & S. Samoilenko (Eds.), *Handbook of Research on Deception, Fake News, and Misinformation Online* (pp. 439–458). Hershey, PA: IGI Global. doi:10.4018/978-1-5225-8535-0.ch023

Chimuanya, L., & Igwebuike, E. (2019). "Type Amen" or Perish!: Religious Deception on Facebook. In I. Chiluwa & S. Samoilenko (Eds.), *Handbook of Research on Deception, Fake News, and Misinformation Online* (pp. 503–518). Hershey, PA: IGI Global. doi:10.4018/978-1-5225-8535-0.ch027

Chong, M., & Choy, M. (2020). An Empirically Supported Taxonomy of Misinformation. In K. Dalkir & R. Katz (Eds.), *Navigating Fake News, Alternative Facts, and Misinformation in a Post-Truth World* (pp. 117–138). Hershey, PA: IGI Global. doi:10.4018/978-1-7998-2543-2.ch005

Çömlekçi, M. F. (2020). Combating Fake News Online: Turkish Fact-Checking Services. In K. Dalkir & R. Katz (Eds.), *Navigating Fake News, Alternative Facts, and Misinformation in a Post-Truth World* (pp. 273–289). Hershey, PA: IGI Global. doi:10.4018/978-1-7998-2543-2.ch013

Cook, J. (2019). Understanding and Countering Misinformation About Climate Change. In I. Chiluwa & S. Samoilenko (Eds.), *Handbook of Research on Deception, Fake News, and Misinformation Online* (pp. 281–306). Hershey, PA: IGI Global. doi:10.4018/978-1-5225-8535-0.ch016

Dale, T. (2019). The Fundamental Roles of Technology in the Spread of Fake News. In I. Chiluwa & S. Samoilenko (Eds.), *Handbook of Research on Deception, Fake News, and Misinformation Online* (pp. 122–137). Hershey, PA: IGI Global. doi:10.4018/978-1-5225-8535-0.ch008

Delellis, N. S., & Rubin, V. L. (2020). 'Fake News' in the Context of Information Literacy: A Canadian Case Study. In K. Dalkir & R. Katz (Eds.), *Navigating Fake News, Alternative Facts, and Misinformation in a Post-Truth World* (pp. 89–115). Hershey, PA: IGI Global. doi:10.4018/978-1-7998-2543-2.ch004

Du, J. (2020). Constructing the Internet Panoptic-Fortification: A Legal Study on China's Internet Regulatory Mechanism. In V. Kumar & G. Malhotra (Eds.), *Examining the Roles of IT and Social Media in Democratic Development and Social Change* (pp. 211–249). Hershey, PA: IGI Global. doi:10.4018/978-1-7998-1791-8.ch009

El Gody, A. (2020). Social Networks, Media, and the Egyptian Revolution: Building Democratic Front? In V. Kumar & G. Malhotra (Eds.), *Examining the Roles of IT and Social Media in Democratic Development and Social Change* (pp. 133–155). Hershey, PA: IGI Global. doi:10.4018/978-1-7998-1791-8.ch006

Flores, J. L. (2020). The Politics of Social Media: Mediating Ambivalences in the Era of Political Populism. In V. Kumar & G. Malhotra (Eds.), *Examining the Roles of IT and Social Media in Democratic Development and Social Change* (pp. 22–54). Hershey, PA: IGI Global. doi:10.4018/978-1-7998-1791-8.ch002

Froehlich, T. J. (2020). Ten Lessons for the Age of Disinformation. In K. Dalkir & R. Katz (Eds.), *Navigating Fake News, Alternative Facts, and Misinformation in a Post-Truth World* (pp. 36–88). Hershey, PA: IGI Global. doi:10.4018/978-1-7998-2543-2.ch003

Gachigua, S. G. (2016). Legislating for a De Jure One-Party State in 1982 and "Party Hopping" in 2012: Reconstructing Elite Discourse on Political Parties in Kenya. In D. Orwenjo, O. Oketch, & A. Tunde (Eds.), *Political Discourse in Emergent, Fragile, and Failed Democracies* (pp. 286–305). Hershey, PA: IGI Global. doi:10.4018/978-1-5225-0081-0.ch016

Gambarato, R. R., & Medvedev, S. (2020). ICT and Transmedia Storytelling for Democratic Development in the Russian Political Landscape. In V. Kumar & G. Malhotra (Eds.), *Examining the Roles of IT and Social Media in Democratic Development and Social Change* (pp. 55–91). Hershey, PA: IGI Global. doi:10.4018/978-1-7998-1791-8.ch003

Georges, A. M. (2016). ISIS Rhetoric for the Creation of the Ummah. In D. Orwenjo, O. Oketch, & A. Tunde (Eds.), *Political Discourse in Emergent, Fragile, and Failed Democracies* (pp. 178–198). Hershey, PA: IGI Global. doi:10.4018/978-1-5225-0081-0.ch010

Gow, G. A. (2020). Alternative Social Media for Outreach and Engagement: Considering Technology Stewardship as a Pathway to Adoption. In M. Adria (Ed.), *Using New Media for Citizen Engagement and Participation* (pp. 160–180). Hershey, PA: IGI Global. doi:10.4018/978-1-7998-1828-1.ch009

Grazulis, A., & Rogers, R. (2019). "Ridiculous and Untrue – FAKE NEWS!": The Impact of Labeling Fake News. In I. Chiluwa & S. Samoilenko (Eds.), *Handbook of Research on Deception, Fake News, and Misinformation Online* (pp. 138–151). Hershey, PA: IGI Global. doi:10.4018/978-1-5225-8535-0.ch009

Groshek, J. (2020). Exploring a Methodological Model for Social Media Gatekeeping on Contentious Topics: A Case Study of Twitter Interactions About GMOs. In M. Adria (Ed.), *Using New Media for Citizen Engagement and Participation* (pp. 97–111). Hershey, PA: IGI Global. doi:10.4018/978-1-7998-1828-1.ch006

Guadagno, R. E., & Guttieri, K. (2019). Fake News and Information Warfare: An Examination of the Political and Psychological Processes From the Digital Sphere to the Real World. In I. Chiluwa & S. Samoilenko (Eds.), *Handbook of Research on Deception, Fake News, and Misinformation Online* (pp. 167–191). Hershey, PA: IGI Global. doi:10.4018/978-1-5225-8535-0.ch011

Hage, H., Aïmeur, E., & Guedidi, A. (2020). Understanding the Landscape of Online Deception. In K. Dalkir & R. Katz (Eds.), *Navigating Fake News, Alternative Facts, and Misinformation in a Post-Truth World* (pp. 290–317). Hershey, PA: IGI Global. doi:10.4018/978-1-7998-2543-2.ch014

Heaton, L., & Días da Silva, P. (2020). Civic Engagement in Local Environmental Initiatives: Reaping the Benefits of a Diverse Media Landscape. In M. Adria (Ed.), *Using New Media for Citizen Engagement and Participation* (pp. 16–34). Hershey, PA: IGI Global. doi:10.4018/978-1-7998-1828-1.ch002

Hesketh, K. A. (2020). Spiritualism and the Resurgence of Fake News. In K. Dalkir & R. Katz (Eds.), *Navigating Fake News, Alternative Facts, and Misinformation in a Post-Truth World* (pp. 222–237). Hershey, PA: IGI Global. doi:10.4018/978-1-7998-2543-2.ch010

Hucks, D., Sturtz, T., & Tirabassi, K. (2018). *Fostering Positive Civic Engagement Among Millennials: Emerging Research and Opportunities* (pp. 1–98). Hershey, PA: IGI Global. doi:10.4018/978-1-5225-2452-6

Ingram, D. P. (2019). On the Alert for Share Price Manipulation and Inadvertent Disclosure in Social Media Channels: An Exploratory Investigation of Nordic Companies. In I. Chiluwa & S. Samoilenko (Eds.), *Handbook of Research on Deception, Fake News, and Misinformation Online* (pp. 265–280). Hershey, PA: IGI Global. doi:10.4018/978-1-5225-8535-0.ch015

Inya, O. (2016). Metaphors for Nation and War in Chinua Achebe's Memoir. In D. Orwenjo, O. Oketch, & A. Tunde (Eds.), *Political Discourse in Emergent, Fragile, and Failed Democracies* (pp. 199–219). Hershey, PA: IGI Global. doi:10.4018/978-1-5225-0081-0.ch011

Iwasaki, Y. (2020). Centrality of Youth Engagement in Media Involvement. In M. Adria (Ed.), *Using New Media for Citizen Engagement and Participation* (pp. 81–96). Hershey, PA: IGI Global. doi:10.4018/978-1-7998-1828-1.ch005

Jakaza, E., & Visser, M. W. (2016). Argumentation and Appraisal in Divergent Zimbabwean Parliamentary Debates. In D. Orwenjo, O. Oketch, & A. Tunde (Eds.), *Political Discourse in Emergent, Fragile, and Failed Democracies* (pp. 126–142). Hershey, PA: IGI Global. doi:10.4018/978-1-5225-0081-0.ch007

Kamalu, I. (2016). Politics and Promises: A Multimodal Social Semiotic Interpretation of Political Party Emblems and Slogans as Discourse of Hope in a Democratic Nigeria. In D. Orwenjo, O. Oketch, & A. Tunde (Eds.), *Political Discourse in Emergent, Fragile, and Failed Democracies* (pp. 112–125). Hershey, PA: IGI Global. doi:10.4018/978-1-5225-0081-0.ch006

Kamga, O. (2020). Social Media as Disruptive Technologies in an Era of Fake News: Examining the Efficacy of Social Media in the Shaping of the Political Landscape in Africa. In V. Kumar & G. Malhotra (Eds.), *Examining the Roles of IT and Social Media in Democratic Development and Social Change* (pp. 250–274). Hershey, PA: IGI Global. doi:10.4018/978-1-7998-1791-8.ch010

Kankara, I. S. (2016). Impediments to Nigerian Democracy: Ambivalent Role of Vigilante Groups in Maintaining Security in the Wake of the Boko Haram Insurgence in Northern Nigeria. In D. Orwenjo, O. Oketch, & A. Tunde (Eds.), *Political Discourse in Emergent, Fragile, and Failed Democracies* (pp. 240–251). Hershey, PA: IGI Global. doi:10.4018/978-1-5225-0081-0.ch013

Karandikar, S. (2019). Persuasive Propaganda: An Investigation of Online Deceptive Tactics of Islamist, White, and Zionist Extremists. In I. Chiluwa & S. Samoilenko (Eds.), *Handbook of Research on Deception, Fake News, and Misinformation Online* (pp. 538–555). Hershey, PA: IGI Global. doi:10.4018/978-1-5225-8535-0.ch029

Kiggins, R. (2017). Smartphone Guns Shooting Tweets: Killing the "Other" in Palestine. In R. Luppicini & R. Baarda (Eds.), *Digital Media Integration for Participatory Democracy* (pp. 22–43). Hershey, PA: IGI Global. doi:10.4018/978-1-5225-2463-2.ch002

Kilhoffer, Z. (2020). Platform Work and Participation: Disentangling the Rhetoric. In M. Adria (Ed.), *Using New Media for Citizen Engagement and Participation* (pp. 1–15). Hershey, PA: IGI Global. doi:10.4018/978-1-7998-1828-1.ch001

Kleim, A. J., Eckler, P., & Tonner, A. (2019). "Too Good to Be True": Semi-Naked Bodies on Social Media. In I. Chiluwa & S. Samoilenko (Eds.), *Handbook of Research on Deception, Fake News, and Misinformation Online* (pp. 65–86). Hershey, PA: IGI Global. doi:10.4018/978-1-5225-8535-0.ch005

Klyueva, A. (2019). Trolls, Bots, and Whatnots: Deceptive Content, Deception Detection, and Deception Suppression. In I. Chiluwa & S. Samoilenko (Eds.), *Handbook of Research on Deception, Fake News, and Misinformation Online* (pp. 18–32). Hershey, PA: IGI Global. doi:10.4018/978-1-5225-8535-0.ch002

Knoblock, N. (2016). Sarcasm and Irony as a Political Weapon: Social Networking in the Time of Crisis. In D. Orwenjo, O. Oketch, & A. Tunde (Eds.), *Political Discourse in Emergent, Fragile, and Failed Democracies* (pp. 11–33). Hershey, PA: IGI Global. doi:10.4018/978-1-5225-0081-0.ch002

Külcü, Ö. (2020). Verification of Information and Evaluation of Approaches of Information Professionals in Accessing Accurate Information. In K. Dalkir & R. Katz (Eds.), *Navigating Fake News, Alternative Facts, and Misinformation in a Post-Truth World* (pp. 162–183). Hershey, PA: IGI Global. doi:10.4018/978-1-7998-2543-2.ch007

Kuzio, A. M. (2019). The Role of Deceptive Communication and Gender in Shaping Online Dating Interactions: A Discursive Approach. In I. Chiluwa & S. Samoilenko (Eds.), *Handbook of Research on Deception, Fake News, and Misinformation Online* (pp. 460–474). Hershey, PA: IGI Global. doi:10.4018/978-1-5225-8535-0.ch024

Lacharite, J. R. (2017). Digital Media, Civic Literacy, and Civic Engagement: The "Promise and Peril" of Internet Politics in Canada. In R. Luppicini & R. Baarda (Eds.), *Digital Media Integration for Participatory Democracy* (pp. 44–65). Hershey, PA: IGI Global. doi:10.4018/978-1-5225-2463-2.ch003

Lamphere, R. D., & Lucas, K. T. (2019). Online Romance in the 21st Century: Deceptive Online Dating, Catfishing, Romance Scams, and "Mail Order" Marriages. In I. Chiluwa & S. Samoilenko (Eds.), *Handbook of Research on Deception, Fake News, and Misinformation Online* (pp. 475–488). Hershey, PA: IGI Global. doi:10.4018/978-1-5225-8535-0.ch025

Lata, M., & Gupta, A. (2020). Role of Social Media in Environmental Democracy. In V. Kumar & G. Malhotra (Eds.), *Examining the Roles of IT and Social Media in Democratic Development and Social Change* (pp. 275–293). Hershey, PA: IGI Global. doi:10.4018/978-1-7998-1791-8.ch011

Luoch, T. O. (2016). The Verbal Fuel for Ethnic Hatred and Political Violence in Kenya. In D. Orwenjo, O. Oketch, & A. Tunde (Eds.), *Political Discourse in Emergent, Fragile, and Failed Democracies* (pp. 1–10). Hershey, PA: IGI Global. doi:10.4018/978-1-5225-0081-0.ch001

Luppicini, R. (2017). Technoethics and Digital Democracy for Future Citizens. In R. Luppicini & R. Baarda (Eds.), *Digital Media Integration for Participatory Democracy* (pp. 1–21). Hershey, PA: IGI Global. doi:10.4018/978-1-5225-2463-2.ch001

Mach, L. T. (2019). The Rise of Professional Facebook Content Generators in Vietnam: A Fake News Campaign Against the Betibuti Founder. In I. Chiluwa & S. Samoilenko (Eds.), *Handbook of Research on Deception, Fake News, and Misinformation Online* (pp. 209–225). Hershey, PA: IGI Global. doi:10.4018/978-1-5225-8535-0.ch013

Margaritis, K. (2016). Are We All Equal?: Immunity of Parliament Members and Criminal Responsibility of Cabinet Members in Greece. In D. Orwenjo, O. Oketch, & A. Tunde (Eds.), *Political Discourse in Emergent, Fragile, and Failed Democracies* (pp. 360–372). Hershey, PA: IGI Global. doi:10.4018/978-1-5225-0081-0.ch020

Martin, P. M., & Onampally, J. J. (2019). Patterns of Deceptive Communication of Social and Religious Issues in Social Media: Representation of Social Issues in Social Media. In I. Chiluwa & S. Samoilenko (Eds.), *Handbook of Research on Deception, Fake News, and Misinformation Online* (pp. 490–502). Hershey, PA: IGI Global. doi:10.4018/978-1-5225-8535-0.ch026

Martínez-Ávila, D., Mello, M. R., Borges, E. V., & Ottonicar, S. L. (2020). Behind the Post-Truth World: A Philosophical Perspective on Information and Media Literacy. In K. Dalkir & R. Katz (Eds.), *Navigating Fake News, Alternative Facts, and Misinformation in a Post-Truth World* (pp. 139–161). Hershey, PA: IGI Global. doi:10.4018/978-1-7998-2543-2.ch006

Maulana, I. (2020). Democracy, Technology, and Human Irresponsibility. In V. Kumar & G. Malhotra (Eds.), *Examining the Roles of IT and Social Media in Democratic Development and Social Change* (pp. 1–21). Hershey, PA: IGI Global. doi:10.4018/978-1-7998-1791-8.ch001

Maulana, I. (2020). Social Media as Public Political Instrument. In M. Adria (Ed.), *Using New Media for Citizen Engagement and Participation* (pp. 181–197). Hershey, PA: IGI Global. doi:10.4018/978-1-7998-1828-1.ch010

Moura, M. A., & Tavares de Paula, L. (2020). Cognitive Authority, Accountability, and the Anatomy of Lies: Experiments to Detect Fake News in Digital Environments. In K. Dalkir & R. Katz (Eds.), *Navigating Fake News, Alternative Facts, and Misinformation in a Post-Truth World* (pp. 259–272). Hershey, PA: IGI Global. doi:10.4018/978-1-7998-2543-2.ch012

Mpiima, D. M. (2016). Multilayered Political Systems and the Politics of Monitoring Local Government Programmes for Engendered Service Delivery: A Case of Apac District in Northern Uganda. In D. Orwenjo, O. Oketch, & A. Tunde (Eds.), *Political Discourse in Emergent, Fragile, and Failed Democracies* (pp. 220–239). Hershey, PA: IGI Global. doi:10.4018/978-1-5225-0081-0.ch012

Musiyiwa, M., & Visser, M. W. (2016). Of Drag and Push Democracies: The Construction of Zimbabwe as a Failed-Partially Resuscitated State in Popular Songs. In D. Orwenjo, O. Oketch, & A. Tunde (Eds.), *Political Discourse in Emergent, Fragile, and Failed Democracies* (pp. 34–60). Hershey, PA: IGI Global. doi:10.4018/978-1-5225-0081-0.ch003

Nielsen, G. (2020). Populism, Fake News, and the Flight From Democracy. In K. Dalkir & R. Katz (Eds.), *Navigating Fake News, Alternative Facts, and Misinformation in a Post-Truth World* (pp. 238–257). Hershey, PA: IGI Global. doi:10.4018/978-1-7998-2543-2.ch011

Noor, R. (2020). Citizen Journalism: New-Age Newsgathering. In M. Adria (Ed.), *Using New Media for Citizen Engagement and Participation* (pp. 135–159). Hershey, PA: IGI Global. doi:10.4018/978-1-7998-1828-1.ch008

Nyam, E. (2016). Revolutionary Politics and Theater of Semiotics: Challenges and Solutions in Northern Nigeria. In D. Orwenjo, O. Oketch, & A. Tunde (Eds.), *Political Discourse in Emergent, Fragile, and Failed Democracies* (pp. 349–359). Hershey, PA: IGI Global. doi:10.4018/978-1-5225-0081-0.ch019

Olajimbiti, E. (2019). The Pragmatics of Political Deception on Facebook. In I. Chiluwa & S. Samoilenko (Eds.), *Handbook of Research on Deception, Fake News, and Misinformation Online* (pp. 308–325). Hershey, PA: IGI Global. doi:10.4018/978-1-5225-8535-0.ch017

Olivera, M. N., & Cogo, D. (2017). Transnational Activism of Young Spanish Emigrants and Uses of ICT. In R. Luppicini & R. Baarda (Eds.), *Digital Media Integration for Participatory Democracy* (pp. 155–187). Hershey, PA: IGI Global. doi:10.4018/978-1-5225-2463-2.ch008

Oluwole, J. O., & Green, P. C. III. (2016). *Censorship and Student Communication in Online and Offline Settings* (pp. 1–622). Hershey, PA: IGI Global. doi:10.4018/978-1-4666-9519-1

Ottonicar, S. L. (2020). Brazilian Policy and Actions to Fight Against Fake News: A Discussion Focused on Critical Literacy. In K. Dalkir & R. Katz (Eds.), *Navigating Fake News, Alternative Facts, and Misinformation in a Post-Truth World* (pp. 204–221). Hershey, PA: IGI Global. doi:10.4018/978-1-7998-2543-2.ch009

Pal, A., & Banerjee, S. (2019). Understanding Online Falsehood From the Perspective of Social Problem. In I. Chiluwa & S. Samoilenko (Eds.), *Handbook of Research on Deception, Fake News, and Misinformation Online* (pp. 1–17). Hershey, PA: IGI Global. doi:10.4018/978-1-5225-8535-0.ch001

Paruthi, M., Mendiratta, P., & Gupta, G. (2020). Young Citizen's Political Engagement in India: Social Media Use by Political Parties. In V. Kumar & G. Malhotra (Eds.), *Examining the Roles of IT and Social Media in Democratic Development and Social Change* (pp. 115–132). Hershey, PA: IGI Global. doi:10.4018/978-1-7998-1791-8.ch005

Rajan, B. (2019). New Mythologies of Fake News: WhatsApp and Misrepresented Scientific Achievements of Ancient India. In I. Chiluwa & S. Samoilenko (Eds.), *Handbook of Research on Deception, Fake News, and Misinformation Online* (pp. 192–208). Hershey, PA: IGI Global. doi:10.4018/978-1-5225-8535-0.ch012

Reynard, L. J. (2019). Troll Farm: Anonymity as a Weapon for Online Character Assassination. In I. Chiluwa & S. Samoilenko (Eds.), *Handbook of Research on Deception, Fake News, and Misinformation Online* (pp. 392–419). Hershey, PA: IGI Global. doi:10.4018/978-1-5225-8535-0.ch021

Sabao, C. (2016). Shades of the GNU in Zimbabwe (2009 – 13): Linguistic Discourse Analyses of Representations of Transitional Politics in Zimbabwean Newspapers. In D. Orwenjo, O. Oketch, & A. Tunde (Eds.), *Political Discourse in Emergent, Fragile, and Failed Democracies* (pp. 306–327). Hershey, PA: IGI Global. doi:10.4018/978-1-5225-0081-0.ch017

Sabao, C., & Visser, M. (2016). Tearing up Nationalist Discourses?: Appraisal Analysis of Representations of Joice Mujuru and the ZANU PF Factionalism Dialectic in Zimbabwean Newspapers. In D. Orwenjo, O. Oketch, & A. Tunde (Eds.), *Political Discourse in Emergent, Fragile, and Failed Democracies* (pp. 88–111). Hershey, PA: IGI Global. doi:10.4018/978-1-5225-0081-0.ch005

Salvati, E. (2017). E-Government and E-Democracy in the Supranational Arena: The Enforcing of Transparency and Democratic Legitimacy in the European Union. In R. Luppicini & R. Baarda (Eds.), *Digital Media Integration for Participatory Democracy* (pp. 101–129). Hershey, PA: IGI Global. doi:10.4018/978-1-5225-2463-2.ch006

Samoilenko, S. A., & Miroshnichenko, A. (2019). Profiting From the "Trump Bump": The Effects of Selling Negativity in the Media. In I. Chiluwa & S. Samoilenko (Eds.), *Handbook of Research on Deception, Fake News, and Misinformation Online* (pp. 375–391). Hershey, PA: IGI Global. doi:10.4018/978-1-5225-8535-0.ch020

Shan, Z., & Tang, L. (2020). Social Media and Public Sphere in China: A Case Study of Political Discussion on Weibo After the Wenzhou High- Speed Rail Derailment Accident. In M. Adria (Ed.), *Using New Media for Citizen Engagement and Participation* (pp. 280–295). Hershey, PA: IGI Global. doi:10.4018/978-1-7998-1828-1.ch015

Song, M. Y. (2020). Public Engagement and Policy Entrepreneurship on Social Media in the Time of Anti-Vaccination Movements. In M. Adria (Ed.), *Using New Media for Citizen Engagement and Participation* (pp. 60–80). Hershey, PA: IGI Global. doi:10.4018/978-1-7998-1828-1.ch004

Spada, P., & Allegretti, G. (2020). When Democratic Innovations Integrate Multiple and Diverse Channels of Social Dialogue: Opportunities and Challenges. In M. Adria (Ed.), *Using New Media for Citizen Engagement and Participation* (pp. 35–59). Hershey, PA: IGI Global. doi:10.4018/978-1-7998-1828-1.ch003

Stacey, E. (2018). *Nationalism, Social Movements, and Activism in Contemporary Society: Emerging Research and Opportunities* (pp. 1–135). Hershey, PA: IGI Global. doi:10.4018/978-1-5225-5433-2

Strelluf, C. (2016). Media Coverage of the 2009 Afghan Presidential Election. In D. Orwenjo, O. Oketch, & A. Tunde (Eds.), *Political Discourse in Emergent, Fragile, and Failed Democracies* (pp. 143–164). Hershey, PA: IGI Global. doi:10.4018/978-1-5225-0081-0.ch008

Svensson, J. (2020). A Study of Politicians in a Hybrid Media Setting During the 2014 Swedish Elections: A Logic Polarisation and Dissent. In V. Kumar & G. Malhotra (Eds.), *Examining the Roles of IT and Social Media in Democratic Development and Social Change* (pp. 92–114). Hershey, PA: IGI Global. doi:10.4018/978-1-7998-1791-8.ch004

Sylvia, J. J. IV, & Moody, K. (2019). False Information Narratives: The IRA's 2016 Presidential Election Facebook Campaign. In I. Chiluwa & S. Samoilenko (Eds.), *Handbook of Research on Deception, Fake News, and Misinformation Online* (pp. 326–348). Hershey, PA: IGI Global. doi:10.4018/978-1-5225-8535-0.ch018

Tessier, D. (2020). The Needle in the Haystack: How Information Overload Is Impacting Society and Our Search for Truth. In K. Dalkir & R. Katz (Eds.), *Navigating Fake News, Alternative Facts, and Misinformation in a Post-Truth World* (pp. 18–35). Hershey, PA: IGI Global. doi:10.4018/978-1-7998-2543-2.ch002

Tiwari, A., & Gupta, T. (2020). Role of IT and Social Media in Democratic Change: Paraphernalia Around Information Technology and Social Media. In V. Kumar & G. Malhotra (Eds.), *Examining the Roles of IT and Social Media in Democratic Development and Social Change* (pp. 294–319). Hershey, PA: IGI Global. doi:10.4018/978-1-7998-1791-8.ch012

Towner, T. L. (2020). Information Hubs or Drains?: The Role of Online Sources in Campaign Learning. In M. Adria (Ed.), *Using New Media for Citizen Engagement and Participation* (pp. 112–134). Hershey, PA: IGI Global. doi:10.4018/978-1-7998-1828-1.ch007

Tunde, A. H., & Orwenjo, D. O. (2016). On The Threshold of Democratic Fragility: A Macrospeech Act Explication of Media Representation of the Nigerian 2011 Post-Presidential Election News Reports. In D. Orwenjo, O. Oketch, & A. Tunde (Eds.), *Political Discourse in Emergent, Fragile, and Failed Democracies* (pp. 328–348). Hershey, PA: IGI Global. doi:10.4018/978-1-5225-0081-0.ch018

Villanueva-Mansilla, E. (2020). Salience, Self-Salience, and Discursive Opportunities: An Effective Media Presence Construction Through Social Media in the Peruvian Presidential Election. In M. Adria (Ed.), *Using New Media for Citizen Engagement and Participation* (pp. 240–255). Hershey, PA: IGI Global. doi:10.4018/978-1-7998-1828-1.ch013

Wendo, N. (2016). Ethnic Stereotyping on Kenyan Blog Sites in the 2013 Political Elections: A Spurious Harbinger of Ethnic Discord. In D. Orwenjo, O. Oketch, & A. Tunde (Eds.), *Political Discourse in Emergent, Fragile, and Failed Democracies* (pp. 252–264). Hershey, PA: IGI Global. doi:10.4018/978-1-5225-0081-0.ch014

Xu, W., & Hu, H. (2019). Government Regulation on the Flourishing Network Audio-Visual Entrepreneurship: Experience From the Administration in Beijing. *Journal of Media Management and Entrepreneurship*, *1*(2), 1–13. doi:10.4018/JMME.2019070101

Yang, K. C., & Kang, Y. (2016). Real-Name Registration Regulation in China: An Examination of Chinese Netizens' Discussions about Censorship, Privacy, and Political Freedom. In D. Orwenjo, O. Oketch, & A. Tunde (Eds.), *Political Discourse in Emergent, Fragile, and Failed Democracies* (pp. 61–87). Hershey, PA: IGI Global. doi:10.4018/978-1-5225-0081-0.ch004

Yang, K. C., & Kang, Y. (2020). Political Mobilization Strategies in Taiwan's Sunflower Student Movement on March 18, 2014: A Text-Mining Analysis of Cross-National Media Corpus. In M. Adria (Ed.), *Using New Media for Citizen Engagement and Participation* (pp. 256–279). Hershey, PA: IGI Global. doi:10.4018/978-1-7998-1828-1.ch014

Yang, K. C., & Kang, Y. (2020). Will Microblogs Shape China's Civil Society Under President's Xi's Surveillance State?: The Case of Anti-Extradition Law Protests in Hong Kong. In V. Kumar & G. Malhotra (Eds.), *Examining the Roles of IT and Social Media in Democratic Development and Social Change* (pp. 156–184). Hershey, PA: IGI Global. doi:10.4018/978-1-7998-1791-8.ch007

Yin, Y., & Fung, A. (2017). Youth Online Cultural Participation and Bilibili: An Alternative Form of Democracy in China? In R. Luppicini & R. Baarda (Eds.), *Digital Media Integration for Participatory Democracy* (pp. 130–154). Hershey, PA: IGI Global. doi:10.4018/978-1-5225-2463-2.ch007

Yuan, Y. (2020). A Gradual Political Change?: The Agenda-Setting Effect of Online Activism in China 1994-2011. In M. Adria (Ed.), *Using New Media for Citizen Engagement and Participation* (pp. 198–218). Hershey, PA: IGI Global. doi:10.4018/978-1-7998-1828-1.ch011

About the Authors

Nikolaos Koumartzis is a PhD graduate from the School of Journalism & Mass Communication at the Aristotle University of Thessaloniki. He received his BSc in Computer Science from Aristotle University of Thessaloniki, Ma in Publications from University of the Arts London, and MSc in Strategic Product Design from International Hellenic University. His research interests include Internet regulation and online cencorship, ancient Greek musical instruments, 3d design and 3d analysis. He has authored seven mainstream books with various Greek publishers (in Greek and in English), while his researches were published in journals (such as the *International Journal of E-Politics, Computer Technology and Application, First Monday Journal, Journal of New Music Research* etc.) and being presented in conferences (such as the *First International Congress on the Internet, Trolling and Addiction (ITA15), Hellenic Conference of Acoustics, Sixteenth IEEE Symposium on Computers and Communications (ISCC11), Euro-NF International Workshop on Traffic and Congestion Control for the Future Internet* etc.). He is the co-founder of a series of companies focusing on different cultural aspect such as cultural events, ancient music, book publishing etc. Currently, he works as an Art Director at Luthieros Music Instruments and SEIKILO Museum.

Andreas Veglis is Professor, head of the Media Informatics Lab at the School of Journalism & Mass Communication at the Aristotle University of Thessaloniki. He received his BSc in Physics, MSc in Electronics and Communications, and PhD in Computer Science, all from Aristotle University. His research interests include information technology in journalism, new media, course support environments, data journalism, open data and distance learning. He has published in books and international journals like *Journal of Applied Journalism & Media Studies, Journal of Greek Media & Culture, Digital Journalism, Studies in Media and Communication, Computers in Human Behavior, International Journal of Monitoring and Surveillance*

Technologies Research, International Journal of Advanced Computer Science and Information Technology, International Journal of Computers and Communications, International Journal of E-Politics, Journalism & Mass Communication Educator, International Communication Gazette, Publishing Research Quarterly, International Journal of Electronic Governance, Journalism, Austral Comunicación. He is the author or co-author of 12 books, he has published 70 papers on scientific journals and he has presented 110 papers in international and national Conferences. Professor Veglis has been involved in 25 national and international research projects.

Index

B

banned websites 10, 19, 40, 58, 60, 63, 74

C

circumventing techniques 62, 64-65, 68, 70-74
circumvention methods 155, 159
CleanFeed 10, 13-14, 19-21, 29-32, 35-40, 51-54, 56-71, 73-74, 78, 182, 185, 188
Content Blocking 6, 10-12, 14-15, 19, 21, 30, 32, 56-57, 61-62, 89
copyright infringement 9, 98, 115, 147, 176, 183, 185
Cypriot Internet 135, 141, 144, 147-148

F

fair internet regulation system (FIRS) 153, 162, 181
free speech 108, 148, 167, 176

G

global phenomenon 1, 93, 98, 101, 107, 110, 114-115, 118, 123-124, 126, 132, 135, 141, 146, 164, 168, 176, 183, 188

H

hate-speech 9, 96, 98, 104, 108, 113, 115, 123-124, 132, 140-141, 147-149, 164, 170, 175-177, 183, 185

I

internet censorship 4, 7, 32, 35, 42, 44, 53, 81, 95, 102-103, 111
Internet regulation 1-2, 4-7, 9-11, 16, 19-21, 29-32, 40, 42, 44, 53, 77-79, 81-82, 87, 93, 96-98, 101, 103-105, 107-108, 110-115, 118, 120-124, 126, 128-132, 135-139, 141, 143, 146-148, 153-155, 160, 162-165, 167-168, 170-173, 176-179, 181-183, 185-188
Internet users 1, 4, 6-7, 9, 11, 14, 21, 29-32, 34-35, 38-39, 51, 53, 77-78, 81, 85, 92-93, 101, 106-108, 110, 118, 126, 132, 135, 141, 144, 146-149, 153-155, 159-160, 162-163, 168, 170, 176-179, 182-183, 185-186

K

Kruskal-Wallis 143-144

M

Mann-Whitney 143-144

N

non-governmental organisations 97, 105, 148, 155, 164, 167, 176

O

online citizens 78-79, 84, 185
online filtering 1

P

Pearson chi-square 85, 106, 114, 123, 130-131, 139-140, 143, 173-175
Peter Robbins 56, 61

S

significant association 106, 114, 123, 130-131, 139-140, 143, 173-175, 183
smooth transition 106, 108, 147
standardised residuals 106, 114, 123, 130-131, 139-140, 173-175
statistical analysis 9, 85, 87, 92, 97, 100, 106, 108-109, 114-115, 117, 123-125, 130-131, 134, 139-141, 143-144, 148, 167, 172-176, 183-184, 186-187

T

technical weaknesses 61-62, 74

U

university-based institutes 148, 154-155

www.ingramcontent.com/pod-product-compliance
Lightning Source LLC
LaVergne TN
LVHW061539290926
849162LV00004B/845